A Practical Approach
to Software Quality

Springer

New York
Berlin
Heidelberg
Barcelona
Hong Kong
London
Milan
Paris
Singapore
Tokyo

Gerard O'Regan

A Practical Approach to Software Quality

With 155 Illustrations

 Springer

Gerard O'Regan
SQC Consulting
80 Upper Friars Rd.
Turners Cross
Cork
Ireland
oregang@yahoo.com
http://sqc.netfirms.com

Library of Congress Cataloging-in-Publication Data
O'Regan, Gerard (Cornelius Gerard).
    A practical approach to software quality / Gerard O'Regan.
      p. cm.
    Includes bibliographical references and index.

    1. Computer software—Quality control.   I. Title.
QA76.76.Q35 O83 2002
005.1'0685—dc21   2001059797

Printed on acid-free paper.

Manufacturing supervised by Joe Quatela.
Photocomposed copy prepared from Microsoft Word files supplied by the author.

9 8 7 6 5 4 3 2 1

ISBN 978-1-4419-2951-8   e-ISBN 978-0-387-22454-1

Springer-Verlag New York Berlin Heidelberg
A member of BertelsmannSpringer Science+Business Media GmbH

To my mother Eileen O'Regan.

Preface

Overview

The aim of this book is to provide a practical introduction to software quality in an industrial environment and is based on the author's experience in working in software engineering and software quality improvement with leading industrial companies. The book is written from a practitioner's viewpoint, and the objective is to include both theory and practice. The reader will gain a grasp of the fundamentals as well as guidance on the practical application of the theory.

The principles of software quality management and software process improvement are discussed, and guidance on the implementation of maturity models such as the CMM, SPICE, or the ISO 9000:2000 standard is included.

Organization and Features

The first chapter provides an introduction to the fundamentals of quality management. Later chapters consider software inspections and testing, ISO 9000, the CMM, the evolving SPICE standard, metrics and problem solving, and the final chapter on formal methods and design considers some advanced topics, including configuration management, UML, software usability, and formal methods. The reader may find the material heavy going in places, especially in the section on formal methods, and this section may be skipped.

The book includes a chapter on software inspections and testing, and this includes material on Fagan inspections to build quality into the software product. The software testing section includes material on test planning and tracking, test metrics, test reporting, test case definition, the various types of testing performed, and testing in an e-commerce environment. There are separate chapters on ISO 9000, the CMM, and SPICE, and these chapters provide background material and an appropriate level of material to support the implementation of the model or standard.

The new ISO 9000:2000 standard is discussed as well as practical implementation issues, and the new CMMI model from the software Engineering Institute is described in the chapter on the CMM. There is a chapter on metrics and problem solving, and this includes a discussion of the balanced score card which assists in identifying appropriate metrics for the organization, GQM for relating metrics to organization goals, and a collection of sample metrics for the various functional areas in an organization.

The final chapter discusses advanced topics and includes material on software configuration management, UML, software usability, and formal methods. The section on formal methods provides an introduction to this field in software engineering and it is the most difficult section. It includes some elementary mathematics to give the reader a flavor of the discipline, but most of the text is in prose. This section may be skipped by readers who are uncomfortable with mathematical notation.

Audience

This book is suitable for software engineers and managers in software companies as well as software quality professionals and practitioners.

It is an introductory textbook and is suitable for software engineering students who are interested in the fundamentals of quality management as well as software professionals. The book will also be of interest to the general reader who is curious about software engineering.

Acknowledgments

I am deeply indebted to friends and colleagues in academia and in industry who supported my efforts in this endeavor. My thanks to Rohit Dave of Motorola for sharing his in-depth knowledge of the software quality field with me, for camaraderie, and for introducing me to many of the practical subtleties in quality management. The staff of Motorola in Cork, Ireland, provided an excellent working relationship.

John Murphy of DDSI, Ireland, supported my efforts in the implementation of a sound quality system in DDSI, and my interests in the wider software process improvement field. The formal methods group at Trinity College, Dublin, were an inspiration, and my thanks to Mícheál Mac An Airchinnigh, and the Trinity formal methods group.

My thanks to Richard Messnarz of ISCN for sharing his sound practical approach to assessment planning and execution, and his pragmatic approach to the improvement of organizations.

Finally, I must thank my family and friends in the Cork area. I must express a special thanks to Liam O'Driscoll for the unique Hop Island school of motivation and horse riding, and to my friends at the Hop Island Equestrian Centre. Finally, my thanks to personal friends such as Kevin Crowley and others too numerous to mention, and to the reviewers who sent many helpful comments and suggestions.

Gerard O'Regan
Cork, Ireland
November 2001

Contents

1
Introduction to Software Quality

The mission of a software company is to provide innovative products or services at a competitive price to its customers and to do so ahead of its competitors. This requires a clear vision of the business, a culture of innovation, detailed knowledge of the business domain, and a sound product development strategy.

It also requires a focus on customer satisfaction and software quality to ensure that the desired quality is built into the software product and to ensure that customers remain loyal to the company. Customers in the new millennium have very high expectations on quality and expect high-quality software products to be delivered on time and every time. The focus on quality requires that the organization define a sound software development infrastructure to enable quality software to be produced.

This book describes approaches used in current software engineering to build quality into software. This involves a discussion of project planning and tracking, software lifecycles, software inspections and testing, configuration management, software quality assurance, etc. Maturity models such as the capability maturity model (CMM) and the software process improvement and capability determination (SPICE) model are discussed in detail, as these provide a model for organizations to assess their current maturity and to prioritize improvements.

The assessments of organizations against a model such as the CMM reveals strengths and weaknesses of the organization. The output from the assessment is used to formulate an improvement plan, which is then tracked to completion. The execution of the plan may take one to two years of effort.

Quality improvement also requires that the organization be actively aware of industrial best practices as well as the emerging technologies from the various European or US research programs. Piloting or technology transfer of innovative technology is a key part of continuous improvement.

The history of quality and some of the key people who have contributed to the quality movement are included in this chapter. This list includes well-known people such as Shewhart, Deming, Juran, and Crosby. The ideas of these grandfathers of quality are discussed, as is the application of their ideas to software maturity models such as the CMM.

1.1 The Software Engineering Challenge

The challenge in software engineering is to deliver high-quality software on time to customers. The Standish Group research [Std:99] (Fig. 1.1) on project cost overruns in the US during 1998 indicate that 33% of projects are between 21% and 50% over estimate, 18% are between 51% and 100% over estimate, and 11% of projects are between 101% and 200% overestimate.

Project management and estimating project cost and schedule accurately are among the major software engineering challenges. Consequently, organizations need to determine how good their estimation process actually is and to make improvements as appropriate. The use of software metrics is one mechanism to determine how good software estimation actually is. This may involve computing actual project effort versus estimate project estimate, and actual project schedule versus projected project schedule. Risk management is a key part of project management, and the objective is to identify potential risks to the project at initiation, determine the probability of the risks occurring and to assess its impact if it materializes, then to eliminate or reduce the risk and to have contingency plans in place to address the risk if it materializes, and finally to track risks throughout the project.

The Taurus project at the London stock exchange is an infamous case of a project that was abandoned and never completed. The original budget was £6 million and by the time that the project was abandoned, the project was 11 years late, i.e., 13,200% late and had cost the city of London over £800 million [Man:95].

The software engineering domain is characterized by changing requirements or the introduction of new requirements late in the software development lifecycle. This makes the estimation process more difficult, as often there is little choice but to accept a late requirement change if it is demanded by a customer. However, a good requirements process will ensure that changes to the requirements are minimized and controlled, and the requirements process may include

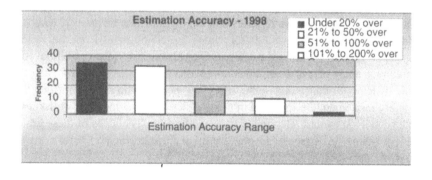

Figure 1.1: Managing Projects - Estimation Accuracy

prototyping or joint user reviews to ensure that they match the needs of the customer.

The implementation of the requirements involves design, coding, and testing activities. User manuals, technical documentation, and training materials may be required also. Challenges to be faced include the technical activities of the project, communication of changes to the project team, building quality into the software product, verifying that the software is correct and corresponds to the requirements, ensuring that the project is delivered on time, and, where appropriate, taking corrective action to recover if the project is behind schedule.

The challenges in software engineering are also faced in many other disciplines. Bridges have been constructed by engineers for several millennia and bridge building is a mature engineering activity. However, civil engineering projects occasionally fall behind schedule or suffer design flaws, for example, the infamous Tacoma Narrows bridge (or Galloping Gertie as it was known) collapsed in 1940 owing to a design flaw.

The Tacoma Narrows Bridge was known for its tendency to sway in windstorms. The shape of the bridge was like that of an aircraft wing and under windy conditions it would generate sufficient lift to become unstable. On November 7, 1940, a large windstorm caused severe and catastrophic failure. The significance of the Tacoma bridge is derived from this collapse, the subsequent investigation by engineers, and the realization that aero-dynamical forces in suspension bridges were not sufficiently understood or addressed in the design of the bridge. New research was needed and the recommendation from the investigation was to use wind tunnel tests to aid in the design of the second Tacoma Narrows bridge. New mathematical theories of bridge design also arose from these studies.

Software engineering is a less mature field than civil engineering, and it is only in more recent times that investigations and recommendations from software projects have become part of the software development process. The study of software engineering has led to new theories and understanding of software development. This includes the use of mathematics to assist in the modeling or understanding of the behavior or properties of a proposed software system. The use of mathematics is an integral part of the engineer's work in other engineering disciplines. The software community has piloted the use of formal specification of software systems, but to date formality has been mainly applied to safety critical software. Currently, the industrial perception is that formal methods are difficult to use, and their widespread deployment in industry is unlikely at this time.

1.2 History of Software Failures

There is quite a catalog of software failures in the literature. These include the Y2K problem, the Intel microprocessor bug, the Ariane 5 disaster, etc. Software failures may cause major problems for the customer and adversely affect the customer's business. This leads to potential credibility issues for the software company, and damage to the customer relationship, with subsequent loss of market share.

The Y2K bug is now a part of history and computer science folklore. The event itself on January 1, 2000 had minimal impact on the world economy and was, in effect, a non-event. Much has been written about the background to theY2K bug and the use of two digits for recording dates rather than four digits. The solution to the Y2K problem involved finding and analyzing all code with a Y2K impact, planning and making the necessary changes, and verifying the correctness of the changes. The cost in the UK alone is estimated to have been approximately $38 billion.

The Intel response to the famous microprocessor mathematical bug back in 1994 inflicted damage on the company and its reputation. The Intel corporation was slow to acknowledge the floating point problem in the Pentium microprocessor and to provide adequate information on the potential impact of the problem to its customers. This damaged its reputation and credibility at the time and involved a large financial cost in replacing microprocessors.

The Ariane 5 failure caused major embarrassment and damage to the credibility of the European Space Agency (ESA). The maiden flight of the Ariane launcher ended in failure on June 4, 1996, after a flight time of 40 seconds. The first 37 seconds of flight proceeded normal. The launcher then veered off its flight path, broke up, and exploded. An independent inquiry board investigated the cause of the failure, and the report and recommendations to prevent a future failure are described in [Lio:96].

The inquiry noted that the failure of the inertial reference system was followed immediately by a failure of the backup inertial reference system. The origin of the failure was narrowed down to this specific area quite quickly. The problem was traced to a software failure owing to an operand error, specifically, the conversion of a 64 bit floating point number to a 16 bit signed integer value number. The floating point number was too large to be represented in the 16 bit number and this resulted in an operand error. The inertial reference system and the backup reference system reported failure owing to the software exception. The operand error occurred owing to an exceptionally high value related to the horizontal velocity, and this was due to the fact that the early part of the trajectory of the Ariane 5 was different from that of the earlier Ariane 4, and required a higher horizontal velocity. The inquiry board made a series of recommendations to prevent a reoccurrence of similar problems.

These failures indicate that software quality needs to be a key driving force in any organization. The effect of software failure may result in huge costs to correct the software (e.g., Y2K), negative perception of a company and possible loss of market share (e.g., Intel microprocessor problem), or the loss of a valuable communications satellite (e.g., Ariane 5).

1.3 Background to Software Quality

Customers today have very high expectations regarding quality and reliability of products and expect the highest of standards from all organizations within the economy. This includes manufacturing companies, service companies, and the software sector. There are many quality software products in the marketplace produced by leading-edge software development companies. However, the task of producing high-quality software products consistently on time is non-trivial. Occasionally flaws are discovered in products developed by the most respected of organizations, or occasionally products are shipped late owing to quality problems. These errors may cause minor irritation to a customer, loss of credibility for the software company, or in a worst case scenario may lead to injury or loss of life.

A late delivery of a product leads to extra costs to the organization and may adversely affect the revenue, profitability, or business planning of the customer. Consequently, organizations seek an infrastructure and framework to develop high-quality software consistently, within time and within budget. The influential papers by Fred Brooks in [Brk:75, Brk:86] suggests that there is no silver bullet that will ensure software quality and project timeliness within an organization. Instead an incremental improvement approach is adopted and this is achieved by small but sustainable improvements in methodologies, tools, models, design, requirements, etc. Quality improvements may take the form of organization or technical improvements.

1.3.1 What is Software Quality?

In later sections the work of Deming, Shewhart, Juran, and Crosby will be discussed. The Crosby definition of quality is narrow and states that quality is simply "conformance to the requirements". This definition does not take the intrinsic difference in quality of products into account in judging the quality of the product or in deciding whether the defined requirements are actually appropriate for the product. Juran defines quality as "fitness for use" and this is a better definition, although it does not provide a mechanism to judge better quality when two products are equally fit to be used.

The ISO 9126 standard for information technology [ISO:91] provides a framework for the evaluation of software quality. It defines six product quality characteristics which indicate the extent to which a software product may be judged to be of a high quality. These include:

Table 1.1: ISO 9126–Quality Characteristics

Characteristic	Description
Functionality	This characteristic indicates the extent to which the required functions are available in the software.
Reliability	This characteristic indicates the extent to which the software is reliable.
Usability	This indicates the usability of the software and indicates the extent to which the users of the software judge it to be easy to use.
Efficiency	This characteristic indicates the efficiency of the software.
Maintainability	This characteristic indicates the extent to which the software product is easy to modify and maintain.
Portability	This characteristic indicates the ease of transferring the software to a different environment.

The extent to which the software product exhibits these quality characteristics will judge the extent to which it will be rated as a high-quality product by customers. The organization will need measurements to indicate the extent to which the product satisfies these quality characteristics, and metrics for the organization are discussed in chapter 6.

1.3.2 Early Quality Management

In the middle ages a craftsman was responsible for the complete development of a product from conception to delivery to the customer. This lead to a very strong sense of pride in the quality of the product by the craftsman. Apprentices joined craftsmen to learn the trade and skills, and following a period of training and working closely with the master they acquired the skills and knowledge to be successful craftsmen themselves.

The industrial revolution involved a change to the traditional paradigm and labor became highly organized with workers responsible for a particular part of the development or manufacture of a product. The sense of ownership and the pride of workmanship in the product were diluted as workers were now responsible only for their portion of the product and not the product as a whole.

This lead to a requirement for more stringent management practices, including planning, organizing, implementation, and control. It inevitably lead to a hierarchy of labor with various functions identified, and a reporting structure for the various functions. Supervisor controls were needed to ensure quality and productivity issues were addressed.

1.3.3 Total Quality Management

The modern approach to quality management by organizations is total quality management (TQM). This is a management philosophy and involves customer focus, process improvement, developing a culture of quality within the organization and developing a measurement and analysis program in the organization. It emphasizes that customers have rights and quality expectations which should be satisfied, and that everyone in the organization is both a customer and has customers.

It is a holistic approach and requires that all functions, including development, marketing, sales, distribution, and customer support, follow very high standards. The framework for total quality management within the organization requires that quality be built into the product by ensuring that quality is addressed at each step by individuals at all levels within the organization.

It involves defining internal and external customers, recognizing that internal and external customers have rights and expectations, identifying the requirements that they have, and meeting these first time and every time. It requires total commitment from the top management, training all staff in quality management, and ensuring that all staff participate in quality improvement. It requires that a commitment to quality be instilled in all staff, and that the focus within the organization change from fire fighting to fire prevention.

Fire prevention involves problem solving to address root causes and taking appropriate corrective action. Project plans for quality may include inspections and testing and independent audits of the work products. Quantitative quality measurements are maintained and monitored to ensure that the required quality level is achieved.

1.3.4 Software Quality Control

Software quality control may involve extensive inspections and testing. Inspections typically consist of a formal review by experts who critically examine a particular deliverable, for example, a requirements document, a design document, source code, or test plans. The objective is to identify defects within the work product and to provide confidence in its correctness. Inspections play a key role in achieving process quality, and one well known inspection methodology is the Fagan inspection methodology developed by Michael Fagan [Fag:76].

Inspections in a manufacturing environment are quite different in that they take place at the end of the production cycle, and in effect, do not offer a mechanism for quality assurance of the product; instead the defective products are removed from the batch and reworked. There is a growing trend towards quality sampling at the early phases of a manufacturing process to minimize reworking of defective products.

Software testing consists of "white box" or "black box" testing techniques, including unit testing, functional testing, system testing, performance testing, and acceptance testing. The testing is quite methodical and includes a comprehensive set of test cases produced manually or by automated means. The validation of the product involves ensuring that all defined tests are executed, and that any failed or blocked tests are corrected. In some cases, it may be impossible to be fully comprehensive in real time testing, and only simulation testing may be possible. In these cases, the simulated environment will need to resemble the real time environment closely to ensure the validity of the testing.

The cost of correction of a defect is directly related to the phase in which the defect is detected in the lifecycle. Errors detected in phase are the least expensive to correct, and defects, i.e., errors detected out of phase, become increasingly expensive to correct. The most expensive defect is that detected by the customer. This is because a defect identified by a customer will require analysis to determine the origin of the defect; it may affect requirements, design and implementation. It will require testing and a fix release for the customer. There is further overhead in project management, configuration management, and in communication with the customer.

It is therefore highly desirable to capture defects as early as possible in the software lifecycle, in order to minimize the effort required to re-work the defect. Modern software engineering places emphasis on defect prevention and in learning lessons from the actual defects. This approach is inherited from manufacturing environments and consists of formal causal analysis meetings to brainstorm and identify root causes and corrective actions necessary to prevent reoccurrence. The actions are then implemented by an action team and tracked to completion.

Next, some of the ideas of the key individuals who have had a major influence on the quality field are discussed. These include people such as Shewhart, Deming, Juran, and Crosby.

1.4 History of Quality

1.4.1 Shewhart

Walter Shewhart was a statistician at AT&T Bell Laboratories (or Western Electric Co. as it was known then) in the 1920s and is regarded as the founder of statistical quality improvement, and modern process improvement is based on the concepts of process control developed by Shewhart. Deming and Juran worked with Shewhart at Bell Labs in the 1920s.

The Shewhart model is a systematic approach to problem solving and process control. It consists of four steps which are used for continuous process improvement. These steps are plan, do, check, act, and it is known as the *"PDCA model"* or Shewhart's model (Fig. 1.2).

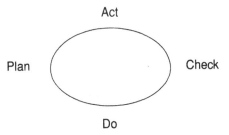

Figure 1.2: Shewhart PDCA Cycle

Table 1.2: Shewhart Cycle

Step	Description
Plan	This step identifies an improvement opportunity and outlines the problem or process that will be addressed. • Select the problem to be addressed. • Describe current process. • Identify the possible causes of the problem. • Find the root cause of problems. • Develop an action plan to correct the root cause.
Do	This step involve carrying out the improved process and involves following the plan. This step may involve a pilot of the proposed changes to the process.
Check	This step involves reviewing and evaluating the result of the changes and determining the effectiveness of the changes to the process.
Act	This step involves acting on the analysis and recommended changes. It results in further plans for improvement.

Shewhart argued that quality and productivity improve as process variability is reduced. His influential book, *The Economic control of quality of manufactured product* [Shw:31], was published in 1931, and outlines the methods of statistical process control to reduce process variability. The book prophesized that productivity would improve as process variability was reduced, and this was verified by Japanese engineers in the 1950s.

This lead to a paradigm shift in quality management in Japanese companies and a focus on quality. It lead to productivity improvements, increased market share, and dominance of world markets by Japanese companies until American and European companies responded to the Japanese challenge, and awarded quality management the place it deserves in the organization.

1.4.2 Deming

W. Edwards Deming was one of the major figures in the quality movement. He was influenced by the work of Shewhart, the pioneer of statistical process control. Deming's ideas on quality management were embraced by the industrial community in post second world war Japan, and played a key role in achieving the excellence in quality that Japanese manufactured output is internationally famous for.

Deming argued that it is not sufficient for everyone in the organization to be doing his best: instead, what is required is that there be a consistent purpose and direction in the organization. That is, it is first necessary that people know what to do, and there must be a constancy of purpose from all individuals in the organization to ensure success.

Deming argued that there is a very strong case for improving quality as costs will decrease owing to less reworking of defective products and productivity will increase as less time is spent in reworking. This will enable the company to increase its market share with better quality and lower prices and to stay in business. Conversely, companies which fail to address quality issues will lose market share and go out of business. Deming was highly critical of the American management approach to quality, and the lack of vision of American management in quality. Deming also did pioneering work on consumer research and sampling.

Deming's influential book *Out of the Crisis* [Dem:86], proposed 14 principles or points of action to transform the western style of management of an organization to a quality and customer focused organization. This transformation will enable it to be in a position to be successful in producing high-quality products. The 14 points of action include:

- Constancy of purpose
- Quality built into the product
- Continuous improvement culture

Statistical process control is employed to minimize variability in process performance as the quality of the product may be adversely affected by process variability. This involves the analysis of statistical process control charts so that the cause of variability can be identified and eliminated. All staff receive training on quality and barriers are removed. Deming's ideas are described in more detail below:

Table 1.3: Deming–14 Step Programme

Step	Description
Constancy of Purpose	Companies face short-term and long-term problems. The problems of tomorrow require long-term planning on new products, training, and innovation. This requires resources invested in research and development and continuous improvement of existing products and services.
Adopt new Philosophy	Deming outlined the five deadly diseases which afflicted US companies. These included lack of purpose and an excessive interest in short-term profits.
Build quality in	Deming argued that performing mass inspections is equivalent to planning for defects and are too late to improve quality. Consequently, it is necessary to improve the production process to build the quality into the product.
Price and Quality	Deming argued against the practice of awarding business on the basis of price alone, as the price of a product or service is meaningless unless there is an objective measure of the quality of the product or service being purchased.
Continuous Improvement	Continuous improvement is a fundamental part of Deming's program. There must be continuous improvement in all areas, including understanding customer requirements, design, manufacturing and test methods. The organization must be a learning organization with the employees and development processes continuously improving.
Institute Training	This involves setting up a training program to educate management and staff about the company, customer needs, and pride of workmanship in the products or services. Supervisors and managers need training on the 14 point program to ensure they fully understand the enhanced contribution that their staff can make if inhibitors to good work are removed.
Institute Leadership	Deming argues that management is about leadership and not supervision. Management should work to remove barriers, know the work domain in depth, and seek innovative solutions to resolve quality and other relevant issues.
Eliminate Fear	The presence of fear is a barrier to an open discussion of problems and the identification of solutions or changes to prevent problems from arising.
Eliminate Barriers	The objective here is to break down barriers between different departments and groups. It is not enough for each group to optimize its own area: instead, what is required is for the organization to be working as one team.

Table 1.3 (*continued*): Deming – 14 Step Programme

Step	Description
Eliminate Slogans	Deming argued that slogans do not help anyone to do a better job. Slogans may potentially alienate staff or encourage cynicism. Deming criticized slogans such as "Zero defects" or "Do it right the first time" as inappropriate, as how can it be made right first time if the production machine is defective. The slogans take no account of the fact that most problems are due to the system rather than the person. A slogan is absolutely inappropriate unless there is a clearly defined strategy to attain it, and Deming argued that numerical goals set for people without a road map to reach the goals have the opposite effect to that intended, as it contributes to a loss of motivation.
Eliminate Numerical Quotas	Deming argued that quotas act as an impediment to improvement in quality, as quotas are normally based on what may be achieved by the average worker. People below the average cannot make the rate and the result is dissatisfaction and turnover. Thus, there is a fundamental conflict between quotas and pride of workmanship.
Pride of Work	The intention here is to remove barriers that rob people of pride of workmanship, for example, machines that are out of order and not repaired.
Self Improvement	This involves encouraging education and self-improvement for everyone in the company, as an organization requires people who are improving all the time.
Take Action	This requires that management agree on direction using the 14 principles, communicate the reasons for changes to the staff, and train the staff on the 14 principles. Every job is part of a process, and the process consists of stages. There is a customer for each stage, and the customer has rights and expectations of quality. The objective is to improve the methods and procedures and thereby improve the output of the phase. The improvements may require a cross- functional team to analyze and improve the process

The application of Deming's 14 points for quality management transforms the conventional western management paradigm. However, Deming argued that there are several diseases that afflict companies in the western world. The *"five deadly diseases"* noted by Deming include the following:

Table 1.4: Deming – Five Deadly Diseases

Disease	Description
Lack of Constancy of Purpose	Management is too focused on short term thinking rather than long-term improvements.
Emphasis on Short Term profit	A company should aim to become the world's most efficient provider of product/service. Profits will then follow.
Evaluation of performance	Deming is against annual performance appraisal and rating.
Mobility of Management	Mobility of management frequently has a negative impact on quality.
Excessive Measurement	Excessive management by measurement.

Comment (Deming):

Deming's program has been quite influential and has many sound points. His views on slogans in the workplace are in direct opposition to the use of slogans like Crosby's "Zero defects". The key point for Deming is that a slogan has no value unless there is a clear method to attain the particular goal described by the slogan.

1.4.3 Juran

Joseph Juran is another giant in the quality movement and he argues for a top down approach to quality. Juran defines quality as *"fitness for use"*, and argues that quality issues are the direct responsibility of management, and that management must ensure that quality is planned, controlled, and improved.

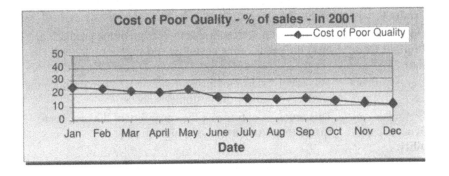

Figure 1.3: Cost of Poor Quality - % of Sales

The trilogy of quality planning, control, and improvement is known as the *"Juran Trilogy"*, and is usually described by a diagram with time on the horizontal axis and the cost of poor quality on the vertical axis (Fig. 1.3).

Quality planning consists of setting quality goals, developing plans, and identifying resources to meet the goals. Quality control consists of evaluating performance, setting new goals, and taking action. Quality improvement consists of improving delivery, eliminating wastage and improving customer satisfaction. The 10 step quality planning roadmap is in [Jur:51].

Table 1.5: Juran's Ten Step Programme

Step	Description
Identify Customers	This includes the internal and external customers of an organization, e.g., the testing group is the internal customer of the development group, and the end user of the software is the external customer.
Determine Customer Needs	Customer needs are generally expressed in the language of the customer's organization. There may be a difference between the real customer needs and the needs as initially expressed by the customer. Thus there is a need to elicit and express the actual desired requirements, via further communication with the customer, and thinking through the consequences of the current definition of the requirements.
Translate	This involves translating the customer needs into the language of the supplier.
Establish Units of Measurement	This involves defining the measurement units to be used.
Establish Measurement	This involves setting up a measurement program in the organization and includes internal and external measurements of quality and process performance.
Develop Product	This step determines the product features to meet the needs of the customer.
Optimize Product Design	The intention is to optimize the design of the product to meet the needs of the customer and supplier.
Develop Process	This involves developing processes which can produce the products to satisfy the customer's needs.
Optimize Process capability	This involves optimizing the capability of the process to ensure that products are of a high quality.
Transfer	This involves transferring the process to normal product development operations.

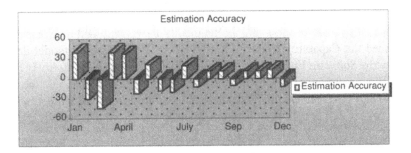

Figure 1.4: Estimation Accuracy - Breakthough and Control

Juran defines an approach to achieve a new quality performance level that is termed *"Breakthrough and Control"*. It is described pictorially by a control chart showing the old performance level with occasional spikes or random events; what is needed is a breakthrough to a new and more consistent quality performance, i.e., a new performance level and control in performance at that level.

The example in Fig. 1.4 presents the breakthrough in developing a more accurate estimation process, and initially the variation in estimation accuracy is quite large, but as breakthroughs and a better estimation process is put in place, the control limits are narrowed and more consistent estimation accuracy is achieved.

The breakthrough is achieved by a sustained and coordinated effort, and the old performance standard becomes obsolete. The difference between the old and the new performance level is known as the *"chronic disease"* which must be diagnosed and cured.

Juran's approach to breakthrough and control is summarized as follows:

Table 1.6: Juran's Ten Breakthrough and Control

Step	Description
Breakthrough in attitude	This involves developing a favorable attitude to quality improvement.
Pareto	This involves concentrating on the key areas affecting quality performance.
Organization	This involves analyzing the problem and coordinating a solution.
Control	This involves ensuring that performance is controlled at the new level.
Repeat	This leads to continuous improvement with new performance levels set and breakthroughs made to achieve the new performance levels.

1.4.4 Crosby

Philip Crosby is one of the giants in the quality movement, and his ideas have influenced the Capability Maturity Model (CMM), the maturity model developed by the Software Engineering Institute. His influential book *Quality is Free* [Crs:80] outlines his philosophy of doing things right the first time, i.e., the zero defects (ZD) program. Quality is defined as *"conformance to the requirements"*, and he argues that people have been conditioned to believe that error is inevitable.

Crosby argues that people in their personal lives do not accept this: for example, it would not be acceptable for nurses to drop a certain percentage of newly born babies. He further argues that the term *"Acceptable Quality Level"* (AQL) is a commitment to produce imperfect material. Crosby notes that defects are due to two main reasons: lack of knowledge or a lack of attention of the individual.

He argues that lack of knowledge can be measured and addressed by training, but that lack of attention is a mindset that requires a change of attitude by the individual. The net effect of a successful implementation of a zero defects program is higher productivity due to less reworking of defective products. Thus, quality, in effect, is free.

Crosby's approach to achieve the desired quality level of zero defects was to put a quality improvement program in place. He outlined a 14 step quality improvement program. The program requires the commitment of management to be successful and requires an organization-wide quality improvement team to be set up. A measurement program is put in place to determine the status and cost of quality within the organization. The cost of quality is then shared with the staff and corrective actions are identified and implemented. The zero defect program is communicated to the staff and one day every year is made a zero defects day, and is used to emphasize the importance of zero defects to the organization.

Table 1.7: Crosby's 14 Step Programme

Step	Description
Management Commitment	Management commitment and participation is essential to ensure the success of the quality improvement program. The profile of quality is raised within the organization.
Quality Improvement Team	This involves the formation of an organization-wide cross-functional team consisting of representatives from each of the departments. The representative will ensure that actions for each department are completed.
Quality Measurement	The objective of quality measurements is to determine the status of quality in each area of the company and to identify areas where improvements are required.

Table 1.7 (*continued*): Crosby's 14 Step Programme

Step	Description
Cost of Quality Evaluation	The cost of quality is an indication of the financial cost of quality to the organization. The cost is initially high, but as the quality improvement program is put in place and becomes effective there is a reduction in the cost of quality.
Quality Awareness	This involves sharing the cost of poor quality with the staff, and explaining what the quality problems are costing the organization. This helps to motivate staff on quality and on identifying corrective actions to address quality issues.
Corrective Action	This involves resolving any problems which have been identified, and bringing any problems which cannot be resolved to the attention of the management or supervisor level.
Zero Defect Program	The next step is to communicate the meaning of zero defects to the employees. The key point is that it is not a motivation program: instead, it means doing things right the first time, i.e., zero defects.
Supervisor Training	This requires that all supervisors and managers receive training on the 14 step quality improvement program.
Zero Defects Day	This involves setting aside one day each year to highlight zero defects, and its importance to the organization. Supervisors and managers will explain the importance of zero defects to the staff.
Goal Setting	This phase involves getting people to think in terms of goals and achieving the goals.
Error Cause Removal	This phase identifies any roadblocks or problems which prevent employees from performing error-free work. The list is produced from the list of problems or roadblocks for each employee.
Recognition	This involves recognizing employees who make outstanding contributions in meeting goals or quality improvement.
Quality Councils	This involves bringing quality professionals together on a regular basis to communicate with each other and to share ideas on action.
Do it over again	The principle of continuous improvement is a key part of quality improvement. Improvement does not end; it is continuous.

Crosby's Quality Management Maturity Grid measures the maturity of the current quality system with respect to various quality management categories, and highlights areas which require improvement. Six categories of quality management are considered: *management understanding and attitude towards quality, quality organization status, problem handling, the cost of quality, quality improvement actions and summation of company quality posture.*

Each category is rated on a 1 to 5 maturity scale and this indicates the maturity of the particular category. Crosby's maturity grid has been adapted and applied to the CMM. The five maturity ratings are:

Table 1.8: Crosby's Maturity Grid

Level	Name	Description
1.	Uncertainty:	Management has no understanding of quality, and is likely to blame quality problems on the quality department. Fire fighting is evident and problems are fought as they occur. Root causes of problems are not investigated. There are no organized quality improvement activities, no measurements of cost of quality, and inspections are rarely done.
2.	Awakening:	Management is beginning to recognize that quality management may be of value, but is unwilling to devote time and money to it. Instead, the emphasis is on appraisal rather than prevention. Teams are set up to address major problems, but long-term solutions are rarely sought.
3.	Enlightenment:	Management is learning more about quality from the quality improvement program, and is becoming more supportive of quality improvement. The quality department reports to senior management, and implementation of the 14 step quality improvement program is underway. There is a culture of openness where problems are faced openly and resolved in an orderly way.
4.	Wisdom:	Management is fully participating in the program, and fully understands the importance of quality management. All functions within the organization are open to suggestions for improvement, and problems are identified earlier. Defect prevention is now part of the culture.
5.	Certainty:	The whole organization is involved in continuous improvement

Comment (Crosby):

Crosby's program has been quite influential and his maturity grid has been applied in the software CMM. The ZD part of the program is difficult to apply to the complex world of software development, where the complexity of the systems to be developed are often the cause of defects rather than the mindset of software professionals who are dedicated to quality. Slogans may be dangerous and potentially unsuitable to some cultures and a zero defects day may potentially have the effect of de-motivating staff.

1.4.5 Miscellaneous Quality Gurus

There are other important figures in the quality movement including *Shingo* who developed his own version of zero defects termed *"Poka yoke"* or *defects = 0*. This involves identifying potential error sources in the process and monitoring these sources for errors. Causal analysis is performed on any errors found, and the root causes are eliminated. This approach leads to the elimination of all errors likely to occur, and thus only exceptional errors should occur. These exceptional errors and their causes are then eliminated. The failure mode and effects analysis (FMEA) methodology is a variant of this. Potential failures to the system or sub-system are identified and analyzed, and the causes and effects and probability of failure documented.

Genichi Taguchi's definition of quality is quite different. Quality is defined as *"the loss a product causes to society after being shipped, other than losses caused by its intrinsic function"*. Taguchi defines a loss function as a measure of the cost of quality; $L(x) = c(x-T)^2 + k$. Taguchi also developed a method for determining the optimum value of process variables which will minimize the variation in a process while keeping a process mean on target.

Kaoru Ishikawa is well known for his work in quality control circles (QCC). A quality control circle is a small group of employees who do similar work and arrange to meet regularly to identify and analyze work-related problems, to brainstorm, and to recommend and implement solutions. The problem solving uses tools such as pareto analysis, fishbone diagrams, histograms, scatter diagrams, and control charts. A facilitator will train the quality circle team leaders and a quality circle involves the following activities:

- Select problem
- State and re-state problem
- Collect facts
- Brain-storm
- Build on each others ideas
- Choose course of action
- Presentation

Armand Feigenbaum is well known for this work in total quality control which concerns quality assurance applied to all functions in the organization. It is distinct from total quality management: total quality control is concerned with controlling quality throughout, whereas TQM embodies a philosophy of quality management and improvement involving all staff and functions throughout the organization. Total quality management was discussed earlier.

1.5 Software Engineering

The pre-70s approach to software development has been described as the "Mongolian Hordes Approach" by Ince and Andrews [InA:91]. The "method" or lack of method is characterized by the following belief system:

> The completed code will always be full of defects.
> The coding should be finished quickly to correct these defects.
> Design as you code approach.

This is the *"wave the white flag approach"*, i.e., accepting defeat in software development, and suggests that irrespective of a scientific or engineering approach, the software will contain many defects, and that it makes sense to code quickly and to identify the defects to ensure that the defects can be corrected as soon as possible.

The motivation for software engineering came from what was termed the "software crisis", a crisis with software being delivered over budget and much later than its original delivery deadline, or not been delivered at all, or a product being delivered on time, but, with significant quality problems. The term "software engineering" arose out of a NATO conference held in Germany in 1968 to discuss the critical issues in software [Bux:75].

The NATO conference led to the birth of software engineering and to new theories and understanding of software development. software development has an associated lifecycle, for example, the waterfall model, which was developed by Royce [Roy:70], or the spiral lifecycle model, developed by Boehm [Boe:88]. These models detail the phases in the lifecycle for building a software product.

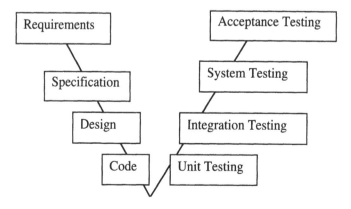

Figure 1.5: Waterfall Lifecycle Model

The waterfall model (Fig. 1.5) starts with requirements, followed by specification, design, implementation, and testing. It is typically used for projects where the requirements can be identified early in the project lifecycle or are known in advance. The waterfall model is also called the "V" life cycle model, with the left-hand side of the "V" detailing requirements, specification, design, and coding and the right-hand side detailing unit tests, integration tests, system tests and acceptance testing. Each phase has entry and exit criteria which must be satisfied before the next phase commences. There are many variations to the waterfall model.

The spiral model is another lifecycle model and is useful where the requirements are not fully known at project initiation, and where the evolution of the requirements is a part of the development lifecycle. The development proceeds in a number of spirals where each spiral typically involves updates to the requirements, design, code, testing, and a user review of the particular iteration or spiral.

The spiral is, in effect, a re-usable prototype and the customer examines the current iteration and provides feedback to the development team to be included in the next spiral. This approach is often used in joint application development for web-based software development. The approach is to partially implement the system. This leads to a better understanding of the requirements of the system and it then feeds into the next cycle in the spiral. The process repeats until the requirements and product are fully complete. There are several variations of the spiral model including the RAD / JAD models, DSDM models, etc. The spiral model is shown in Fig. 1.6.

There are other life-cycle models, for example, the iterative development process which combines the waterfall and spiral lifecycle model. The cleanroom approach to software development includes a phase for formal specification and its approach to testing is quite distinct from other models as it is based on the predicted usage of the software product.

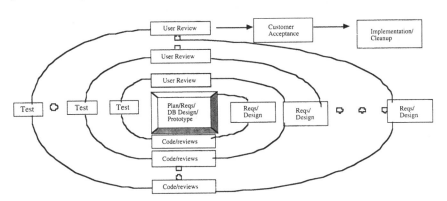

Figure 1.6: SPIRAL Lifecycle Model

The choice of a particular software development lifecycle is determined from the particular needs of the specific project. The phases of a typical lifecycle and software development project are described in the following sections.

1.5.1 Requirements Analysis

The requirements detail what the software system should do as distinct from how this is to be done. The requirements area is the foundation for the system. If the requirements are incorrect, then irrespective of the best programmers in the world the system will be incorrect. Prototyping may be employed to assist in the definition of the requirements, and the prototype may be thrown away after the prototyping phase is complete. In some cases the prototype will be kept and used as the foundation for the system. The prototype will include key parts of the system and is useful in determining the desired requirements of the system.

The proposed system will typically be composed of several sub-systems, and the system requirements are composed of sub-system requirements. The sub-system requirements are typically broken down into requirements for several features or services. The specification of the requirements needs to be unambiguous to ensure that all parties involved in the development of the system understand fully what is to be developed and tested. There are two categories of requirements: namely, functional requirements and non-functional requirements. The functional requirements are addressed via the algorithms, and non-functional requirements may include hardware or timing requirements.

The implications of the proposed set of requirements needs to be considered, as the choice of a particular requirement may affect the choice of another requirement. For example, one key problem in the telecommunications domain is the problem of feature interaction. The problem is that two features may work correctly in isolation, but when present together interact in an undesirable way. Feature interactions should be identified and investigated at the requirements phase to determine how the interaction should be resolved, and the problem of feature interaction is discussed again in chapter 7.

- Requirement Gathering
  This involves the collection of all relevant information for the creation of the product.
- Requirement Consolidation
  This involves the consolidation of the collected information into a coherent set of requirements.
- Requirement Validation
  This involves validation to ensure that the defined requirements are actually those desired by the customer.
- Technical Analysis
  This involves technical analysis to verify the feasibility of the product.

- Developer/Client Contract
  This involves a written contract between the client and the developer.

1.5.2 Specification

This phase of the lifecycle involves a detailed specification of the requirements of the product. The specification is written in a natural language, a modeling language such as UML [Rum:99] for specifying and visualizing the proposed system, or possibly a formal specification of the system using a formal specification language such as Z or *VDM*.

The specification is typically produced by the requirements group in the organization. A formal specification has the advantage that it is amenable to proof and mathematical analysis to debug the requirements and thus to provide increased confidence in the correctness and validity of the requirements. The advantages and disadvantages of a formal specification are discussed in chapter 7.

1.5.3 Design

Architectural Design

This involves a description of the architecture or structure of the product using flow charts, sequence diagrams, state charts, or a similar methodology.

Functional Design

This describes the algorithms and operations to implement the specification.

Object-oriented reuse

This sub-phase identifies existing objects that may be reused in the implementation.

Verification of Design

This involves verification to ensure that the design is valid with respect to the specification of the requirements. The verification may consist of a review of the design using a methodology similar to Fagan inspections. Formal methods may be employed for verification of the design and this involves a mathematical proof that the design is a valid refinement of the specification.

1.5.4 Implementation

This phase involves translating the design into the target implementation language. This involves writing or generating the actual code. The code is divided among a development team with each programmer responsible for one or more modules. The implementation may involve code reviews or walkthroughs to verify the correctness of the software with respect to the design, and to ensure that maintainability issues are addressed. The reviews generally include verification that coding standards are followed and verification that the implementation satisfies the software design.

The implementation may use software components either developed internally or commercial off-the-shelf software (COTS). There may be some risks from the COTS component as the supplier may decide to no longer support it, and an organization needs to consider the issues with the use of COTS before deciding to employ components. The issues with COTS are described in [Voa:90], and research into COTS is being conducted by international research groups such as the SEI and ESI.

The main benefits are increased productivity and a reduction in cycle time, and as long as the issues with respect to COTS can be effectively managed there is a good case for the use of COTS components.

1.5.5 Testing

Unit Test

Unit testing is performed by the programmer on the unit that has been completed, and prior to handover to an independent test group for verification. Tests are restricted to the particular unit and interaction with other units is not considered in this type of testing. Unit tests are typically written to prove that the code satisfies the design, and the test cases describe the purpose of the particular test. Code coverage and branch coverage give an indication of the effectiveness of the unit testing as it is desirable that the test cases execute as many lines of code as possible and that each branch of a condition is covered by a test case. The test results are executed and recorded by the developer and any defects are corrected prior to the handover to the test group. In some software development models, e.g., the cleanroom model, the emphasis is on the correctness of the design, and the use of unit testing is considered to be an unnecessary step in the lifecycle.

Integration Test

This type of testing is performed by the development team on the integrated system, and is performed after it has been demonstrated that the individual units all work correctly in isolation. The problem is that often units may work correctly in isolation but may fail when integrated with other modules. Consequently, the purpose of integration testing is to verify that the modules and their interfaces work correctly together and to resolve any integration issues.

Sub-system Test

This testing is performed in some organizations prior to system testing, and in large systems the objective is to verify that each large sub-system works correctly prior to the system test of the entire system. It is typically performed by a dedicated test group independent of the development group. The purpose of this testing is to verify the correctness of the sub-system with respect to the sub-system requirements, and to identify any areas requiring correction, and to verify that corrections to defects are fully resolved and preserve the integrity of the sub-system.

System Test

The purpose of this testing is to verify that the system requirements are satisfied, and it is usually carried out by an independent test group. The system test cases will need to be sufficient to verify that all of the requirements have been correctly implemented, and traceability of the requirements to the test cases will usually be employed. Any requirements which have been incorrectly implemented will be identified, and defects reported. The test group will verify that the corrections to the defects are valid and that the integrity of the system is maintained. The system testing may include security testing or performance testing also, or they may be separate phases where appropriate.

Performance Test

The purpose of this testing is to ensure the performance of the system is within the bounds specified in the requirements. This may include load performance testing, where the system is subjected to heavy loads over a long period of time (soak testing), and stress testing, where the system is subjected to heavy loads during a short time interval. This testing generally involves the simulation of many users using the system and measuring the various response times. Performance requirements may refer to the future growth or evolution of the system, and the performance of projected growth of the system will need to be measured also. Test tools are essential for performance testing as often, for example, soak performance testing will need to proceed for 24 to 48 hours, and automated tests are therefore required to run the test cases and record the test results.

Acceptance test

This testing is performed by a dedicated group with customer involvement in the testing. The objective is to verify that the product exhibits the correct functionality and fully satisfies the customer requirements, and that the customer is happy to accept the product. This testing is usually performed under controlled conditions at the customer site, and the testing therefore matches the real life behavior of the system. The customer is in a position to see the product in operation and to verify that its behavior and performance is as agreed and meets the customer requirements.

1.5.6 Maintenance

This phase continues after the release of the software product. The customer reports problems which require investigation by the development organization. These may include enhancements to the product or may consist of trivial or potentially serious defects which negatively impact the customer's business. The development community is required to identify the source of the defect and to correct and verify the correctness of the defect. Mature organizations will place emphasis on post mortem analysis to learn lessons from the defect and to ensure corrective action is taken to improve processes to prevent a repetition of the defect.

The activities are similar to those in the waterfall lifecycle model. The starting point is requirements analysis and specification, next is the design, followed by implementation and testing. Often, requirements may change at a late stage in a project in the software development cycle. This is often due to the fact that a customer is unclear as to what the exact requirements should be, and sometimes further desirable requirements only become apparent to the customer when the system is implemented. Consequently, the customer may identify several enhancements to the product once the implemented product has been provided. This highlights the need for prototyping to assist in the definition of the requirements and to assist the customer in requirements elicitation.

The emphasis on testing and maintenance suggests an acceptance that the software is unlikely to function correctly the first time, and that the emphasis on inspections and testing is to minimize the defects that will be detected by the customer. There seems to be a certain acceptance of defeat in current software engineering where the assumption is that defects will be discovered by the test department and customers, and that the goal of building a correct and reliable software product the first time is not achievable.

The approach to software correctness almost seems to be a "brute force" approach, where quality is achieved by testing and re-testing, until the testing group can say with confidence that all defects have been eliminated. Total quality management suggests that to have a good-quality product quality will need to be built into each step in the development of the product. The more effective the in-phase inspections of deliverables, including reviews of requirements, design and code, the higher the quality of the resulting implementation, with a corresponding reduction in the number of defects detected by the test groups.

There is an inherent assumption in the approach to quality management. The assumption is that formal inspections and testing are in some sense sufficient to demonstrate the correctness of the software. This assumption has been challenged by the eminent computer scientist E. Dijkstra who argued in [Dij:72] that

> "Testing a program demonstrates that it contains errors, never that it is correct."

The implication of this statement, if it is correct, is that irrespective of the amount of time spent on the testing of a program it can never be said with absolute confidence that it is correct, and, at best all that may be done is to employ statistical techniques as a measure of the confidence that the software is correct. Instead, Dijkstra and C.A.R Hoare argued that in order to produce correct software the programs ought to be derived from their specifications using mathematics, and that mathematical proof should be employed to demonstrate the correctness of the program with respect to its specification. The formal methods community have argued that the formal specification of the requirements and the step-wise refinement of the requirements to produce the implementation accompanied by mathematical verification of each refinement step offers a rigorous framework to develop programs adhering to the highest quality constraints.

Many mature organizations evaluate methods and tools, processes, and models regularly to determine their suitability for their business, and whether they may positively impact quality, cycle time, or productivity. Studies in the US and Europe have suggested that there are difficulties in scalability with formal methods and that some developers are uncomfortable with the mathematical notation. Formal methods may be employed for a part or all of the lifecycle and one approach to the deployment of formal methods in an organization is to adopt a phased approach to implementation.

An organization needs to consider an evaluation or pilot formal methods to determine whether there is any beneficial impact for its business. The safety-critical area is one domain to which formal methods have been successfully applied: for example, formal methods may be used to prove the presence of safety properties such as *"when a train is in a level crossing, then the gate is closed"*. In fact, limited testing may only be possible in some safety critical domains, hence the need for further quality assurance and confidence in the correctness of the software via simulation, or via mathematical proof of the presence or absence of certain desirable or undesirable properties for these domains. Formal methods is discussed in more detail in chapter 7.

Many software companies may consider one defect per thousand lines of code (KLOC) to be reasonable quality. However, if the system contains one million lines of code this is equivalent to a thousand post-release defects, which is unacceptable. Some mature organizations have a quality objective of three defects per million lines of code.

This goal is known as six sigma and is used as a quality objective by organizations such as Motorola. Six sigma (6σ) was originally applied by Motorola to its manufacturing businesses, and subsequently applied to the software businesses. The intention was to reduce the variability in manufacturing processes, and to therefore ensure that the manufacturing processes performed within strict quantitative process control limits. It has since been applied to software organizations outside of Motorola, and the challenge is to minimize and manage the variablity in software processes. There are six steps to six sigma:

- Identify the product (or service) you create.
- Identify your customer and your customer's requirements.
- Identify your needs to satisfy the customer.
- Define the process for doing the work.
- Mistake-proof the process and eliminate waste.
- Ensure continuous improvement by measuring, analyzing, and controlling the improved process.

Motorola was awarded the first Malcom Baldridge Quality award in 1988 for its commitment to quality as exhibited by the six sigma initiative.

One very important measure of quality is customer satisfaction with the company, and this feedback may be determined by defining an external customer satisfaction survey and requesting customers to provide feedback in this structured survey form. The information may be used to determine the overall level of customer satisfaction with the company and the loyalty of the customer to the company. It may also be employed to determine the perception of the customer of the quality and reliability of the product, the usability of the product, the ability of the company to correct defects in a timely manner, the perception of the testing capability of the organization, etc.

1.6 Modern Software Quality Management

The lifecycle for software development has been described earlier in this chapter, and the cost of correction of a defect increases the later that it is detected in the life cycle. Consequently, it is desirable to detect errors as early as possible and preferably within the phase in which it was created. This involves setting up a software quality infrastructure to assist in error detection within the phase in which the defect is created or at worst to detect the defect shortly after it exits the particular phase. The development of high quality software requires a good infrastructure for software development to be in place, and this includes best practices in software engineering for:

- Project planning and tracking, estimation processes.
- Risk management process.
- Software development lifecycles
- Quality assurance / management
- Software inspections
- Software testing
- Configuration management
- Customer satisfaction process
- Continuous improvement

Mature software organizations are learning organizations and there is an emphasis on learning from defects in order to improve software processes to more effectively prevent defects from occurring or to enhance defect detection techniques. One key part of the infrastructure to identify errors in the phase in which they are created is software inspections, and this is described in the next section.

1.6.1 Software Inspections

The Fagan Inspection Methodology was developed by Michael Fagan of IBM [Fag:76], and it is a seven-step process to identify and remove errors in work products, and to identify and remove systemic defects in the processes which lead to the defects in the work products. There is a strong economic case, as discussed previously, for identifying defects as early as possible, as the cost of correction of increases the later a defect is discovered in the lifecycle. The Fagan inspection proposes that requirement documents, design documents, source code, and test plans all be formally inspected by experts independent of the author of the deliverable, and the experts represent the different areas in software engineering.

There are various *roles* defined in the inspection process including the *moderator* who chairs the inspection. The moderator is highly skilled in the inspection process and is responsible for ensuring that all of the participants receive the appropriate materials for the inspection, and that sufficient preparation is done by all for the inspection. The moderator will ensure that any major or minor errors identified are recorded and that the speed of the inspection does not exceed the recommended guidelines. The *reader's* responsibility is to read or paraphrase the particular deliverable, and the *author* is the creator of the deliverable and has a special interest in ensuring that it is correct. The *tester* role is concerned with the test viewpoint.

The inspection process will consider whether a design is correct with respect to the requirements, and whether the source code is correct with respect to the design. There are seven stages in the inspection process and these are described in detail in chapter 2:

- Planning
- Overview
- Prepare
- Inspect
- Process improvement
- Re-work
- Follow-up

The errors identified in an inspection are classified into various types as defined by the Fagan methodology. There are other classification schemes of defect types including the scheme defined by orthogonal defect classification (ODC). A mature organization will record the inspection data in a database and this will enable analysis to be performed on the most common types of errors. The analysis will yield actions to be performed to minimize the re-occurrence of the most common defect types. Also, the data will enable the effectiveness of the organization in identifying errors in phase and detecting defects out of phase to be determined and enhanced. Software inspections are described in more detail in chapter 2.

1.6.2 Software Testing

Software testing has been described earlier in this chapter and two key types of software testing are black box and white box testing. White box testing involves checking that every path in a module has been tested and involves defining and executing test cases to ensure code and branch coverage. The objective of black box testing is to verify the functionality of a module or feature or the complete system itself. Testing is both a constructive activity in that it is verifying the correctness of functionality, and it may be a destructive activity in that the objective is to find defects in the implementation of the defined functionality. The requirements are verified and the testing yields the presence or absence of defects.

The various types of testing have been discussed previously and these typically include test cases which are reviewed by independent experts to ensure that they are sufficient to verify the correctness of the software. There may also be a need for usability type testing, i.e., the product should be easy to use with respect to some usability model. One such model is SUMI developed by Jurek Kirakowski [Kir:00]. The testing performed in the cleanroom approach is based on a statistical analysis of the predicted usage of the system, and the emphasis is on detecting the defects that the customer is most likely to encounter in daily operations of the system. The cleanroom approach also provides a certificate of reliability based on the mean time between failure.

The effectiveness of the testing is influenced by the maturity of the test process in the organization. Testing is described in the software product engineering key process area on the CMM. Statistics are typically maintained to determine the effectiveness of the testing process and metrics are maintained, e.g., the number of defects in the product, the number of defects detected in the testing phase, the number of defects determined post testing phase, the time period between failure, etc. Testing is described in more detail in chapter 2.

1.6.3 Software Quality Assurance

The IEEE definition of software quality assurance is "the planned and systematic pattern of all actions necessary to provide adequate confidence that the software performs to established technical requirements" [MaCo:96]. The software quality assurance department provides visibility into the quality of the work products being built, and the processes being used to create them. The quality assurance group may be just one person operating part time or it may be a team of quality engineers. The activities of the quality assurance group typically include software testing activities to verify the correctness of the software, and also quality audits of the various groups involved in software development. The testing activities have been discussed previously, and the focus here is to discuss the role of an independent quality assurance group.

The quality group promotes quality in the organization and is independent of the development group. It provides an independent assessment of the quality of the product being built, and this viewpoint is quite independent of the project manager and development viewpoint. The quality assurance group will act as the voice of the customer and will ensure that quality is carefully considered at each development step.

The quality group will perform audits of various projects, groups and departments and will identify any deficiencies in processes and non-compliance to the defined process. The quality group will usually have a reporting channel to senior management, and any non-compliance issues which are not addressed at the project level are escalated to senior management for resolution. Software quality assurance is a level 2 key process area on the Capability Maturity Model (CMM). The key responsibilities of the quality assurance group are summarized as follows:

- Independent reporting to senior management
- Customer Advocate
- Visibility to Management
- Audits to verify Compliance
- Promote Quality awareness
- Promote process improvement
- Release sign-offs

The quality audit provides visibility into the work products and processes used to develop the work products. The audit consists of an interview with several members of the project team, and the auditor interviews the team, determines the role and responsibilities of each member, considers any issues which have arisen during the work, and assesses if there are any quality risks associated with the project based on the information provided from team members.

The auditor requires good written and verbal communication skills, and will need to gather data via open and closed questions. The auditor will need to observe behavior and body language and be able to deal effectively with any potential conflicts. The auditor will gather data with respect to each participant and the role that the participant is performing, and relates this to the defined process for their area. The entry and exit criteria to the defined processes are generally examined to verify that the criteria has been satisfied at the various milestones. The auditor writes a report detailing the findings from the audit and the recommended corrective actions with respect to any identified non-compliance to the defined procedures. The auditor will perform follow-up activity at a later stage to verify that the corrective actions have been carried out by the actionees. The audit activities include planning activities, the audit meeting, gathering data, reporting the findings and assigning actions, and following the actions through to closure. The audit process is described in more detail in chapter 3.

1.6.4 Problem Solving

There is a relationship between the quality of the process and the quality of the products built from the process. The defects identified during testing are very valuable in that they enable the organization to learn and improve from the defect. Defects are typically caused by a mis-execution of a process or a defect in the process. Consequently, the lessons learned from a particular defect should be used to correct systemic defects in the process.

Problem-solving teams are formed to analyze various problems and to identify corrective actions. The approach is basically to agree on the problem to be solved, to collect and analyze the facts, and to choose an appropriate course of action to resolve the problem. There are various tools to assist problem solving and these include fishbone diagrams, histograms, trend charts, pareto diagrams, and bar charts. Problem solving is described in detail in chapter 6.

Fishbone Diagrams

This is the well-known cause-and-effect diagram and is in the shape of the backbone of a fish. The approach is to identify the causes of some particular quality effect. These may include people, materials, methods, and timing. Each of the main causes may then be broken down into sub-causes. The root cause is then identified, as often 80% of problems are due to 20% of causes (the 80:20 rule).

Histograms

A histogram is a way of representing data via a frequency distribution in a bar chart format and displays data spread over a period of time, and illustrating the shape, variation, and centering of the underlying distribution. The data is divided into a number of buckets where a bucket is a particular range of data values, and the relative frequency of each bucket is displayed in bar format. The shape of the process and its spread from the mean is evident from the histogram.

Pareto Chart

The objective of a pareto chart is to identify the key problems and to focus on these. Problems are classified into various types or categories, and the frequency of each category of problem is then determined. The chart is displayed in a descending sequence of frequency, with the most significant category detailed first, and the least significant category detailed last. The success in problem-solving activities over a period of time may be judged from the old and new pareto chart, and if problem solving is successful, then the key problem categories in the old chart should show a noticeable improvement in the new pareto chart.

Trend Graph

A trend graph is a graph of a variable over time and is a study of observed data for trends or patterns over time.

Scatter Graphs

The scatter diagram is used to measure the relationship between variables, and to determine whether there is a correlation between the variables. The results may be a positive correlation, negative correlation or no correlation between the data. The scatter diagram provides a means to confirm a hypothesis that two variables are related, and provides a visual means to illustrate the potential relationship.

Failure Mode Effect Analysis

This involves identifying all of the modes of failures of the system and the impact or effect of such a failure. It involves documenting in each case the possible failure mode, the effect of failure, the cause of failure, the frequency of occurrence, its severity, the estimate of detection of the failure, the risk and corrective action to minimize the risk. FMEAs are usually applied at the design stage.

The problem solving techniques discussed here are tools for the teams to analyze and identify corrective actions. Problem-solving teams may be formed to solve a particular problem and may dissolve upon successful problem resolution.

1.6.5 Modeling

The world is dominated by models: for example, models of weather systems as used by meteorologists, models of the economy as used by Economists: models of population growth: and models of the solar system, for example, the Ptolemaic model and the Copernican model of the solar system. Modeling can play a key role in computer science, as computer systems tend to be highly complex, whereas a model allows simplification or abstraction of the underlying complexity, and enables a richer understanding of the underlying reality to be gained.

There may be more than one model of a particular entity, for example, the Ptolemaic model and the Copernican model are different models of the solar system. This leads to the question as to which is the best or most appropriate model to use, and to what criteria should be employed to determine whether a model is good. The choice is generally influenced by the ability of the model to explain the behavior, its simplicity, and its elegance.

The importance of models is that they serve to explain the behavior of a particular entity and may also be used to predict future behavior in other cases. Different models may differ in their ability to explain aspects of the entity under study. Some models are good at explaining some parts of the behavior, other models are good at explaining other aspects. The adequacy of a model is a key concept in modeling, and the adequacy is determined by the effectiveness of the model in representing the underlying behavior, and its ability to predict future behavior. Model exploration consists of asking questions, and determining whether the model is able to give an effective answer to the particular question. A good model is chosen as a representation of the real world, and is referred to whenever there are questions in relation to the aspect of the real world.

The model is a simplification or abstraction of the real world and will contain only the essential details. For example, the model of an aircraft is hardly likely to include the color of the aircraft and instead the objective may be to model the aerodynamics of the aircraft. The principle of 'Ockham's Razor' is used extensively in modeling and in model simplification. The objective is to choose only those entities in the model which are absolutely necessary to explain the behavior of the world.

The software domain has applied models of software development to assist with the complexities in software development, and these include the software maturity models such as the Capability Maturity Model (CMM), which is employed as a framework to enhance the capability of the organization in software development, to modeling requirements with graphical notations such as UML, or mathematical models derived from formal specifications.

1.6.6 Cost of Quality

Crosby argues that the most meaningful measurement of quality is the cost of quality, and the emphasis on the improvement activities in the organization is therefore to reduce the cost of poor quality (COPQ). The cost of quality includes the cost of external and internal failure, the cost of providing an infrastructure to prevent the occurrence of problems and an infrastructure to verify the correctness of the product. The cost of quality was divided into the following four subcategories by A.V. Feigenbaum in the 1950s, and evolved further by James Harrington of IBM.

Table 1.9: Cost of Quality Categories

Type of Cost	Description
Cost External	This includes the cost of external failure and includes engineering repair, warranties, and a customer support function.
Cost Internal	This includes the internal failure cost and includes the cost of reworking and re-testing of any defects found internally.
Cost Prevention	This includes the cost of maintaining a quality system to prevent the occurrence of problems, and includes the cost of software quality assurance, the cost of training, etc.
Cost Appraisal	This includes the cost of verifying the conformance of a product to the requirements and includes the cost of provision of software inspections and testing processes.

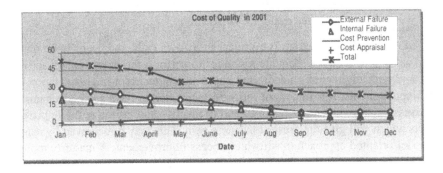

Figure 1.7: Cost of Quality

The cost of quality graph (Fig. 1.7) will initially show high external and internal costs and very low prevention costs, however, the total quality costs will be high. However, as an effective quality system is put in place and becomes fully operational there will be a noticeable decrease in the external and internal cost of quality and a gradual increase in the cost of prevention and appraisal. The total cost of quality will substantially decrease, as the cost of provision of the quality system is substantially below the savings gained from lower cost of internal and external failure. The COPQ curve will indicate where the organization is in relation to the cost of poor quality, and the organization will need to derive a plan to achieve the desired results to minimize the cost of poor quality.

1.6.7 Process Improvement

Software process improvement (SPI) offers an effective means of improving the capability of an organization in delivering high-quality software on time consistently and in reducing the cost of quality in an organization. The implementation of process improvements is achieved by launching an improvement program in the organization [Mag:00, Pri:00], and this typically involves:

- Management awareness of benefits of SPI.
- Formation of an improvement team.
- Alignment of SPI goals to business goals.
- Assessment of current strengths/weaknesses of organization.
- Improvement plan.
- Improvement suggestions from staff.
- Customer satisfaction feedback.
- Improvements identified during an audit.
- Project post mortem recommendations.
- Measuring improvement
  - Enhanced project cycle time, quality, productivity
  - Increased customer satisfaction

An improvement program is a project in its own right and needs to be managed as such. It requires adequate resources to perform the improvement activities, and typically requires a dedicated improvement team for implementation of the improvements. It is important for the organization to have some mechanism to assess its current state of maturity and to identify and prioritize the improvements which will give the greatest business gain. This may be achieved by using a model-oriented approach to software process improvement. A maturity model provides a set of best practices in software engineering and an internal or external assessment of the organization against the model will yield the current strengths and weaknesses of the organization with respect to the model.

Suggestions for improvement may come from various sources, including feedback from customer satisfaction surveys, the lessons learned from the various project post mortems, issues noted during independent quality audits, and suggestions for improvement made by the employees of the company.

The employees of the company are, in effect, the owners of the process infrastructure within the organization, as they work with the processes and procedures on a daily basis, and have an interest in having the best possible processes and templates for the organization. A good improvement program will empower employees to make suggestions for continuous improvement, and a reward and recognition mechanism helps to make process improvement part of the organization culture.

The improvement plan typically has a long-term focus and a short-term focus. The long-term plan includes activities to achieve particular improvement goals over a longer term period, i.e., typically one to two years. The short-term plan typically includes activities to be performed over a three to six-month period and represents a detailed plan for an individual phase of the improvement program.

There may come a stage where decreasing returns come from improvement activities, and the cost benefit analysis of improvement activities needs to be considered. The appropriate time to be spent on improvement activities varies depending on organization size, the nature of its business, and the current maturity of the organization.

Improvement tends to be most successful when performed in small steps rather than trying to do too much initially. It is generally easier for an organization to adjust to a series of small changes rather than one big major change. Changes within an organization need to be carefully planned and controlled. Training for the existing employees may be required to ensure that they fully understand the rationale for the proposed changes and are in a position to implement the proposed changes in the organization.

1.6.8 Metrics

The use of measurement is an integral part of science and engineering disciplines and is gradually being applied to software engineering. The term "*software metric*" was coined by Tom Gilb in his influential book on software measurement [Glb:76]. The purpose of measurements in software engineering is to provide visibility and an objective indication of the effectiveness of the organization in achieving its key goals and objectives.

There is, of course, no point in measuring for the sake of measuring itself and care is required to ensure that the measurements to be made are closely related to the particular goal. The well-known approach of Goal, Question, Metric (GQM) suggests that the organization first needs to identify the key goals which it is trying to achieve; then it identifies relevant questions which need to be answered to assess the extent to which the goal is being satisfied, and then to formulate a metric to give an objective answer to the particular question. This approach was formulated by Victor Basilli and is described in [Bas:88].

The use of measurement is invaluable in determining whether an organization has actually improved, as actual quantitative data before and after the improvement initiative can be compared and used to determine the extent of the improvements. The initial measurements prior to the improvement program serves as a baseline measurement. The baseline measurement gives a precise indication of the actual ability of the organization and the results achieved by the organization. A successful improvement programs will lead to improvements within the organization, and this will be reflected in the metrics.

- Business goals
- Questions related to goals
- Metrics

- Data gathering
- Presentation of charts
- Trends
- Action plans

Software metrics are discussed in chapter 6, and sample metrics for the various functional areas in the organization are included. The metrics are only as good as the underlying data, and data gathering is a key part of a metrics program.

1.6.9 Customer Satisfaction

The effectiveness of the quality management system in the organization will ultimately be judged by the customer. The extent to which the organization has been successful in delivering high-quality products will influence the level of customer satisfaction and ultimately the decision by the customer to re-purchase again from the company or to recommend the company. Consumer research and customer satisfaction surveys are an important part of determining the level of customer satisfaction with the company.

The customer is requested to rate the organization in several key areas such as the quality of the software, its reliability, the timeliness of the project, and so on. The customer satisfaction process takes the form of a closed feedback loop, and an organization dedicated to customer satisfaction will analyze and act appropriately on the feedback received.

The approach is to survey, prepare and execute an action plan, and survey again. A simple customer satisfaction process is described in graphical format below (Fig. 1.8):

The customer surveys are analyzed and where appropriate follow-up activity takes place. This may involve a telephone conversation with the customer or a visit to the particular customer to discuss the specific issues. The issues are shared with engineering groups as appropriate. The objective is to ensure that

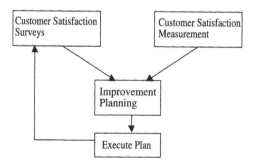

Figure 1.8: Customer Satisfaction Process

customers are totally satisfied with the product and service and to develop loyalty in customers. A loyal customer will re-purchase and recommend the company to other potential customers. The customer satisfaction process is summarized as follows:

- Define customer surveys
- Send customer surveys
- Analysis and ratings
- Customer meeting and key issues
- Action plans and follow-up
- Metrics for customer satisfaction

The definition of a customer satisfaction survey is dependent on the nature of the business; however, the important thing is that the questionnaire employed in the survey is usable and covers the questions that will enable the organization to identify areas in which it is weak and in need of improvement, and also to identify areas where it is strong. The questions typically employ a rating scheme to allow the customer to give quantitative feedback on satisfaction, and the survey will also enable the customer to go into more detail on issues.

Software companies will be interested in the customer's perception of the quality of software, reliability, usability, timeliness of delivery, value for money, etc., and a sample customer satisfaction survey form is included in Table 1.10.

Table 1.10 includes 10 key questions and may be expanded to include other relevant questions that the organization wishes to measure its performance on. The survey form will typically include open-ended questions to enable the customer to describe in more detail areas where the organization performed well, and areas where the customer is unhappy with the performance.

Customer satisfaction metrics provide visibility into the level of customer satisfaction with the software company. The objective of the software company is to provide a very high level of customer satisfaction, and the feedback from the customer satisfaction surveys provide an indication of the level of customer satisfaction. Metrics are produced to provide visibility into the customer satisfaction feedback and to identify trends in the customer satisfaction measurements.

A sample customer satisfaction metric is included in Figure 1.9, and the metric is derived from the data collected in Table 1.10. The metric provides a quantitative understanding of the level of customer satisfaction with the company, and the company will need to analyze the measurements for trends. Customer satisfaction is discussed again in chapter 3 as it is an important part of ISO 9000:2000.

Table 1.10: Sample Customer Satisfaction Questionnaire

No	Criteria /Question	Unacceptable	Poor	Fair	Satisfied	Excellent	N/A
1.	Quality of software	❑	❑	❑	❑	❑	❑
2.	Ability to meet committed dates	❑	❑	❑	❑	❑	❑
3.	Timeliness of projects	❑	❑	❑	❑	❑	❑
4.	Effective testing of software	❑	❑	❑	❑	❑	❑
5.	Expertise of staff	❑	❑	❑	❑	❑	❑
6.	Value for money	❑	❑	❑	❑	❑	❑
7.	Quality of support	❑	❑	❑	❑	❑	❑
8.	Ease of installation of software	❑	❑	❑	❑	❑	❑
9.	Ease of use	❑	❑	❑	❑	❑	❑
10.	Timely resolution of problems	❑	❑	❑	❑	❑	❑

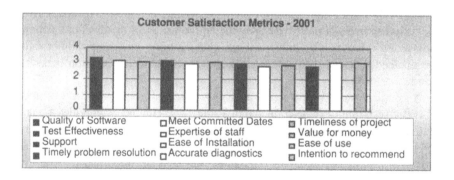

Figure 1.9: Customer Satisfaction Metrics

1.6.10 Assessments

The objective of an assessment is to rate an organization with respect to a standard or model. This may include assessing the maturity of the organization with respect to a maturity model such as the CMM or SPICE, or an assessment of the organization with respect to an international quality standard such as ISO 9000:2000.

Many organizations aspire to excellence and the assessment against some maturity or excellence model yields strengths and weaknesses of the organization. The assessment may be performed by an external assessment team or by a trained internal assessment team. The assessment team typically interviews project managers, software developers, senior management, etc., and there is a detailed review of project documentation. The result of an assessment includes an assessment report which details the strengths and weaknesses of the organization with respect to the particular model.

The organization then uses the assessment report to plan and prioritize future improvements. The assessment needs to be carefully planned, and the assessment team needs to have sufficient expertise and experience to objectively rate the organization. The assessment is a major review of the organization and is typically one to two weeks in duration. The assessment team publishes a plan and schedule of the activities to be performed during the assessments, and these typically involve a kick-off meeting, interviews with project managers, software developers, the quality and testing personnel, reviews of documentation, presentation of preliminary findings, presentation of final findings, and a written assessment report. The assessment will determine the extent to which the organization relates to the model or international standard, and any gaps will be noted as potential improvement opportunities.

The IDEAL model [Pet:95] is a model for continuous improvement, and it includes a diagnosing phase, in which a CMM assessment is employed. The CMM based appraisal for internal process improvement (CBA IPI) is described in [Dun:96]. Each key process area (KPA) within the scope of the assessment is rated, and the findings for each KPA are presented. The emphasis is on continuous improvement and the findings of the assessment are used to generate further improvement plans. Assessments with ISO 9000, CMM and SPICE are described in chapters 3 through 5.

1.6.11 Total Quality Management

Total quality management (TQM) is a management philosophy to focus attention on quality and to develop a culture of quality within the organization. Quality is addressed company-wide and the organization goal is total customer satisfaction. The objective is to ensure that the organization delivers products and services that totally satisfy the customer needs. It is a holistic approach and it applies to all levels and functions within the organization.

TQM employs many of the ideas of the famous names in the quality movement, including Deming, Juran, and Crosby and follows the culture and attitude of delivering what is promised. Senior management are required to take charge of the implementation of quality management, and all staff will need to be trained in quality management and to take part in quality improvement activities. Quality improvement is continuous.

There are four main parts of TQM (Table 1.11)

The implementation of TQM involves a focus on all areas within the organization, and in identifying areas for improvement. The problems in the particular area are evaluated and data is collected and analyzed. An action plan is then derived and the actions implemented and monitored. This is then repeated for continuous improvement. The implementation is summarized as follows:

- Identify improvement area
- Problem evaluation
- Data collection
- Data analysis
- Action plan
- Implementation of actions
- Monitor effectiveness
- Repeat

Table 1.11: Total Quality Management

Part	Description
Customer Focus	This involves identifying internal and external customers and recognizing that all customers have expectations and rights which need to be satisfied first time and every time. Quality must be considered in every aspect of the business, and the focus is on fire prevention.
Process	This involves a focus on the process and improvement to the process via problem solving. The improvements will reduce waste and eliminate error.
Measurement and Analysis	This involves setting up a measurement program within the organization to enable objective and effective analysis of the quality of the process and product.
Human Factors	This involves developing a culture of quality and customer satisfaction throughout the organization. The core values of quality and customer satisfaction need to be instilled in the organization. This requires training for the employees on quality, customer satisfaction, and continuous improvement.

The ISO 9000 standard is a structured approach to the implementation of TQM. Its clauses are guidelines for what needs to be done, and include requirements to be satisfied for the organization to satisfy TQM and ISO 9000.

1.7 Miscellaneous

Software quality management is, in essence, according to this author, the application of common sense to software engineering. Clearly, it is sensible to plan and track a project, identify potential risks early and attempt to eliminate or reduce their impact, determine the requirements, produce a design, obtain feedback from customers and peers for planning, requirements, design, and implementation of the software. It is sensible to test the software against the requirements, to record any problems identified, and to correct them. It is sensible to have objective criteria to determine if the software is ready to be released to the customer, and sensible to have a post-mortem at the end of a project to determine the lessons learned from the project and to do things slightly differently the next time for improvement, and to survey customers to obtain valuable feedback.

1.7.1 The Future of Software Quality

Quality will continue to be fundamental to the success of the company. There will be an increased focus on achieving approved quality systems such as ISO 9000. Many companies are ISO 9000 certified or have ambitious improvement programs in place to achieve the maturity levels of the CMM or other maturity models. Customer expectations are increasing all the time, and in the future it is likely that software companies will need to have a minimal quality standard such as ISO 9000 or CMM level 3 to be taken seriously by potential customers.

The cost of poor quality is currently measured in mature companies. It is likely to be measured in most software companies in the future as driving down the cost of poor quality will become a key goal for most organizations as it will improve the profitability and long-term survival of the organization.

Software components and the verification of software components will become increasingly important, as companies speed up development and thereby shortening the time to market, which is a key driver of most companies. However, software organizations will need to have confidence in the correctness of the components, and there may be an independent certification body in the future to verify that components are correct.

1.7.2 Organization Culture and Change

Every organization has a distinct culture and this reflects the way in which things are done in the organization. Organization culture includes the ethos of the organization, the core values that the organization has, the history of the organization, its success stories, its people, amusing incidents, and many more. The culture of the organization may be favorable or unfavorable to developing high-quality software.

Occasionally, where the culture is such that it is a serious impediment to the development of a high-quality software product, changes may be required to the organization's culture. This may be difficult as it may involve changing core values or changing in a fundamental way the approach to software development, and this is subject to organization psychology, which often manifests as a resistance to change from within an organization. Successful change management, i.e., the successful implementation of a change to the organization culture, will typically involve the following:

- Plan implementation
- Kick-off meeting
- Motivate changes
- Display plan
- Training
- Implement changes
- Monitor implementation
- Institutionalize

The culture of an organization is often illustrated by the well-known phrase of its staff: *"That's the way we do things around here"*. For example, the evolution from one level of the CMM to another often involves a change in organization culture, for example, a software quality assurance process at level 2, and a peer review process at level 3. The focus on prevention requires a change in mindset within the organization to focus on problem solving and problem prevention, rather than on fire fighting.

1.7.3 Law of Negligence

The impact of a flaw in software may be catastrophic, and several infamous software failures in the history of software development have been discussed earlier in this chapter. Clearly, every organization must take all reasonable precautions to prevent the occurrence of defects, especially in the safety critical domain where defects may cause major damage or even loss of life. Reasonable precautions generally consist of having appropriate software engineering practices in place to allow the organization to consistently produce high quality software.

A quality management system is an indication that the organization is taking its duty in providing high quality software seriously. The objective of the quality management system is to put a sound software development process in place that serves the needs of the organization and its customers. Modern quality assurance systems include processes for software inspections, testing, quality audits, customer satisfaction, software development, project planning, etc.

The organization will require evidence or records to prove that the quality management system is in place, that it is appropriate for the organization, and that it is fully operational within the organization. The proof that the quality system is actually operational typically takes the form of records of the various activities. The records also enable the organization to prepare a legal defense to show that it took all reasonable precautions in software development, especially if a customer decides to take legal action for negligence against the software provider following a serious problem in the software at the customer environment.

The presence of records may be used to indicate that all reasonable steps were taken, and the records typically include lists of all the deliverables in the project; minutes of project meetings; records of reviews of requirements, design, and software code, records of test plans and test results; and so on.

1.7.4 Formal Methods

Spivey (cf. chapter 1 of [Spi:92]) describes "formal specifications" as the use of mathematical notation to describe in a precise way the properties which an information system must have, without unduly constraining the way in which these properties are achieved. The formal specification describes *what* the system must do, as distinct from saying *how* it is to be done. This abstraction away from implementation enables questions about what the system does to be answered, independently of the implementation, i.e., the detailed code. Furthermore the unambiguous nature of mathematical notation avoids the problem of speculation about the meaning of phrases in an imprecisely worded natural language description of a system.

The formal specification thus becomes the key reference point for the different parties concerned with the construction of the system. This includes determining customer needs, program implementation, testing of results, and program documentation. It follows that the formal specification is a valuable means of promoting a common understanding for all those concerned with the system.

The term "formal methods" is used to describe a formal specification language and a method for the design and implementation of computer systems. The specification is written in a mathematical language, and this ensures that the problem of ambiguity inherent in a natural language specifications is avoided, owing to the precision of mathematics. The derivation of an implementation from the specification may be achieved via step-wise refinement. Each refinement step makes the specification more concrete and closer to the actual implementation. There is an associated proof obligation that the refinement be valid, and that the concrete state preserves the properties of the more abstract state. Thus, assuming the original specification is correct and the proofs of correctness of each refinement step are valid, then there is a very high degree of confidence in the correctness of the implemented software.

Requirements is the foundation stone from which the system is built and the objective of requirements validation is to confirm that the requirements are correct and are actually those required by the customer. Formal methods may be employed to model the requirements and model exploration yields further desirable or undesirable properties. These properties are consequences of the definition of the requirements, and, where appropriate, the requirements are amended. Thus formal methods may be employed, in a sense, to debug the proposed requirements.

The main advantage of formal methods is that the mathematical models are useful for studying properties of the system, and the use of formal methods generally leads to more robust software, leading to increased confidence in the software. The challenges involved in the deployment of formal methods in an organization include the education of staff in formal specification, as formal specification may be a culture shock to many staff.

Formal methods have been applied to a diverse range of applications, including circuit design, artificial intelligence, specification of standards, specification and verification of programs, etc. Formal methods and a selection of state of the art formal methodologies are described in more detail in chapter 7.

1.7.5 Quality and the WEB

The explosive growth of the world wide web and electronic commerce in recent years has made quality of web sites a key concern for any organization which conducts part or all of its business on the world wide wed. software development for the web is a relatively new technology area, and the web is rapidly becoming ubiquitous in society. A web site is quite distinct from other software systems in that:

- It may be accessed from anywhere in the world.
- It may be accessed by many different browsers.
- The usability and look and feel of the application is a key concern.
- The performance of the web site is a key concern.
- Security is a key concern.
- The web site must be capable of dealing with a large number of transactions at any time.
- The web site has very strict availability constraints (typically 24x365 availability).
- The web site needs to be highly reliable.

Typically, a specific web development software lifecycle is employed for web development. Rapid Application Development (RAD) or Joint Application Development (JAD) lifecycle is employed, and the lifecycle is spiral. That is, there is an acceptance that the requirements will not be fully defined at project initiation and that the requirements will evolve to the final agreed set. It is therefore generally inappropriate to employ the waterfall lifecycle for this domain. Testing issues for web sites is considered in chapter 2.

1.8 Structure of This Book

Chapter 2 describes software inspections and testing. Software inspections are a key approach to defect detection and prevention. Software testing provides confidence in the fitness for use of the software and indicates the risks associated with the release of the software product based on the testing performed. Various types of testing are discussed as well as testing in an e-commerce environment.

Chapter 3 describes the ISO 9000 standard, which is a quality standard for software, manufacturing, and service companies. An ISO 9000 certified quality system has certain minimal practices in place, and places emphasis on customer satisfaction and quality improvement. This chapter includes guidelines on implementing ISO 9000:2000.

Chapter 4 describes the Capability Maturity Model which was developed by the software Engineering Institute at Carnegie Mellon University in Pittsburgh, USA. The CMM is a framework for improvement, and advocates step wise improvement. The architecture of the CMM is described and guidelines for the implementation of the CMM are provided. The CMM was originally written for the Department of Defense (DOD) in the US, and the terminology reflects this domain. This means that companies need to interpret and tailor the CMM for their organization. This chapter includes a section on the new CMMI model, and this model is SPICE compatible and combines the software CMM and the systems CMM.

Chapter 5 describes SPICE, the emerging standard for software process assessment, and provides guidance on implementation. SPICE is a framework for process assessment and improvement but differs from the CMM in that it allows the organization to focus on improvements in selected process areas, rather than focusing on the step-wise improvement approach adopted by the CMM. However, the SEI has released a SPICE compatible version in July 2000, and the two models are expected to coexist harmoniously.

Chapter 6 describes metrics and describes how metrics may be used for problem solving. Guidelines are presented for setting up a metrics program including data gathering, data analysis, and action plans. This chapter describes various tools used in problem solving, including histograms, trend plots, pareto charts, scatter graphs, etc.

Chapter 7 describes formal methods and design and includes advanced topics such as software configuration management, the unified modeling language (UML), software usability, and formal methods.

2
Software Inspections and Testing

Software inspections play a key role in building quality into a software product, and testing plays a key role in verifying that the software is correct and corresponds to the requirements. The objective of inspections is to build quality into the software product as there is clear evidence that the cost of correction of a defect increases the later in the development cycle in which the defect is detected. Consequently, there is an economic argument to employing software inspections as there are cost savings in investing in quality up front rather than adding quality later in the cycle. The purpose of testing is to verify that quality has been built into the product, and in a mature software company the majority of defects (e.g., 80%) will be detected by software inspections with the remainder detected by the various forms of testing conducted in the organization.

There are several approaches to software inspections, and the degree of formality employed in an inspection varies with the particular method adopted. The simplest and most informal approach consists of a walkthrough of the document or code by an individual other than the author. The informal walkthrough generally consists of a meeting of two people, namely, the author and a reviewer. The meeting is informal and usually takes place at the author's desk or in a meeting room, and the reviewer and author discuss the document or code, and the deliverable is reviewed informally.

There are very formal software inspection methodologies and these include the well-known Fagan inspection methodology [Fag:76] and the Gilb methodology [Glb:94], and these typically include pre-inspection activity, an inspection meeting, and post-inspection activity. Several inspection roles are typically employed, including an author role, an inspector role, a tester role, and a moderator role. The Fagan inspection methodology was developed by Michael Fagan of IBM, and the Gilb methodology was developed by Tom Gilb. The formality of the inspection methodology used by an organization is dependent on the type of organization and its particular business. For example, telecommunications companies tend to employ a very formal inspection process, as it is possible for a one-line software change to create a major telecommunications outage. Consequently, a telecommunications company needs to assure the quality of its software, and a key part of building the quality in is the use of software inspections. The organization needs to devise an inspection process which is suitable for its particular needs.

The quality of the delivered software product is only as good as the quality at the end each particular phase. Consequently, it is desirable to exit the phase only when quality has been assured in the particular phase. Software inspections assist in assuring that quality has been built into each phase, and thus assuring that the quality of the delivered product is good. Software testing verifies the correctness of the software. Customer satisfaction is influenced by the quality of the software and its timely delivery.

2.1 Overview Fagan Inspections

The Fagan methodology is a well known software inspection methodology. It is a seven-step process, including planning, overview, preparation, inspection, process improvement, re-work, and follow-up activity. Its objectives are to identify and remove errors in the work products, and also to identify any systemic defects in the processes used to create the work products. A defective process may lead to downstream defects in the work products.

There is a strong economic case for identifying defects as early as possible, as the cost of correction increases the later a defect is discovered in the lifecycle. The Fagan inspection process stipulates that requirement documents, design documents, source code and test plans all be formally inspected by experts independent of the author, and the experts typically inspect the deliverable with different viewpoints, for example, requirements, design, test, customer support, etc.

There are various roles defined in the inspection process, including the moderator, who chairs the inspection, the reader, who paraphrasing the particular deliverable and gives an independent viewpoint, the author, who is the creator of the deliverable; and the tester, who is concerned with the testing viewpoint. The inspection process will consider whether a design is correct with respect to the requirements, and whether the source code is correct with respect to the design. There are seven stages in the Fagan inspection process:

Table 2.1: Overview Fagan Inspection

Step	Description
Planning	This includes identifying the inspectors and their roles, providing copies of the inspection material to the participants, and booking rooms for the inspection.
Overview	The author provides an overview of the deliverable to the inspectors.
Prepare	All inspectors prepare for the inspection and the role that they will perform.
Inspection	The actual inspection takes place and the emphasis is on finding major errors and not solutions.
Process Improvement	This part is concerned with continuous improvement of the development process and the inspection process.
Rework	The defects identified during in the inspection are corrected, and any items requiring investigation are resolved.
Follow Up Activity	The moderator verifies that the author has made the agreed-upon corrections and completed any investigations.

2.1.1 Economic Benefits of Software Inspections

The successful implementation of a software inspection program has demonstrated tangible benefits to organizations in terms of positive impacts on productivity, quality, time to market, and customer satisfaction. For example, IBM Houston employed software inspections for the Space Shuttle missions: 85% of the defects were found by inspections and 15% were found by testing. Thus there have been no defects found in the space missions. This project includes about 2 million lines of computer software. IBM, North Harbor in the UK quoted a 9% increase in productivity with 93% of defects found by software inspections.

Software inspections are also useful for educating new employees on the product and the standards and procedures employed in the organization, and in ensuring that the knowledge in the organization is shared among the employees rather than understood by just one individual, thereby reducing dependencies on key employees. Inspections thus play a valuable role in training new employees. Higher-quality software has an immediate benefit on productivity, as less time and effort are devoted to re-working the defective product, and thus productivity is improved.

The cost of correction of a defect increases the later the defect is identified in the lifecycle. Boehm [Boe:81] states that a requirements defect identified in the field is over 40 times more expensive to correct than if it were detected at the requirements phase. It is most economical to detect and fix the defect in phase.

The cost of a requirements defect which is detected in the field includes the cost of correcting the requirements, and the cost of design, coding, unit testing, system testing, regression testing, and so on. There are other costs also: for example, it may be necessary to send an engineer on site on short notice to implement the corrections. There may also be hidden costs in the negative perception of the company and a subsequent loss of sales. Thus there is a powerful economic argument to identify defects as early as possible, and software inspections serve as a cost beneficial mechanism to achieve this.

There are various estimates of the cost of quality in an organization, and the cost has been estimated to be between 20% to 40% of revenue. The exact calculation may be determined by a time sheet accountancy system which details the cost of internal and external failure and the cost of appraisal and prevention. The precise return on investment from introducing software inspections into the software development lifecycle needs to be calculated by the organization; however, the economic evidence available suggests that software inspections are a very cost-effective way to improve quality and productivity.

2.2 Software Inspection Methodology

The organization needs to define a precise software inspection methodology. This may be close to the Fagan or Gilb approach or may be tailored to its own environment and needs. It may not be possible to have an inspection methodology where all of the participants are present in a room, and participation by conference call or video link may be employed. For some organizations, the formality of a meeting may not suit its culture, and a methodology similar to an e-mail review may be the appropriate approach.

The software inspection methodology needs to suit the culture of the organization, and the degree of formality in the software inspection is influenced by the particular business domain of the organization and the potential impact of a software defect on the customer's business. The impact of a defect may have a major adverse effect on the customer's business: for example, a software defect may cause a telecommunications outage and lead to major disruption to the customers. There may also be penalty clauses specified in service level agreements to detail the appropriate level of compensation relating to an outage. In such environments a very formal inspection process tends to be employed and requirement documents, high-level, detailed design documents, and code are inspected, and generally inspections are explicitly planned in the project schedule.

The effectiveness of an inspection is influenced by the expertise of the inspectors, the preparation for the inspection being done by the inspectors, the speed of the inspection, and the steps in the inspection process being followed. The inspection methodology provides guidelines on the inspection and preparation rates for an inspection, and guidelines on the entry and exit criteria for an inspection.

There are typically at least two roles in the inspection methodology. These include the *author* role and the *inspector* role. The *moderator, tester,* and the *reader* roles may not be present in the methodology. The next section describes a very simple review methodology where there is no physical meeting of the participants, and where instead the reviewers send comments directly to the author. Then, a slightly more formal inspection process is described, and finally the Fagan inspection process is described in detail.

2.3 E-Mail/Fax Reviews

There is no physical meeting of the reviewers, and instead the reviewers participate by sending comments directly to the author. This approach lacks the formality of the Fagan inspection process, but works effectively for many organizations. It is described as follows:

Table 2.2: E-mail / Fax Review Process

Step	Description
1.	The author circulates the deliverable either physically or electronically to the review audience.
2.	The author advises the review audience of the due date for comments on the deliverable to be submitted.
3.	The due date for comments is reasonable (typically one week or longer).
4.	The author checks that comments have been received from all reviewers by the due date.
5.	Any reviewers who have not provided feedback by the due date are contacted by the author, and comments are requested.
6.	The author analyzes all comments received and implements the appropriate changes.
7.	The deliverable is circulated to the review audience for sign-off.
8.	The reviewers signoff with comments indicating that the document has been correctly amended by the author
9.	The author / project leader stores the e-mail or fax comments.

The author is responsible for making sure that the review happens, and advising the participants that comments are due by a certain date. The author then analyzes the comments, makes the required changes, and circulates the document for approval.

> COMMENT: The e-mail / fax review process may work for an organization. It is dependent on the participants sending comments to the author, and the author can only request the reviewer to send comments. There is no independent monitoring of the author to ensure that the review actually happens and that comments are requested, received, and implemented.

2.4 Semi Formal Review Meeting

The next type of inspection process is slightly more formal, and includes an actual review meeting, with an option to have the participation of a leader or moderator to chair the meeting. The review leader is responsible for verifying that the follow-up activity has been carried out. In the absence of an actual leader, the author takes responsibility for the review leader role. The material in this section is adapted from [OHa:98]:

The author selects the appropriate participants prior to the review, and appoints a review leader, who may be the author. The documentation/code to be reviewed is distributed to the reviewers by the author and the author may provide a brief overview to the participants.

The review meeting consists of a meeting with the review participants, and possibly remote participation via a conference call. The review meeting is chaired by the review leader. The leader is responsible for keeping the meeting focused and running smoothly, resolving any conflicts, completing the review form, recording actions, etc.

The review leader checks that all participants, including conference call participants are present, and that all have done adequate preparation for the review. Each reviewer is invited to give general comments, as this will indicate whether the material is ready for the review, and whether it makes sense to continue with the review. Participants who are unable to attend are required to send their comments to the review leader prior to the review, and the review leader will present the comments for the absent participant. The material is typically reviewed page per page for a document review, and each reviewer is invited to comment on the current page. Code reviews may focus on coding standards only or may focus on finding defects in the software code. The issues noted during the review are recorded and these may include items requiring further investigation.

At the end of the review a decision is taken as to whether the deliverable is to be re-reviewed or not. The author then carries out the necessary corrections and investigation, and this is verified by the review leader. The document is then circulated to the audience for sign-off.

> COMMENT: The semi-formal review process may work well for an organization when there is a review leader other than the author to ensure that the review is conducted effectively, and to verify that the follow up activity takes place. It may work with the author acting as review leader provided the author has received the right training on software inspections, and follows the inspection process.

Table 2.3 in section 2.4.1 summarizes the process for semi-formal reviews. Section 2.4.2 includes a template to record the issues identified during a semi-formal review.

2.4.1 Checklist for Review Meetings – Guidance for Reviews

Table 2.3: Checklist for review meetings

Phase	Review Task	Roles
Planning	Ensure document/code is ready to be reviewed. Appoint review leader (may be author) Select reviewers with appropriate knowledge/experience and assign roles The author may reserve a room or it may take place at the author's desk	Author
Distribution	Check document / code is ready for review Distribute document/code and other material to reviewers at least 3 days before the meeting Schedule the meeting	Author / leader
Informal meeting (Optional)	Summarize the purpose of the review Allow reviewers to ask any questions and to request any further information	Author
Preparation	The reviewers read the document/code, marking up issues/problems and questions Reviewers mark minor issues on their copy of the document/code	Reviewers

Table 2.3 (*continued*): Checklist for review meetings

Phase	Review Task	Roles
Review meeting	Sole responsibility for chairing review meeting	Leader
	Opening address: Introduce document/code for review and how meeting will proceed	(may be author)
	Review document page by page	
	Set time limit for meeting	
	Keep review meeting focused and moving	
	Code reviews may focus on standards/defects	
	Resolve any conflicts or defer as investigates	
	Note comments/shortcomings on review forms	
	Propose review outcome	
	Complete review summary form / return to Author. Keep a record of the review form	
	Respond to any questions or issues raised	Author
	Present comments/suggestions/questions. Raise issues – *(Do not fix them)* Pass review documents/code with marked up minor issues directly to the author	Reviewers
Post review	Issues/shortcomings identified at review are investigated and addressed The leader verifies that the corrections are made	Author / leader

2.4.2 Template for Minutes and Actions of Review

Item Under Review _____   **Review Reference** _____

Date_____

Document Name _____   **Version No.**_____

Author _____   **No. of Previous Reviews**_____

Reviewers_____

NOTES_____

_____

Minutes / Actions from the Review

Issue No	Raised By	Page/ Section/ Line/	Description	Action

Unresolved Issues/Investigates

Issue No.	Reason why Issue is unresolved	Checked

Review Outcome (Tick one of the following)

No change required   _____
Resolve issues (with review by leader only)   _____
Resolve issues, with another full review required   _____
Review incomplete. Reason/Action   _____

_____

Review Summary (Optional)

\# Major Defects Discovered (Customer Defects if Undetected)   _____
\# Minor Defects Discovered   _____
Authors Estimate of Rework Time   (Hours)   _____
\# Hours Preparation (total)_____   \# Hours review (total)   _____
Amount Reviewed (pages / LOC)   _____

2.5 Fagan Inspection Methodology

The objective of an inspection is to identify as many defects as possible, and to confirm the correctness of a particular deliverable. Inspection data is recorded and may be analyzed in detail. It will enable the organization to assess its effectiveness in detecting and preventing defects, and in learning from defects. An overview of the Fagan Inspection methodology was provided in section 2.1. This section goes into more detail on the methodology. The seven step Fagan inspection process is summarized in Table 2.4.

Table 2.4: Fagan Inspection Process

Step	Role/ Responsibility	Activity	Objective
1.	Moderator	Planning/ overview	Identify inspectors and roles. Verify materials are ready for inspection. Distribute inspection material to the inspector(s). Book a room for the inspection. The materials must meet the entry requirements.
2.	Moderator / author	Overview	Brief participants on material, and give background information.
3.	Inspectors	Preparation	The inspector(s) prepare for the meeting and especially for the role that the participant will be performing at the inspection. The moderator is responsible for ensuring that the participants have prepared sufficiently, and may need to cancel the inspection where inadequate preparation is done. The preparation involves reading through the deliverable and any other relevant documentation.
4.	Inspectors (moderator, author, reader and tester)	Inspection	The inspection meeting is held and defects are recorded and classified. The emphasis is on identifying major defects and not on solutions. The duration of the inspection is recorded. The inspectors may use checklists as a guide for the more common errors that may escape detection.
5.	Inspectors	Analysis / process improve- ment	This part of the inspection is concerned with continuous improvement of development and inspection process. The causes of major defects are recorded and a root cause analysis to identify any systemic defect within the software process or inspection process. Recommendations are made to the process improvement team.
6.	Author	Re-work	The author re-works the defective material listed any carries out any necessary investigations.
7.	Moderator / author	Follow-up	The moderator verifies that the author has successfully resolved the items requiring correction and investigation.

The moderator records the defects identified during the inspection, and the defects are classified according to their type and severity. Mature organizations typically enter defects into an inspection database to allow metrics to be generated, and to allow historical analysis. The severity of the defect is recorded, and the major defects are classified according to the Fagan defect classification scheme. Some organizations use other classification schemes, e.g., the orthogonal defect classification scheme (ODC).

The next section describes the Fagan inspection guidelines and these detail the recommended time to be spent on the inspection activities, including preparation for the actual inspection meeting. Often, the organization may need to tailor the Fagan inspection process to suit its needs, and the recommended times in the Fagan process may need to be adjusted accordingly. However, the tailoring will need empirical evidence to confirm that the tailored guidelines are effective in defect detection.

2.5.1 Fagan Inspection Guidelines

The Fagan inspection guidelines are based on studies by Michael Fagan and provide recommendations for the appropriate time to spend on the various inspection activities. The aim is to assist the performance of an effective inspection and to thereby identify as many major defects as possible. There are two tables presented here: the strict Fagan guidelines as required by the Fagan inspection methodology, and tailoring of the strict guidelines to more relaxed criteria to meet the needs of organizations that cannot devote the effort demanded by the strict guidelines.

The effort involved in a strict adherence to the Fagan guidelines is substantial and the tailored guidelines presented here are based on observations by the author of effective software inspection methodologies in leading industrial companies. Empirical evidence of the effectiveness of the tailoring is not presented. Tailoring any methodology requires care, and the effectiveness of the tailoring should be proved by a pilot prior to its deployment in the organization. This would generally involve quantitative data of the effectiveness of the inspection and the number of escaped customer reported defects.

It is important to comply with the guidelines once they are deployed in the organization, and trained moderators and inspectors will ensure awareness and compliance. Audits can be employed to verify compliance.

Table 2.5: Strict Fagan Inspection Guidelines

Activity	Area	Amount/Hr	Max / Hr
Preparation Time	Requirements	4 pages	6 pages
	Design	4 pages	6 pages
	Code	100 LOC	125 LOC
	Test Plans	4 pages	6 pages
Inspection Time	Requirements	4 pages	6 pages
	Design	4 pages	6 pages
	Code	100	125 LOC
	Test Plans	4 pages	6 pages

The relaxed guidelines detailed in Table 2.6 do not conform to the strict Fagan inspection methodology.

Table 2.6: Tailored (Relaxed) Fagan Inspection Guidelines

Activity	Area	Amount / Hr	Max / Hr
Preparation Time	Requirements	10–15 pages	30 pages
	Design Code	10–15 pages	30 pages
	Test Plans	300 LOC	500 LOC
		10–15 pages	30 pages
Inspection Time	Requirements	10–15 pages	30 pages
	Design	10–15 pages	30 pages
	Code	300	500 LOC
	Test Plans	10–15 pages	30 pages

2.5.2 Inspectors and Roles

There are four inspector roles identified in a Fagan Inspection and these include:

Table 2.7: Inspector Roles

Role	Description
Moderator	The moderator manages the inspection team through the seven-step process. The moderator plans the inspection, chairs the meeting, keeps the meeting focused, keeps to the Fagan guidelines, resolves any conflicts, ensures that the deliverables are ready to be inspected, and that the inspectors have done adequate preparation. The moderator records the defects on the inspection sheet, and verifies that all agreed follow-up activity has been successfully completed. The moderator is highly skilled in the inspection process and is required to have received appropriate training in software inspections. The moderator needs to be skillful, diplomatic, and occasionally forceful
Reader	The reader paraphrases the deliverable, gives an independent view of the product, and participates actively in the inspection.
Author	The author is the creator of the work product being inspected, and has an interest in ensuring that the inspection finds all defects present in the deliverable. The author ensures that the work product is ready to be inspected and informs the moderator, and gives background or an overview to the team if required. The author answers all questions and participates actively during the inspection, and resolves all defects identified and any items which require investigation.
Tester	The tester role focuses on how the product would be tested, and the tester role is typically employed as part of a requirements inspection and as part of the inspection of a test plan. The tester participates actively in the inspection.

2.5.3 Inspection Entry Criteria

There are explicit entry (Table 2.8) and exit criteria (Table 2.10) associated with the various types of inspections. The entry and exit criteria need to be satisfied to ensure that the inspection is effective. The entry criteria (Table 2.8) for the various inspections include the following:

Table 2.8: Fagan Entry Criteria

Inspection Type	Mandatory/ Optional	Entry Criteria	Inspectors/ Roles
Requirements	M	1. Inspector(s) with sufficient expertise available to review the document 2. Preparation done by inspectors 3. Requirements template used to produce the requirements	Author Moderator Reader Tester
Design Inspection	M	1. Requirements inspected and signed off 2. Design template used to produce the design 3. Inspector(s) have sufficient knowledge of the domain 4. Preparation done by inspectors	Author Reader Inspector Moderator
Code Inspection	M	1. Requirements are inspected / signed off 2. Design inspected and signed off 3. Overview provided 4. Inspector(s) have done preparation. 5. Code Listing available 6. Clean compile of source code 7. Code satisfies coding standards 8. Inspector(s) have sufficient knowledge of the domain	Author Reader Inspector Moderator
Test Plan	M	1. Requirements signed off 2. Design Signed off 3. Overview provided 4. Inspector(s) have done preparation. 5. Inspector(s) have sufficient knowledge of the domain.	Author Reader Moderator Tester

2.5.4 Preparation

Preparation is a key part of the inspection process, as the inspection will be ineffective if the inspectors are insufficiently prepared for the inspection The moderator is required to cancel the inspection if any of the inspectors has been unable to do appropriate preparation.

2.5.5 The Inspection Meeting

The inspection meeting (Table 2.9) consists of a formal meeting between the author and at least one inspector. The inspection is concerned with finding major defects in the particular deliverable, and verifying the correctness of the inspected material. The effectiveness of the inspection is influenced by

- The expertise and experience of the inspector(s)
- Preparation done by inspector(s)
- The speed of the inspection

These factors are quite clear since an inexperienced inspector will lack the appropriate domain knowledge to understand the material in sufficient depth. Second, an inspector who has inadequately prepared will be unable to make a substantial contribution during the inspection. Third, the inspection is ineffective if it tries to cover too much material in a short space of time.

Table 2.9: Inspection Meeting

Inspection Type	Purpose	Procedure
Require-ments	1. Find requirements defects 2.Confirm requirements correct and reflect customer's needs	Author and inspector(s) review each page of the requirements The inspector(s) raise questions or objections on each page based on preparation and author's explanation. Defects are recorded by the moderator
Design	1. Find design defects 2. Confirm design correct with respect to the requirements.	Author and inspector(s) review each page of the design The inspector(s) raise questions or objections on each page based on preparation (including a comparison to the requirements) and the author's explanation Defects are recorded by the moderator
Code	1. Find coding defects 2. Confirm code is correct with respect to the design and re-quirements	Author and inspector(s) review the code; the inspector(s) raise questions or objections based on preparation (including a comparison of the design and requirements) and the author's explanation Defects are recorded by the moderator
Test	1. Find defects in test cases 2. Confirm test cases sufficient to verify the design and require-ments	Author and inspector(s) review each page of the test plan; the inspector(s) raise questions or objections on each page based on prepara-tion (including a comparison to requirements and design to ensure all will be sufficiently tested) and author's explanation Defects are recorded by the moderator

The final part of the inspection is concerned with process improvement. The inspector(s) and author examine the major defects, identify the main root causes of the defect, and determine corrective action to address any systemic defects in the software process. The moderator is responsible for completing the inspection summary form and the defect log form, and for entering the inspection data into the inspection database. The moderator will give the process improvement suggestions directly to the process improvement team.

2.5.6 Inspection Exit Criteria

Table 2.10: Fagan Exit Criteria

Inspection Type	Mandatory/ Optional	Exit Criteria
Requirements	M	1. Requirements satisfy the customer's needs 2. All requirements defects are corrected
Design inspection	M	1. Design satisfies the requirements. 2. All defects in the inspection are corrected 3. Design satisfies the design standards
Code inspection	M	1. Code satisfies the design and requirements 2. Code follows coding standards 3. Code compiles cleanly 4. All defects from inspection removed
Test plan	M	1. Test plan sufficient to test the requirements 2. Test plan follows test standards 3. All defects from the inspection removed

2.5.7 Issue Severity

The severity of the issue identified in the Fagan inspection may be classified as major, minor, a process improvement item, or an investigate item. The issue is classified as major if non-detection of the issue would lead to a defect report being raised later in the development cycle, whereas a minor issue would not result in a defect report being raised. An issue classified as investigate requires further study before it is classified, and an issue classified as process improvement is used to improve the software development process.

Table 2.11: Issue Severity

Issue Severity	Definition
Major (M)	A defect in the work product that would lead to a customer reported problem if undetected
Minor (m)	A minor issue in the work product
Process Improvement (PI)	A process improvement suggestion based on analysis of major defects
Investigate (INV)	An item to be investigated. It is not clear whether it is a defect or not

2.5.8 Defect Type

There are various defect-type classification schemes employed in software inspections. These include the Fagan inspection defect classification (Table 2.12) and the Orthogonal Defect Classification scheme (Table 2.13).

Table 2.12: Classification of Defects Fagan Inspections

Code Inspection	Type	Design	Type	Requirements	Type
Logic (code)	LO	Usability	UY	Product objectives	PO
Design	DE	Requirements	RQ	Documentation	DS
Requirements	RQ	Logic	LO	Hardware interface	HI
Maintainability	MN	Systems interface	IS	Competition analysis	CO
Interface	IF	Portability	PY	Function	FU
Data usage	DA	Reliability	RY	Software Interface	SI
Performance	PE	Maintainability	MN	Performance	PE
Standards	ST	Error handling	EH	Reliability	RL
Code comments	CC	Other	OT	Spelling	GS

The Orthogonal Defect Classification (ODC) scheme is an alternate defect classification scheme developed by IBM [Bha:93], and the defect is classified according to three (orthogonal) viewpoints: i.e., the defect trigger is the catalyst that lead the defect to manifest itself, the defect type indicates the change required for correction, and the defect impact indicates the impact of the defect at the phase in which it was identified. The ODC classification yields a rich pool of information about the defect, but requires effort in recording the data for each defect. The ODC classification scheme for defect types is described in Table 2.13.

Table 2.13: Classification of ODC Defect Types

Defect Type	Code	Definition
Checking	CHK	Omission or incorrect validation of parameters or data in conditional statements
Assignment	ASN	Value incorrectly assigned or nor assigned at all
Algorithm	ALG	Efficiency or correctness issue in algorithm
Timing	TIM	Timing/serialisation error between modules, shared resources
Interface	INT	Interface error (error in communications between modules, operating system, etc)
Function	FUN	Omission of significant functionality
Documentation	DOC	Error in user guides, installation guides or code comments
Build/Merge	BLD	Error in build process / library system or version control
Miscellaneous	MIS	None of the above

The approach of ODC is to classify defects from the three orthogonal viewpoints [Chi:95]. The defect impact provides a mechanism to relate the impact of the software defect to customer satisfaction. The defect impact of a defect identified pre-release to the customer is viewed as the impact of the defect being detected by an end-user, and for a customer-reported defect, the impact is the actual information reported by the customer.

The inspection data is typically recorded in the inspection database; this will enable analysis to be performed on the most common types of defects, and enable actions to be identified to minimize reoccurrence. The data will enable the phase containment effectiveness to be determined, and will allow the company to determine if the software is ready for release to the customer.

The use of the ODC classification scheme can give early warning on the quality and reliability of the software, as experience with the ODC classification scheme will enable an expected profile of defects to be predicted for the various phases. The expected profile may then be compared to the actual profile, and clearly it is reasonable to expect problems if the actual defect profile at the system test phase resembles the defect profile of the unit testing phase, as the unit testing phase is expected to identify a certain pool of defect types with system testing receiving higher-quality software with unit testing defects corrected. Consequently, ODC may be applied to make predictions of product quality and performance.

Date_____   Project _____   Project Leader _____

Inspection Type: ☐ Requirements   ☐ Design   ☐ Code   ☐ Test

Document ID_____   **Document Size**_____

Programming Language_____   **Code Size**_____

Entry Criteria Satisfied   ☐ **Preparation Time**_____ **Meeting Time** _____

Amount Inspected (Pages / LOC) _____

Author_____   **Reader** _____

Moderator_____   **Inspector** _____

Inspection Summary   #Major Defects_____   ☐

                                 #Minor Defects_____   ☐

                                 #Process Improvements_____   ☐

ODC Defect Type Summary (Major Defects only)

CHK ☐   ASN ☐   ALG ☐   TIM ☐   INT ☐   FUN ☐   DOC ☐   BLD ☐

Checking Assignment Algorithm Timing   Interface Function   Documentation Build

Top Three Root Causes of Major Defects / Process Improvement

No	Root Cause of Major Defects/Process Improvement	Action	Owner
1.			
2.			
3.			

Author's Estimate of Re-Work Time _____ Defects per page / per KLOC _____

Verification of Re-Work by Inspector_____ Date _____

Inspection Data Entered in Database ☐

Inspection Guidelines

Activity	Area	Amount / Hr	Max / Hr
Inspection Time	Requirements	10–15 pages	30 pages
	Design	10–15 pages	30 pages
	Code	300	500 LOC
	Test Plans	10–15 pages	30 pages

Defect Log Form

Iss No	Line No/ Location	Issue Severity (Maj/Min/PI)	Defect Type	Description of Issue

Summary of Findings:

#Major Issues Logged ☐   #Minor Issues Logged ☐   #Process Improvement Issues Logged ☐

2.6 Software Testing

The objective of software testing is to verify the correctness of the software system and to identify any defects that are present. The successful testing of a software product provides confidence that the product is ready for release to potential customers, and the recommendation of the testing department is crucial in the decision as to whether the software product is ready to be released. The advice of the test manager highlights any risks associated with the product, and the risks are considered prior to its release. The test manager and test department can be influential in an organization by providing strategic advice on product quality and by encouraging organization change to improve the quality of the software product by the use of best practices in software engineering.

The team of testers need to understand the system and software requirements to be in a position to test the software. Test planning commences at the early stages of the project and testers play a role in building quality into the software product as well as verifying its correctness. The testers typically participate in a review of the requirements and thus play a key role in ensuring that the requirements are correct and are testable. They need to develop the appropriate testing environment to enable effective testing to take place and to identify the human resources, hardware, and various testing tools required. The plan for testing the project is typically documented and includes the resources required, the definition of the test environment and the test tools, and the test cases to validate the requirements. The test cases need to be sufficient to verify the requirements and generally include the purpose of the test case, the inputs and expected outputs, and the test procedure for the particular test case.

The testing that is typically performed in a project generally consists of unit testing, integration, system, regression, performance, and acceptance testing. The unit testing is performed by the software developers, and the objective is to verify the correctness of a module. This type of testing is termed *"white box"* testing. White box testing involves checking that every path in a module has been tested and involves defining and executing test cases to ensure code and branch coverage. The objective of *"black box"* testing is to verify the functionality of a module or feature or the complete system itself. Testing is both a constructive activity in that it is verifying the correctness of the functionality, and it also serves as a destructive activity in that another objective is to find defects in the software. Test reporting is a key part of the project, as this enables all project participants to understand the current quality of the software, and indicates what needs to be done to ensure that the product is meets the required quality criteria.

An organization may have an independent test group to carry out the various types of testing. The test results are reported regularly throughout the project, and once the test department discovers a defect, a problem report is opened, and the problem is analyzed and corrected by the software development community. The problem report may indicate a genuine defect, a misunderstanding by the tester, or a request for an enhancement. An influential test department concerned with quality improvement will ensure that the collection of defects identified during the testing phase are analyzed at the end of the project to identify recommendations to prevent or minimize reoccurrence. The testers typically write a test plan for the project, and the plan is reviewed by independent experts. This ensures that it is of a high quality and that the test cases are sufficient to confirm the correctness of the requirements. Effective testing requires sound test planning and execution, and a mature test process in the organization. Statistics are typically maintained to determine the effectiveness of the software testing.

The testing effort is often complicated by real world issues such as late delivery of the software from the development community which may arise in practice owing to challenging, deadline-driven software development. This could potentially lead to the compression of the testing cycle as the project manager may wish to stay with the original schedule. There are risks associated with shortening the test cycle as it may mean that the test department is unable to gather sufficient data to make an informed judgment as to whether the software is ready for release with the obvious implication that a defect-laden product may be shipped. Often, test departments may be understaffed, as management may consider additional testers to be expensive and wish to minimize costs. Sound guidelines on becoming an influential test manager are described in [Rot:00] and include an explicit description of the problem context, the identification of what the other person wants, the value that you as a test manager have and what you want, how you will provide the value that the other person wants, and what to ask for in return.

2.6.1 Test Planning

Effective testing requires good planning and execution. The IEEE 829 standard includes a template for test planning. Testing is a sub-project of a project and needs to be managed as a project. This involves detailing the scope of the work to be performed; estimating the effort required to define the test cases and to perform the testing; identifying the resources needed (including people, hardware, software, and tools); assigning the resources to the tasks; defining the schedule; identifying any risks to the schedule or quality and developing contingency plans to address them; tracking progress and taking corrective action; re-planning as appropriate where the scope of the project has changed; providing visibility of the test status to the full project team including the number of test planned, executed, passed, blocked and failed; re-testing corrections to failed or blocked test cases; taking corrective action to ensure quality and schedule are achieved; and providing a final test report with a recommendation to go to acceptance testing.

- Identify the scope of testing to be done
- Estimates of time, resources, people, hardware, software and tools
- Provide resources needed
- Provide test environment
- Assign people to tasks
- Define the schedule
- Identify risks and contingency plans
- Track progress and take corrective action
- Provide regular test status of passed, blocked, failed tests
- Re-plan if scope of the project changes
- Conduct post mortem to learn any lessons

The scope of the testing to be performed is dependent on the requirements of the proposed system. Estimates for the effort required to define and execute the test cases will need to be provided, and these become part of the schedule for the testing sub-project. The test cases are defined in such a way to ensure that the successful execution of the test cases will provide adequate confidence in the correctness of the implementation of the requirements. The test cases are typically traced back to the requirements as described in section 2.6.6, as this provides the confidence that all of the requirements have been sufficiently tested. The test environment needs to be defined early in the project to ensure that all the required hardware and software is available and configured to enable testing to commence on the scheduled date.

The following is a sample plan for testing the software, and a Microsoft schedule Gantt chart is typically employed for test planning and tracking. The test plan is tracked and updated to indicate that tasks have been completed, and dates are re-scheduled as appropriate. Testing is a critical sub-project of the main project and the main project plan will include the key testing milestones, and will track them to completion. The project manager and testing manager will generally maintain daily contact.

Table 2.14: Sample Test Plan

Activity	Resource Name(s)	Start Date	End/Re-Plan Date	Comments
Review requirements	Test Team	15.02.2001	16.02.2001	Complete
Overall test plan & Review	Test Manager	15.02.2001	28.02.2001	Complete
System test plan and Review	Tester 1	01.03.2001	22.03.2001	Complete
Performance test plan and review	Tester 2	15.03.2001	31.03.2001	Complete
Usability test plan and review	Tester 2	08.03.2001	31.03.2001	Complete
Regression plan and review	Tester 1	01.03.2001	15.03.2001	Complete
Test environment setup	Tester 1	15.03.2001	31.03.2001	Complete

Table 2.14 (*continued*): Sample Test Plan

Activity	Resource Name(s)	Start Date	End/Re-Plan Date	Comments
System testing and re-test defects	Tester 1	01.04.2001	31.05.2001	In progress
Performance testing and re-test defects	Tester 2	15.04.2001	07.05.2001	
Usability testing	Tester 2	01.04.2001	15.04.2001	Complete
Regression testing	Tester 2	07.05.2001	31.05.2001	
Test reporting	Test Manager	01.04.2001	31.05.2001	In progress

The test schedule above (Table 2.14) is a simple example of various possible tasks in a testing project and a more detailed test plan will require finer granularity. Tracking the plan to completeness is essential and the actual and estimated completion dates are tracked and the testing project rescheduled accordingly. It is prudent to consider risk management early in test planning, and the objective is to identify risks that could potentially materialize during the project, estimate the probability and impact if a risk does materialize, and identify as far as is practical a contingency plan to address the risk.

2.6.2 Test Process

The quality of the testing is dependent on the maturity of the test process, and a good test process will include:

- Test planning and risk management
- Dedicated test environment and test tools
- Test case definition
- Test automation
- Formality in handover to test department
- Test execution
- Test result analysis
- Test reporting
- Measurements of test effectiveness
- Post mortem and test process improvement.

A simplified test process is sketched in Figure 2.1.

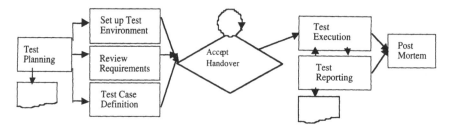

Figure 2.1: Simplified Test Process

The test planning process has been described in detail in section 2.6.1 and generally consists of a documented plan identifying the scope of testing to be performed, the definition of the test environment, the sourcing of any required hardware or software for the test environment, the estimation of effort and resources for the various activities, risk management, the deliverables to be produced, the key milestones, the various types of testing to be performed, the schedule, etc. The test plan is generally reviewed by the affected parties to ensure that it is of high quality, and that everyone understands and agrees to their responsibilities. The test plan may be revised in a controlled manner during the project.

The test environment varies according to the type of organization and the business and project requirements. In safety critical domains where there are high quality constraints, a dedicated test laboratory with lab engineers may be employed, and booking of lab time by the software testers may be required. In a small organization for a small project a single workstation may be sufficient to act as the test environment. The test environment is there to support the project in verifying the correctness of the software and a dedicated test environment may require significant capital investment. However, a sound test environment will pay for itself by providing an accurate assessment of the quality and reliability of a software product.

The test environment includes the required hardware and software to verify the correctness of the software. The test environment needs to be fully defined at project initiation so as to ensure that any required hardware or software may be sourced to ensure availability of the test environment for the scheduled start date for testing. Testing tools for simulation of parts of the system may be required, regression and performance test tools may be required, as well as tools for defect reporting and tracking.

The development organization typically produces a software build under software configuration management, and the software build is verified for integrity to ensure that testing is ready to commence with the software provided. This ensures that the content of the software build is known, that the build is formally handed over to the test department, and that the testers are testing with the correct version of the software. The testers are required to have their test cases defined and approved prior to the commencement of the testing. The test process generally includes a formal handover meeting prior to the acceptance of the development build for testing. The handover meeting typically includes objective criteria to be satisfied prior to the acceptance of the build by the test department.

Effective testing requires a good test process, and the test process details the various activities to be performed during testing, including the roles and responsibilities, the inputs and outputs of each activity, and the entry and exit criteria. The various types of testing employed to verify the correctness of the software may include the following:

Table 2.15: Types of Testing

Test Type	Description
Unit Testing	This testing is performed by the software developers and it verifies the correctness of the module.
Component Testing	This testing is used to verify the correctness of software components to ensure that the component is correct and may be reused. It is carried out by developers or by an independent test group.
System Testing	This type of testing is usually carried out by an independent test group, and the objective is to verify the correctness of the complete system.
Performance Testing	This testing is typically carried out by an independent test group, and the objective is to ensure that the performance of the system is within the defined performance limits. This usually requires tools to simulate many clients and heavy loads, and precise measurements of performance are made.
Load/Stress Testing	Load / stress testing is employed to verify that the system performance is within the agreed limits for heavy system loads over long or short periods of time. Tools may be required to obtain precise measurements.
Browser Compatibility Testing	This testing is specific to web based applications and involves verifying that the web site functions correctly with the different browsers which are supported.
Usability Testing	The objective is to verify that the software is easy to use and that the look and feel of the application is good.
Security Testing	The objective is to verify confidentiality, integrity and availability requirements are satisfied.
Regression Testing	The objective is to verify that the core functionality is preserved following changes or corrections to the software. Test tools may be employed to increase the productivity and efficiency of the regression testing.

Table 2.15 (*continued*): Types of Testing

Test Type	Description
Test Simulation	The objective of test simulation is to simulate part of the system where the real system currently does not exist or where the real live situation is hard to replicate. The effectiveness of the simulation testing is dependent on the how well the simulator matches the reality.
Acceptance Testing	This testing carried out by the customer and the objective is to verify that the software matches the customer's expectations prior to acceptance.

The definition of good test cases is essential for effective testing. The test cases for testing a particular feature need to be complete in that the successful execution of the test cases will provide confidence in the correctness of the software. Hence, the test cases must relate or be traceable to the software requirements, i.e., the test cases must cover the software requirements. The mechanism for defining a traceability matrix is described in section 2.6.6 and the trace matrix demonstrates the mapping between requirements and test cases. The test cases will usually consist of a format similar to the following:

- Purpose of test case
- Setup required to execute the test case
- Inputs to the test case
- The test procedure
- Expected outputs or results

The test execution will follow the procedure outlined in the test cases, and the tester will record the actual results obtained and compare this with the expected results. There may be a test results summary where each test case will usually have a test completion status of pass, fail, or blocked. The test results summary will indicate which test case could be executed, and whether the test case was successful or not, and which test cases could not be executed.

Test results are generally maintained by the tester, and detailed information relevant to the unsuccessful tests are recorded, as this will assist the developers in identifying the precise causes of failure and will allow the team to identify the appropriate corrective actions. The developers and tester will agree to open a defect in the defect control system to track the successful correction of the defect.

The test status (Fig. 2.2) consists of the number of tests planned, the number of test cases run, the number that have passed, and the number of failed and blocked tests. The test status is reported regularly to management during the testing cycle. The test status and test results are analyzed and extra resources provided where necessary to ensure that the product is of high quality with all defects corrected prior to the acceptance of the product

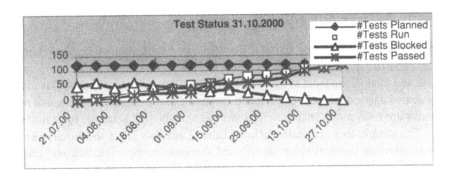

Figure 2.2: Sample Test Status

The test status is reported regularly throughout the project, and the project team agrees the action that is to be taken to ensure that progress is made to assure that the software is of high quality.

Test tools and test automation are described in detail in section 2.6.3 and test tools are there to support the test process in quality, reduced cycle time, and productivity. Tool selection needs to be performed in a controlled manner and it is best to identify the requirements for the tool first and then to examine a selection of tools to determine which best meets the requirements for the tool. Tools may be applied to test management and reporting, test results management, defect management, and to the various types of testing.

A good test process will maintain measurements to determine its effectiveness and will also include a post mortem after testing completion to ensure that any lessons that need to be learned from the project are actually learned. Test process improvement is important as continual improvement of the test process will enhance the effectiveness of the testing group. The testing group will use measures to answer questions similar to the following:

- What is the current quality of the software?
- How stable is the product at this time?
- Is the product ready to be released at this time?
- How good was the quality of the software that was handed over?
- How does the product quality compare to other products?
- How effective was the testing performed on the software?
- How many open problems are there?
- How much testing remains to be done?

2.6.3 Test Tools

The purpose of test tools is to support the test process in achieving its goals more effectively. Test tools can enhance quality, reduce cycle time, and increase productivity. The selection of a tool requires care to ensure that the appropriate tool is selected to meet the requirements. Tool evaluation needs to be planned to be effective and an evaluation plan typically includes the various activities involved in the evaluation, the estimated and actual effort to complete, and the individual carrying out the activity. The structured evaluation and selection of a particular tool typically involves identifying the requirements for the proposed tool, and identifying tools to evaluate against the requirements. Each tool is then evaluated against the tool requirements to yield a tool evaluation profile, and the results are analyzed to enable an informed decision on tool selection to be made.

The sample tool evaluation below (Table 2.16) lists all of the requirements vertically that the tool is to satisfy, and the tools to be evaluated and rated against each requirement are listed horizontally. Various rating schemes may be employed and in the example presented here, a simple rating scheme of good, fair, and bad is employed to rate the effectiveness of the tool under evaluation, to indicate the extent to which the tool satisfies the particular requirement.

Table 2.16: Tool Evaluation Table.

	Tool 1	Tool 2	Tool k
Requirement 1	Good	Bad	Good
Requirement 2	Bad	Fair	Good
Requirement n	Bad	Good	Good

Tool selection is performed in a controlled manner by examining a selection of tools against the set of requirements to determine which tool best meets the requirements for the tool. Tools may be applied to test management and reporting, test automation, test results management, defect management, and to the various types of testing. Tools are available from various vendors such as Compuware, Software Research, Inc., McCabe and Associates, Rational, and many more. The objective here is to give a flavor of the availability of tools and no recommendation of a particular tool or vendor is made.

Test Management Tools

There are various test management tools available from vendors; for example, the QADirector tool is offered as part of the QACenter tool from Compuware. The main features offered by the test management tools typically include the following:

- Management of entire testing process
- Test planning
- Support for building and recording test scripts
- Test status and reporting
- Graphs for presentation
- Defect control system
- Support for many testers
- Support for large volume of test data
- Audit trail proof that testing has been done

- Test automation
- Support for various types of testing

Miscellaneous Testing Tools

There is a wide collection of test tools to support the various types of testing such as static testing, unit testing, system testing, performance testing, regression testing, and so on. Static testing does not involve running the software under test, and instead usually involves inspections or reviews of documentation. We have discussed inspections earlier in this chapter and there are software tools that provide automated software inspections. These tools focus mainly on standards to be satisfied. For example, the CodeRover Caliper tool applies a series of predefined ANSI and industry accepted coding standards to provide a quality assessment report detailing information about the compliance of the software code to the defined rules.

Code coverage tools are useful for unit testing, and, for example, the LDRA testbed is able to analyze source files to report on areas of code that were not executed at run time, thereby facilitating the identification of missing test data. Code coverage tools are useful in identifying the sources of errors as they will typically show the code areas that were executed through textual or graphic reports.

Regression testing requires re-running existing test cases to verify that the core functionality remains once changes to the software have been made. It is usually sensible for regression testing to be automated by capture and playback tools especially for larger projects. There are several tools available to support regression testing. These include, for example, the Winrunner tool from Mercury, which improves the productivity in regression testing. There is work to be done to set up the tests for automation, but the big saving is in the automated running of the regressions tests, which reduces cycle time and increases productivity. The automated testing also reports on any defects identified.

The purpose of performance testing is to effectively test system performance and verify that it is within the agreed performance limits. There are various performance tools available, for example, the Rational Suite Performance TestStudio™. The performance testing will need to verify that the maximum number of concurrent users specified is supported, that any bottlenecks are manageable, and to obtain precise measurements of the response time of the key performance parameters. For example, there is evidence to suggest that the average user will wait approximately 8 seconds for a page to load and after that time they will start thinking about some other action if the page has not loaded. Consequently, it is important that measures are available on the loading of pages. Performance testing will typically require measures on the server side, network side, and client side and will usually include processor speed, disk space used, memory used, etc. There are various kinds of performance testing, including load testing, stress testing, and endurance testing. Performance testing is described in more detail in [Sub:00].

The purpose of stress testing and load testing is to verify that the performance of the system is within the defined quantitative limits whenever the system is placed under heavy loads and that the system performance is acceptable for all loads less than the defined threshold value. The WAS (Web application stress tool) and WCAT (Web capability analysis tool) from Microsoft are useful in performing load or stress testing. These tools simulate multiple clients on one client machine and thus enable heavy loads to be simulated.

The decisions on whether to automate, where to automate, and what to automate are difficult and generally require the involvement of a test process improvement team. The team will need objective data to guide them in making the right decision, and a pilot may be considered. It tends to be difficult for a small organization to make a major investment in test tools especially if the projects are small. However, larger organizations will require a sophisticated testing process to ensure that high-quality software is consistently produced.

2.6.4 E-Commerce Testing

There has been an explosive growth in electronic commerce in the industrial world, and electronic web sites are becoming increasingly sophisticated and ubiquitous throughout the world. Consequently, web site quality and performance is a key concern to web developers and customers. A web site is, of course, a software application; thus, it would seem logical that standard software engineering principles would be sufficient to verify the quality and correctness of a web site. However, the electronic commerce domain is a quite unique software engineering domain, and it is characterized by the following:

- Everything is new
- Distributed system with millions of servers and billions of participants
- Often rapid application development is required
- Design a little, implement a little, and test a little
- Rapidly changing technologies
- Users may be unknown
- Browsers may be unknown
- High availability requirements (24 * 365)
- Look and feel of the web site is highly important
- Performance may be un-predictable
- Security threats may be from anywhere

However, good software development for web-based applications and rigorous web testing require a sound software engineering environment to be in place. The standard waterfall lifecycle model is rarely employed for the front end of a web application, and instead RAD / JAD models are usually employed. The use of rapid application development does not mean that anything goes in software development, and the project team needs to produce similar documentation as the waterfall model, except that the chronological sequence of delivery of the documentation is more flexible. The joint application development is important as it allows early user feedback to be received on the look and feel and correctness of the application, and thus the approach of design a little, implement a little, and test a little is quite suitable and valid for web development.

The various types of web testing include the following:

- Static testing
- Unit testing
- Functional Testing
- Browser compatibility testing
- Usability testing
- Security testing
- Load / performance / stress testing
- Availability testing
- Post deployment testing

Static testing generally involves inspections and reviews of documentation. The purpose of static testing of web sites is to check the content of the web pages for accuracy, consistency, correctness, and usability, and also to identify any syntax errors or anomalies in the HTML. There are tools available (e.g., NetMechanic) for statically checking the HTML for syntax correctness and anomalies. The purpose of unit testing is to verify that the content of the web pages correspond to the design, that the content is correct, that all the links are valid, and that the web navigation operates correctly. The purpose of functional testing is to verify that the functional requirements are satisfied. Functional testing may be extensive and complex as electronic commerce applications can be quite complex, and may involve product catalogue searches, order processing, credit checking and payment processing, and an electronic commerce application may often liase with legacy systems. Also, testing of cookies, whether enabled or disabled, needs to be considered.

The purpose of browser compatibility testing is to verify that the web browsers that are to be supported are actually supported. Different browsers implement the HTML differently; for example, there are differences between the implementation by Netscape and Microsoft. The purpose of usability testing is to verify that the look and feel of the application is good. The purpose of security testing is to ensure that the web site is secure. The purpose of load, performance and stress testing is to ensure that the performance of the system is within the defined parameters. There are tools to measure web server and operating system parameters and to maintain statistics. These tools allow simulation of a large number of users at one time or simulation of the sustained use of a web site over a long period of time. There is a relationship between the performance of a system and its usability. Usability testing includes testing to verify that the look and feel of the application are good, and that performance of loading of web pages, graphics, etc., is good. There are automated browsing tools which go through all of the links on a page, attempt to load each link, and produce a report including the timing for loading an object or page at various modem speeds. Good usability requires attention to usability in design and usability engineering is important for web based or GUI applications.

The purpose of post-deployment testing is to ensure that the performance of the web site remains good, and this is generally conducted as part of a service level agreement (SLA). Service level agreements typically include a penalty clause if the availability of the system or its performance falls below defined parameters. Consequently, it is important to identify as early as possible potential performance and availability issues before they become a problem. Thus post-deployment testing will include monitoring of web site availability, performance, security, etc., and taking corrective action as appropriate. Most web sites are operating 24 hours a day for 365 days a year, and there is the potential for major financial loss in the case of an outage of the electronic commerce web site. This is recognized in service level agreements with a major penalty clause for outages. There is a very good account of e-business testing and all the associated issues by Paul Gerrard of Systeme Evolutif Ltd., and it is described in detail in [Ger:00].

2.6.5 Testing and Quality Improvement

Testing plays a key role in delivering a high-quality software product and is an essential part of the software development process. Testing thus plays a strategic role in decision making and the recommendation of the test manager is critical in the decision to go ahead with the release of the software product. Decision making is based on objective facts, and the test manager will maintain measurements to assess the quality of the software product. The test arrival rate (Fig. 2.3) gives an indication of the stability of the software product, and may be used in conjunction with other measures to make the decision on whether it is appropriate at this time to release the software product, or whether further testing should be performed.

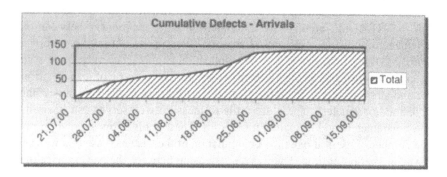

Figure 2.3: Cumulative Defects

The slope of the curve is steep at first as defects are detected; as testing proceeds and defects are corrected and retested, the slope of the curves levels off, and indicates that the software has stabilized and is potentially ready to be released to the customer. However, it is important not to rush to conclusions based on an individual measurement. For example, the above chart could possibly indicate that testing halted on the 25.08.2000; as no testing has been performed since then, and that would explain why the defect arrival rate per week is zero. Careful investigation and analysis needs to be done before the interpretation of a measurement is made, and usually several measurements rather than one are employed in sound decision making.

Test defects are very valuable also, as they offer an organization an opportunity to strengthen its software development process to prevent the defect from reoccurring in the future. Consequently, software testing plays an important part in quality improvement. A mature development organization will perform internal reviews of requirements, design, and code prior to testing. The effectiveness of the internal review process and the test process is demonstrated in the phase containment metric.

Figure 2.4 indicates that the project had a phase containment effectiveness of approximately 56%. That is, the developers identified 56% of the defects, the system testing phase identified approximately 32% of the defects, acceptance testing identified approximately 9% of the defects, and the customer identified approximately 3% of the defects. Mature software organizations set goals with respect to the phase containment effectiveness of their software. For example, some mature organizations aim for their software development department to have a phase defect effectiveness goal of 80%. This means that development has a goal to identify 80% of the defects by software inspections.

The chart above may be used to measure where the organization is with respect to its phase containment, and progress on improvements of phase containment effectiveness may be tracked in this way. There is no point in setting a goal for a particular group or area unless there is a clear mechanism to achieve the goal. Thus in order to achieve the goal of 80% phase containment effectiveness

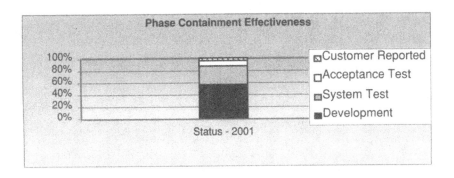

Figure 2.4: Sample Phase Containment Effectiveness Metric

the organization will need to implement a formal software inspection methodology as described earlier in this chapter. Training on inspections will be required and the effectiveness of software inspections monitored. Action plans are defined following problem solving to identify the appropriate actions to improve the software process to enable the organization to achieve its business goals more effectively.

A mature organization will aim to have 0% of defects reported by the customer, and to achieve this goal an organization must improve both its software inspection methodology and software testing methodology. The measurements are useful because they provide an objective status of the current effectiveness of the organization and provide a means to verify that the improvements have been successful. Each defect is potentially very valuable as it, in effect, gives feedback on the software process, and thereby enables the organization to identify weaknesses in the software process and to target corrections.

Defects are typically classified according to some category scheme, for example, the defects may be categorized by the functional area in which they are identified, or via the ODC classification scheme (Fig. 2.5), etc.

The frequency of defects per category is identified and causal analysis to identify appropriate actions to prevent reoccurrence are identified. Often the most problematic areas are targeted first, and an investigation into the particular category is conducted. Action plans are produced and are then tracked to completion. The action plans will identify and carry out improvements to existing processes.

Escaped customer defects offer an opportunity to improve the testing process, as a defect that escapes detection by the testing group, and is subsequently identified by the customer indicates a weakness in the test process. Escaped customer defects are categorized according to a classification scheme, causal analysis is performed, and corrective actions to improve the testing process for more effective defect detection are identified. This helps to prevent a reoccurrence of the defects. Thus software testing offers a mechanism to improve the software development process and to mature the software test process.

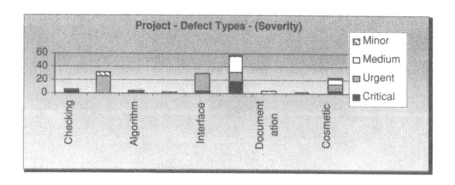

Figure 2.5: Sample–Defect Types in a Project (ODC)

2.6.6 Traceability of Requirements

The objective of requirement traceability is to validate that all of the requirements for the project have been implemented and tested. One way to do this would be to examine each requirement number and to go through every part of the design document to find any reference to the particular requirement number, and similarly to go through the test plan and find any reference to the requirement number. This would demonstrate that the particular requirement number has been implement and tested. A more effective mechanism to do this is to employ a trace matrix for the validation of requirements in the software project. The trace matrix may be maintained as a separate document and the idea is that a mapping between the requirement numbers and sections of the design or test plan is defined. Thus with the test matrix defined there is a high degree of confidence that all of the requirements have been implemented and tested.

Requirements may be numbered or may be detailed in individual sections of the requirements document. A requirement number may map on to several sections of the design or to several test cases, i.e., the mapping may be one to many. Treaceability provides confidence that each requirement number has been implemented in the software design and tested via the test plan.

- The trace matrix (Table 2.17) provides the mapping between individual requirement numbers (or sections) and the sections in the design corresponding to the particular requirement number (or section).
- This mapping will typically be one to many (i.e., a single requirement number will typically be implemented in several design sections).
- The trace matrix will be employed to demonstráte that all of the requirements have been implemented and tested.
- For each requirement number, the associated test cases to verify that the requirement has been correctly implemented will be detailed.
- This mapping will typically be one to many (i.e., for a particular requirement, several test cases will be employed to demonstrate correctness).

2.6.7 Trace Matrix of Requirements

Table 2.17: Sample Trace Matrix

Requirement Section (or Number)	Corresponding Sections in Design	Corresponding Sections in Test Plan	Comments/ Risks
R1.1	D1.4, D1.5, D3.2	T1.2, T1.7	
R1.2	D1.8, D8.3	T1.4	
R1.3	D2.2	T1.3	
R 1.50	D20.1, D30.4	T20.1 T24.2	

2.7 Summary

This chapter considered software inspections and testing in detail and discussed how software inspections may be used to build quality into the software, whereas testing may be used to verify that the software is of a high quality and fit to be released to potential customers. The economic case for software inspections was discussed, and it was pointed out that it makes economic sense to detect defects early as the cost of a late discovery of a defect can be quite expensive. Various types of methodologies for reviews or inspections were discussed ranging from an informal type of inspection, to a semi-formal inspection, and finally to the formal Fagan inspection methodology.

Software testing was considered in detail, including test planning, the test environment setup, test case definition, test execution, defect reporting, and test management and reporting. Various types of testing were discussed including black and white box testing, unit and integration testing, system testing, performance testing, security and usability testing. Testing in an e-commerce environment was considered. Various tools to support the testing process were discussed, and a methodology to assist in the selection and evaluation of tools was considered. Metrics to provide visibility into progress with the testing and the quality of the software were discussed, and also the role of testing in promoting quality improvement was discussed.

3
The ISO 9000 Standard

3.1 Introduction

The ISO 9000 quality standard is a widely employed international standard, and was developed by the International Standards Organization (ISO). The standard was influenced by the British quality standard (BS 5750), and was originally published as a standard in 1987 and revised in 1994. The standard is revised approximately every five years to ensure that it continues to meet the needs of the international community, and submissions for enhancements are invited. The ISO 9000 standards may be applied to various types of organizations including manufacturing, software and service organizations. The achievement of ISO 9000 by a company typically indicates that the company has a sound quality system in place, and that quality and customer satisfaction are core values of the company. ISO 9000 is regarded as a minimal standard that an organization which takes quality seriously should satisfy, and many organizations require that their subcontractors be ISO 9000 certified.

The ISO 9000 standard was developed owing to a need by organizations to assess the capability or maturity of their subcontractors. The approach taken prior to the definition of the standard was that organizations who wished to have confidence in the capability of contractors developed their own internal quality standard, and prior to the selection of a particular subcontractor, a quality representative from the organization visited the proposed subcontractor, and assessed the maturity of the subcontractor with respect to the prime contractor's or subcontractor's own quality system. This became expensive, especially if the organization had many subcontractors, as a visit to each individual subcontractor was required to assess their maturity. Once the international standard became available, it allowed the organization to place the minimal requirement of satisfying the ISO 9000 standard on the subcontractor, and thereby to expect certain minimal quality standards from the subcontractor. ISO 9000 may thereby become a discriminator in the selection of a contractor by a customer or the selection of a subcontractor by the prime contractor. There is no longer any necessity for the organization to assess the quality system of the subcontractor, as the certification of ISO 9000 compliance is checked independently by an ISO 9000 audit of the subcontractor.

The latest revision of ISO 9000 is termed ISO 9000:2000, and it is a significant enhancement over the 1994 version of the standard. It places emphasis on customer satisfaction and continual improvement, and includes a process model. The old 1994 version of the standard placed emphasis on defining procedures for doing the work, whereas the new standard the emphasis is on processes. It is a simpler standard, and is effective from December 2000. The older 1994 ISO 9000 standard is first discussed and then the new ISO 9000:2000 standard and its implementation in an organization.

3.1.1 Motivation for ISO 9000

The previous section discussed how ISO 9000 is useful as a discriminator in the selection of a contractor by a customer, or in the selection of a sub-contractor by a prime contractor. This section includes a more complete justification as to why a company should consider implementing an ISO 9000 certified quality system.

The ISO 9000 standard places requirements on the quality management system of the company, but it is flexible on the mechanism by which the company may satisfy the requirements. The requirements include controls, processes and procedures, and maintaining quality records as evidence.

Table 3.1: ISO 9000 Motivation

Motivation for ISO 9000 Implementation
Enhances the credibility of the company
Marketing benefit of ISO 9000 certificate
Indicates that customer satisfaction and quality are a core value of the company
Indicates that the company is dedicated to continuous improvement
Indicates that the company plans for quality in product development
Higher quality software produced
Indicates that a fire prevention culture rather than a fire fighting culture is in place
The emphasis is on learning lessons from problems
A more capable and effective organization
More loyal customers
Protects the company from litigation. The ISO 9000 requirements on records provide evidence that all reasonable steps were taken
ISO 9000 offers a framework or model to improve. The standard may be used by the organization to improve
Less re-work of defective products
Higher morale in the organization

ISO 9000 offers a structured way for a company to improve. The company can choose the most critical clauses which will yield the greatest business gains and focus on improvements to these first. Then as the company increases in maturity, the other clauses in the standard may be addressed. A standard or model is very useful as a way for an organization to know how good it actually is and to prioritize further improvements.

3.1.2 ISO 9000 and the Quality Group

The ISO 9000 standard places responsibilities on management and staff in the company. This book is on software quality and therefore in this section the impact of the standard on the software quality assurance (SQA) group is considered. The typical responsibilities of the quality group in an ISO 9000 environment are considered. The quality group will generally play a key role in the implementation of the standard.

The quality group plays a key role in the implementation of the quality management system and in monitoring its effectiveness in the organization.

Table 3.2: Quality Group responsibilities

Responsibilities of the Quality Group (SQA)
Perform audits of projects, subcontractors, and departments
Promote awareness and a culture of quality
Communicate Quality System to staff
Support/Champion implementation of ISO 9000
Perform customer satisfaction surveys
Facilitate action/improvement following customer feedback
Review project quality at agreed milestones
Act as a partner in quality to the project
Facilitate improvement and defect prevention activities
Monitor and verify process compliance
Monitor effectiveness of processes
Monitor institutionalisation of processes
Chair organization quality reviews
Facilitate external audits / customer audits of organization
Test Planning, Execution, Reporting and Recommendation
Test Lab management
Support a Metrics culture

3.2 ISO 9000 1994 Version

The ISO 9000:1994 standard consists of a family of standards and guidelines on how to apply the standards. It applied to manufacturing organizations, service organizations, and software organizations. It was written initially for manufacturing companies involved in the design, development, and production of products, and adapted to service and software companies.

The ISO 9001 standard is a superset of ISO 9002 and ISO 9003, and covers the full product lifecycle. ISO 9002 covers the standard for production, installation, and servicing; and ISO 9003 covers the standard for final inspection and test. The full set of standards associated with ISO 9000:1994 are included in Table 3.3.

There are 20 clauses in the 1994 version of the ISO 9001 standard, and an ISO 9000 certified organization must be able to demonstrate that it is satisfying the relevant clauses. The organization needs to choose the appropriate standard to apply for certification, for example, if the organization is a testing company, then it would be applying for ISO 9003. The twenty clauses in the ISO 9001 standard are described in more detail below, and tailored to a software organization interpretation.

Table 3.3: ISO Standards

Standard	Description
ISO 8402	Quality Management /Assurance Vocabulary
ISO 9000 −1	Guidelines for selection and use of ISO 9000
ISO 9000-2	Guidelines of the application ISO 9001/2/3
ISO 9000-3	Guidelines for the application of ISO 9001 to software
ISO 9000-4	Guidelines on planning, organizing and controlling resources to produce reliable products
ISO 9001	ISO Standard for the design, development, test, installation and servicing of the product/service
ISO 9002	ISO Standard for the production, installation and servicing (a subset of ISO 9001)
ISO 9003	Standard for final inspection and test. (a subset of ISO 9001)
ISO 9004-1	Guidelines to implement a quality system
ISO 9004-4	Guidelines for continuous improvement

Table 3.4: ISO 9000:1994 Standard

Clause	Name	Description
4.1	Management Responsibility	Define and communicate quality policy Define responsibility for quality Appoint quality representative Provide sufficient resources, and trained staff Identify, provide, and verify solutions to problems; regular management reviews of the quality system
4.2	Quality System	Quality manual (ISO 100013) Quality System procedures documented Quality planning Controls, inspection and test, quality records
4.3	Contract Review	Review of contract Amendment to contract Records of review
4.4	Design Control	Design and development planning Organizational and technical interfaces Design input and output Design review Design verification and validation (reviews) Design changes (documented and approved)
4.5	Document Control	Review and approval of documents Changes to documents and approval Version control and naming
4.6	Purchasing	Evaluation of subcontractors Managing / control of subcontractor Verification of subcontractor product.
4.7	Purchaser Supplied Product	This is interpreted as referring to software tools, compilers, test data or commercial off the shelf software (COTS) for software companies. It requires that the purchase product be verified via acceptance criteria. Compilers, tools, etc., need to be under version control.
4.8	Product Identification and Traceability	Versions of released product Right constituents for the build This requires a change control mechanism for making changes to the baseline, source code control management and all source code files, data files, etc., that are part of the build of the released software must be clearly identified.
4.9	Process Control	Controlling the process Audits of process fidelity Documented procedures Process measurements and control limits Verified for integrity and performance via measurements and audits

Table 3.4 (*continued*): ISO 9000:1994 Standard

Clause	Name	Description
4.9	Process Control	Controlling the process Audits of process fidelity Documented procedures Process measurements and control limits Verified for integrity and performance via measurements and audits
4.10	Inspection and Testing	Walkthroughs, inspection, and testing Records of inspections and testing Correction of defects
4.11	Inspection Measuring and Test Equipment	This refers to calibration of machines in manufacturing and to test tools and test data in software organizations
4.12	Inspection and Test Status	This requires that the inspection and test status of the project is known and reported throughout the development of the product
4.13	Control of Non-conforming Product	This requires that all defects identified during inspections and testing are assigned to developers for correction prior to the release of the software to the customers
4.14	Corrective Action	The organization performs root cause analysis of problems, and identifies and takes actions to prevent reoccurrence
4.15	Handling, Storage, Packaging and Delivery	This requires the product to be properly handled, stored and packaged prior to delivery. The software is delivered on an agreed media and is accompanied by a release note, an installation guide, a training manual, etc.
4.16	Quality Records	Identify, store, and maintain quality records. This requires a procedure to identify records, length, disposal method, etc. Records provide evidence of performance of QMS.
4.17	Internal Quality Audits (ISO 10011)	This requires an audit program to be in place in the organization. There may be audits of suppliers, projects and the various departments. The audit is independent and the results shared with management
4.18	Training	Establish the training needs of company. Skills to fulfill a particular role identified. Gaps in skills for employee/roles identified Staff are qualified to perform their role. Training records are maintained
4.19	Servicing	This requires a procedure for performing, verifying and reporting that the servicing meets the specified requirements
4.20	Statistical Techniques	Control and verify process. Measure product quality. Data gathering and metrics

3.3 ISO 9000:2000 Version

The ISO 9000:2000 standard is simpler than the 1994 standard, and consists of just three standards: namely, ISO 9000:2000, ISO 9001:2000, and ISO 9004:2000. The ISO 9000 standard covers the fundamentals and vocabulary of quality management systems.

The ISO 9001 standard specifies the requirements of a quality management system and applies to manufacturing, software, and service organizations. It details the requirements which the quality management system of the organization must satisfy to be ISO 9000 compliant. There is a simple process model defined in the standard and there is an emphasis on measurement, continual improvement, and customer satisfaction.

The text in the standard is more friendly and logical than the old ISO 9000:1994 standard. The old ISO 9001, ISO 9002, and ISO 9003 standards have been merged into one standard. There are only five clauses in the new standard as compared to twenty clauses in the old standard, and the standard is very customer focused. The ISO 9004:2000 provides guidance for performance improvement and is helpful in assisting organizations in the implementation of the standard. It includes a simple self-assessment methodology to allow the organization to determine its current maturity with respect to the standard.

The five main clauses in ISO 9000:2000 are described in Table 3.5.

The objective is to elicit the customer requirements and to develop a software product which satisfies the requirements and which matches or exceeds customer expectations, and to continually improve to serve the customer better.

Table 3.5: ISO 9000:1994 Standard

Clause	Description
Quality Management System	This clause refers to the documentation and implementation of the quality management system.
Resource management	This is concerned with the provision of the resources needed to implement the quality management system.
Product or service realisation	The provision of processes to implement the product or service.
Management Responsibility	The responsibility of management in the implementation of the quality management system.
Measurement, analysis and improvement	The establishment of a measurement program to measure the quality management system performance and to identify improvements.

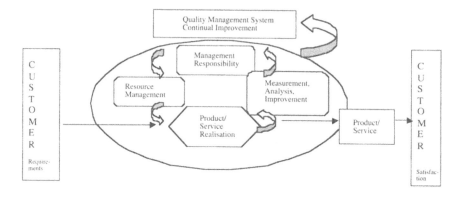

Figure 3.1: ISO 9000:2000 Quality Management System

Quality Management System

This clause includes documenting the quality management system (Fig. 3.1) and defining the procedure for the control of documents and the control of quality records. Its consists of the following sub-clauses:

- Quality manual
- Control of documents
- Control of records

These sub-clauses are described in more detail in section 3.4.1.

Management Responsibility

This clause includes defining the responsibilities of management in the quality system, and includes planning for quality and setting quality objectives, defining a quality policy and reviewing the quality management system. Its consists of the following sub-clauses:

- Management commitment
- Customer focus.
- Quality policy
- Planning
- Responsibility, authority, and communication
- Management review

The results of audits, customer feedback, process performance and product conformity, status of preventive and corrective actions, follow up actions from previous review, planned changes that could affect the QMS, and recommendations for improvement are all considered in the management review of the quality system. The sub-clauses are described in more detail in section 3.4.2.

Resource Management

This clause includes requirements to ensure that appropriate resources are in place to deliver high quality software, and it includes the human and physical infrastructure. This clause addresses human resource management, training, and the work environment and physical infrastructure. It consists of the following sub-clauses:

- Provision of resources
- Human resources
- Infrastructure
- Work environment

The sub-clauses are described in more detail in section 3.4.3.

Product or Service Realization

This clause includes requirements for the organization to define a development process to identify the requirements, create the design, develop and test the software product. It consists of the following sub-clauses:

- Planning of product realization
- Customer related processes
- Customer requirements
- Customer communication
- Design and development
- Control of changes
- Purchasing process (information and verification)
- Production and service provision
- Validation of processes
- Identification and traceability
- Customer property
- Preservation of product
- Control of measuring and monitoring devices

The sub-clauses are described in more detail in section 3.4.4.

Measuring, Analysis, and Improvement

This clause is concerned with the measurement of processes and the analysis of data to plan and verify effective improvement. The measurement provides objective data on the effectiveness of the quality system, and the quantitative data facilitates the performance of a detailed analysis. This includes the use of problem-solving techniques to address the identified issues with improvement actions. The clause is also concerned with customer satisfaction and continuous improvement. It includes the following sub-clauses:

- Measurement of customer satisfaction
- Internal audits
- Measurement and monitoring of processes
- Measurement and monitoring of product
- Control of nonconformity
- Analysis of data
- Continual improvement
- Corrective action
- Preventative action

The sub-clauses are described in more detail in section 3.4.5.

3.4 Implementing ISO 9000:2000

The implementation of ISO 9000 in an organization is closely related to the activities described in section 3.4.1 through section 3.4.5. The objective of the implementation of ISO 9000 is to improve quality and customer satisfaction, and the certification of ISO 9000 is evidence that a sound quality system is in place in the organization. The implementation of ISO 9000:2000 consists of steps similar to the following:

Awareness Training.

This involves briefing management on the ISO 9000:2000 standard and the steps involved in the implementation of the standard. The quality manager or a representative of the management team who is responsible for ISO 9000 implementation will typically attend a course on ISO 9000, and will then share the results with the management team.

Establish a Team

Management will set up a team with responsibility for ISO 9000 implementation. The team will consist of management and employees, and the team chairperson will provide regular progress reports to management. The team members will champion ISO 9000 in the organization, and will receive more detailed training on the standard. The team will work with the employees to implement the standard effectively. Adequate resources and time are required for successful implementation, and a realistic plan is defined. The plan details the activities and the resources and scheduled completion date. The timeframe should be realistic, and take into account that the members of the team have their normal jobs as well as the task of ISO 9000 implementation. The team will need to be motivated and have sufficient influence to deal with roadblocks effectively.

Establish ISO 9000 status

The team will determine the current ISO 9000 status in the organization. The status may be determined by inviting a consultant to examine the quality system and to compare it to the ISO 9000 standard or if the team has sufficient expertise they may be capable of performing a self assessment of the organization against the standard in a manner similar to that described in ISO 9004:2000. The consultant or team will typically provide a report detailing the findings of the examination of the quality system, and the areas that need to be addressed to satisfy the standard. The report is then used by the team to plan the implementation of ISO 9000.

The ISO 9000 status is the baseline for improvements, and if the team is successful in the implementation of improvements, then the next assessment of the organization will demonstrate that the organization has made substantial progress in satisfying the standard.

Prepare Action Plan

The ISO 9000 status is used to prepare the action plan for implementation. Management is responsible for ensuring that the resources needed for implementation are provided. The action plan includes the activities to be performed, the resources for performing the activities, and the estimated completion date of the activity. Often, a high-level plan of the activities to be completed over a 1-2 year period is prepared, and this lists the activities to be performed over a 12 – 18 month period.

The sample high-level plan in Table 3.6 is a high-level timeline of activities to be performed over a 15 month time period. It is a sketch of the activities to be performed, and does not include a detailed breakdown of the tasks to be performed to complete each activity, and the resources and the scheduled completion date for each activity.

Table 3.6: Timeline for ISO 9000:2000 High Level Plan

Q2'01 & Q3 01	Q4'01	Q1'02	Q2'02
Perform mini-ISO 9000 assessment	Document project management process	Perform mini - ISO9000 assessment	Document the disaster recovery plan
Identify actions and owners	Document requirements process	Implement actions from mini assessment	Independent ISO 9000 assessment
Define quality policy	Implement inspections	Define customer satisfaction process	Address actions from Assessment
Document the quality handbook.	Define waterfall and RAD lifecycle.	Formalize post implementation reviews	ISO 9000 `Go/No Go' decision
Draft inspection Process	Implement corrective & preventative action process	Institutionalize monthly quality reviews	Contact certification body
Define documentation control procedure	Revise configuration management	Determine the cost of poor quality (COPQ)	Send handbook to certification body and get feedback
Define which quality records will be kept.	Draft data gathering and quality metrics	Define purchasing procedure	Set date for assessment in Q3'2002
Define workshops on quality	Add trace matrices to the relevant templates	Agree quality metrics for projects	Prepare for assessment
Define training process			
Implement audits			

A detailed plan of activities to be completed over a shorter period (typically six months) is then prepared. The action plan may take the form of a Microsoft project gantt chart, or a similar project planning and tracking mechanism. Each of the activities in the action plan is a project in its own right and needs to be managed as such. A sample detailed action plan is included in Table 3.7 below.

Each activity is a mini project in its own right and needs to be managed as such. The team chairperson will track and report progress to the management team and management will provide the resources needed for successful implementation.

Table 3.7: ISO 9000:2000 Detailed Plan

Action No	Deliver- able	Action Required	Owner	Due- Date	Status
ACT- 001	Quality handbook	Draft quality handbook	Quality manager	24.05.01	Closed
		Team review	Team	13.07.01	Closed
		Updates	Quality manager	27.07.01	Open
		Formal review/updates	Team	04.08.01	Open
		Sign-off and release	Team	11.08.01	Open
		Communicate	Team	31.08.01	Open
ACT- 002	Inspection Process	Draft inspection proc- ess	Quality manager	15.08.01	Open
			Team	22.08.01	Open
		Team review	Quality manager	29.08.01	Open
		Updates	Team	05.09.01	Open
		Formal review	Team	12.09.01	Open
		/updates	Team	31.10.01	Open
		Sign-off and release	Quality manager	31.10.01	Open
		Pilot and feedback	Team	31.12.01	Open
		Communicate	Team	31.12.01	Open
		Training			
		Deployment.			
ACT- 003	RAD Life- cycle	Investigate RAD	S/W Dev Mgr	12.09.01	Open
		Draft RAD lifecycle	S/W Dev Mgr	19.09.01	Open
		Informal review	Team	26.09.01	Open
		Updates/formal review	Team	3.10.01	Open
		Sign off and release	Team	10.10.01	Open
		Pilot and feedback	Team	15.11.01	Open
		Communicate	S/W Dev Mgr	30.11.01	Open
		Training	Team	31.12.01	Open
		Deployment	Team	31.12.01	Open
		Monitor deployment	Quality manager	31.03.02	Open
ACT - 004	Audit Proc- ess	Draft audit process	Quality manager	26.09.01	Open
		Review audit process	Team	10.10.01	Open
		Update/formal review	Team	17.10.01	Open
		Sign-off and release	Team	31.10.01	Open
		Pilot and feedback	Team	30.11.01	Open
		Communicate	Quality manager	15.12.01	Open
		Training	Team	31.12.01	Open
		Deployment	Quality manager	31.12.01	Open

The above plan includes four activities which form part of the ISO 9000 im-plementation program. These activities are mini projects and have associated tasks. The estimates for the completion of each task are included. This enables a judgement to be made on the effort required to complete the implementation of ISO 9000 in the organization, and to determine a realistic completion date.

Track Action Plan

The action plan is the project plan for ISO 9000 implementation, and it is important that the plan be tracked throughout the duration of the project, that the plan be updated to reflect the milestones which have been achieved, and that new dates be provided for any tasks which are behind schedule. The chairperson of the team will need to discuss the progress of the various tasks with the person responsible for the execution of the task. The chairperson may need to take corrective action if the project is behind schedule or at risk of falling behind schedule. The reporting mechanism allows the chairperson to present the actual status of the project to management and to highlight any risks or concerns with the timely completion of the implementation.

Present Status of Action Plan

The status of the action plan is presented regularly to management. The chairperson presents the status of the action plan, and will request more resources if the action plan is falling behind schedule.

ISO 9000 readiness assessment.

It is beneficial to conduct a readiness assessment of the organization prior to applying for ISO 9000 certification. The readiness assessment will indicate whether the organization is ready to go for an ISO 9000 certified assessment, or whether the formal assessment should be postponed to allow for completion of the identified weaknesses in the quality system. The ISO 9000 readiness assessment is carried out by an independent body or consultant and the objective is to compare the quality system to the ISO 9000 requirements, and to identify any issues which an ISO 9000 assessor would regard as non-compliant. The effectiveness of the readiness assessment is dependent on the expertise of the independent assessor. It is an optional step, but an independent view of the quality system is valuable.

Contact Registrar (certification body)

Once the organization is confident that it has implemented an ISO 9000:2000 quality system (Fig. 3.2), it may then apply to the certification body for an ISO 9000 audit of its quality system. The assessment process generally takes the following form:

- Contact the certification body.
- Furnish relevant details about the company.
- Supply the quality manual and any requested processes or procedures to the certification body.
- Arrange a date for when the auditors will visit the company.
- Brief participants in the company on the visit and the expected behavior during the visit.

- Arrange logistics for the visit.
- Arrange interview rooms.
- Facilitate interview schedule.
- Supply any requested documentation that is available.

Official ISO 9000 Audit

Once the auditor(s) are on site they will compare the quality system in the company against the ISO 9000:2000 requirements. The participants are briefed as to what to expect at the assessment, and to understand the expected behavior. They answer all questions openly and honestly. The auditor(s) will stay on site for one to two days depending on the size and complexity of the organization. The standard requires certain processes and procedures, records, and controls to be in place. The auditors will look for evidence of this, and determine the extent to which the written procedures corresponds to the actual observed behavior.

The auditors will publish an evaluation report which will detail the findings of the audit. The auditors may identify corrective actions to be carried out prior to the granting of ISO 9000 certification. The company is required to carry out the corrective actions, and these are then verified. The ISO 9000 registration is then granted. The registration is valid for approximately two years, and follow-up audits are conducted to ensure that the quality system remains ISO 9000 compliant.

Continuous Improvement

The organization will use the feedback from the assessment to continuously improve.

Celebrate

The award of ISO 9000 certification is a major achievement for the organization and merits a celebration. The celebration demonstrates the importance attached to quality and customer satisfaction.

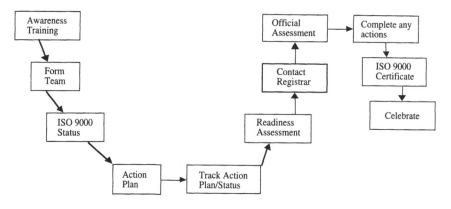

Figure 3.2: ISO 9000:2000 Implementation

3.4.1 Quality Management System Clause

The Quality Management System clause is concerned with the implementation and documentation of the quality management system. This clause requires the production of the documented procedures required by the ISO 9000 standard including the quality manual. It is also concerned with the control of quality records as these are used to provide evidence of conformity to the quality system. The sub-clauses include general requirements of the quality management system, documentation requirements and the use of quality management principles in the organization. The procedures required for ISO 9000:2000 include the following:

Table 3.8: ISO 9000:2000 Procedures

ISO Clause	Procedure
4.2.2	Quality manual
4.2.3	Control of documents
4.2.4	Control of records
8.2.2	Internal audit
8.3	Control of non-conforming product
8.5.2	Corrective action procedure
8.5.3	Preventive action procedure

There is more than one implementation to the specified ISO 9000:2000 requirements. The organization needs to choose an implementation which is tailored to its own needs. Generic guidelines on implementation are provided in this section.

The Quality Manual

The quality manual is a key document in the quality management system. It is advisable to keep the quality handbook as short as possible (approximately 20 pages) as a large quality handbook is likely to remain unopened on a bookshelf. The quality manual normally refers to other procedures or processes for the finer details on implementation of the various ISO 9000 clauses. The standard quality manual will include each ISO 9000:2000 clause, and provide details as to how the organization is satisfying the particular clause. Justification is provided if the clause is not applicable to the organization, and this may be applied only to section 7 of the standard.

A short paragraph may be sufficient to indicate how the clause is being satisfied, or a reference to a process, documented procedure, or records maintained by the organization. The references may be to the software development lifecycles employed in the organization, e.g., waterfall and RAD lifecycles, the customer satisfaction process, the software inspection process, the testing process, the audit process, the improvement program, the monthly review mechanism, and the purchasing procedure.

The quality manual will also provide details of the quality policy, the key goals and initiatives of the organization to achieve customer satisfaction, an organization chart to show where quality fits into the organization, etc. The quality manual is the starting off point for the external ISO 9000 assessor, as it documents how the quality management system has been implemented in the organization.

Control of Documents

The implementation of this clause requires that the organization define a procedure, namely, the Document Control Procedure. This procedure specifies the layout that the document must conform to, and that the document is under version control. Controls need to be in place to ensure that the document is written to high quality standards, and the procedure will specify that the document will need to be reviewed by experts prior to its approval.

The review may be conducted according to the Review/Inspection process employed in the organization, or via an electronic work flow where each reviewer makes comments on the deliverable before it is then passed to the next reviewer. The approval of a document may take the form of physical signatures confirming agreement or via electronic sign-off. The document control procedure specifies how current revisions are identified, and the changes from one version of a document to another are clearly identified. This is typically achieved via revision bars in the document.

Control of Records

Quality records provide evidence that the quality system conforms to requirements and indicate the effectiveness of the quality system. ISO 9000:2000 requires certain records to be maintained, and these may be maintained in electronic or physical form. The organization maintains a procedure which stipulates the type of records that will be maintained, the length of time that they will be maintained for, the means by which they will be maintained, and the method of disposal of the quality records. The records include the following:

Table 3.9: ISO 9000:2000 Records

ISO Clause	Records to be maintained
5.6	Management review records
6.2.2	Training, education and skills records
7.1	Project deliverables
7.2.2	Records of reviews of requirements
7.3.4	Records of design and development review
7.3.5	Records of verification
7.3.6	Records of validation
7.3.7	Records of review of design and development changes
7.6	Records of control and measuring devices
8.2.2	Records of audits
8.2.4	Records of authorization of release of product
8.3	Records on non-conformities and actions
8.5.2	Records of results of corrective action
8.5.3	Records of results of preventive action

3.4.2 Management Responsibility Clause

This clause includes defining the responsibilities of management in the quality system, planning for quality and setting quality objectives, defining a quality policy, and a quality manual. Management plays a key role in creating an environment in which a quality management system can operate effectively. The management is required to promote the quality policy and quality objectives in the organization, and to increase the awareness of the importance of quality throughout the organization. The implementation of this clause involves the implementation of the following sub-clauses.

Management Commitment

The top management in the organization need to play a key role in the development and implementation of the quality management system in the organization, and in continuously improving the quality system. The management need to be committed to establishing and communicating the quality policy, establishing the quality objectives, and participating in the management reviews. The commitment of management is fundamental, and a quality improvement program or quality management system will fail without the commitment of senior management in the company.

Customer Focus

This clause is concerned with a focus on determining the right customer requirements and achieving a high level of customer satisfaction. It is related to the ISO 7.2.1 customer requirements clause, and the ISO 8.2.1 customer satisfaction clause. It requires a focus on customers and end users, and identifying their needs and expectations.

The organization needs to understand the needs of its customers, including those of potential customers, and this may include the competition in the field. The customer needs include price, performance, safety, functional requirements, etc. The requirements gathering process needs to be effective in gathering the correct requirements, and the software development process needs to be effective in delivering high quality software which matches or exceeds the customer expectations.

Quality Policy

The quality policy (Fig. 3.3) expresses the core values that the company has on software quality, and the company's commitment to quality. The employees need to be familiar with the quality policy and are required to actively implement the policy. The quality policy is usually displayed in a prominent location in the organization. It typically expresses the commitment of the company to customer satisfaction and to continuous improvement.

The quality policy of the organization places responsibility on management and employees, and the quality policy needs to be actively implemented. This involves planning for quality, customer satisfaction, and continuous improvement. The quality policy is periodically reviewed to ensure that it continues to meet the needs of the organization.

QUALITY POLICY

It is the policy of *Company X* to provide software products that match or exceed our customer expectations.

Customer satisfaction is a core value of our company.

We are dedicated to continuous improvement to serve our customers better.

Figure 3.3: Sample Quality Policy

Planning

The quality policy and organization strategy are employed to set the quality objectives for the organization. It is important to have measurable objectives, as this provides an objective status for management. The future needs of the organization need to be considered when setting quality objectives. The quality objectives includes quantitative goals similar to the following:

Table 3.10: Quantitative Quality Goals

Planning for Quality–Quantitative Goals
3.4 defects per million lines of software code
Overall customer satisfaction >= 8.2 (out of 10)
Phase Containment Effectiveness of 80%.
100% of critical customer problems addressed in 24 hours
100% of all serious customer problems addressed in 2 days
100% of projects delivered on time to customers.
100% compliance to defined lifecycle
100% of audits planned conducted.
100% of audit actions completed.
100% of deliverables inspected.
Over 80% staff involved in improvement initiatives

Management is responsible for quality planning in the organization. The quality objectives are identified, and include delivering high quality and reliable software on time to its customers, and to match or exceed customer needs and expectations. The planning will typically include the following:

Table 3.11: Planning for Quality

Planning for Quality
Develop state of the art software process
Develop a review/inspection process
Implement an improvement program
Develop a rigorous test process
Implement an audit program
Implement a customer satisfaction program
Perform reviews and inspections
Measure customer satisfaction
Introduce a mentor program for new employees
Promote core values on quality to all employees
Implement configuration management system

Customer satisfaction is measured and action plans are devised. Quality is built into the software project and there is an awareness of the importance of quality in the organization. The quality management system will include a software development lifecycle which will include activities for requirements analysis and definition, templates for design and project planning, standards for the various coding languages employed, a software review or inspection methodology, a testing process to verify that the software is correct and satisfies the customer requirements, quality audits to verify that the software process has been followed, and software configuration management.

Lessons are learned from the projects via a post-implementation review of the project and the lessons are acted upon in future projects. There is an emphasis on improvement and employees are actively encouraged to participate in improvement activities to serve the customer better. The software development process is improved periodically based upon feedback on its effectiveness.

Responsibility, Authority, and Communication

The implementation of this clause is concerned with assigning responsibility and authority to people in order to implement and maintain the quality system. The software development process will outline the responsibilities of the various roles involved in software development. The ISO 9000:2000 standard requires that a management representative be appointed with responsibility for monitoring, evaluating and improving the quality management system.

The management representative will usually be the quality manager, or in the absence of a quality manager, a representative is appointed. The responsibilities include liaising with the customers and others on all matters relating to the quality management system. Large companies will normally have a quality manager, whereas a small company will normally appoint a management representative to manage the quality system in a part-time capacity. There is an ISO 9000 requirement on internal communication of quality policy, objectives, and accomplishments. This usually takes the form of induction to new employees by the management representative, and notice boards with up-to-date information on the quality system. The organization needs a process for the internal communication on quality.

Management reviews

The purpose of the management review of the quality system is to assess the adequacy of the quality system and to address any weaknesses in the system. The quality manager is responsible for the introduction of the quality review in the organization. The review will typically include customer satisfaction, human resources, training, finance, networks, project management and development, process improvements, quality audits, preventive and corrective action status, follow-up actions from previous reviews, etc (Fig. 3.4).

QUALITY REVIEW AGENDA

09:00 Customer Satisfaction	Quality Manager
09:20 HR / Training	HR Manager
09:40 Networks / Facility	Networks Manager
10:00 Project Management	Project Manager
10:20 Development/Test	Dev/Test Leaders
11:00 Quality Audits	Quality Manager
11:20 Process Improvement	Quality Manager
11:40 Feedback	Managing Director
11:45 Action Summary and Close	

Fig 3.4 : Sample Management Review Meeting agenda

Each group in the organization will provide visibility into their area, e.g., via metrics or objective facts, at the quality review. The quality manager is responsible for working with the various groups to facilitate the introduction of metrics, as metrics enable trends and analysis to take place.

Each group will have an allocated period of time to provide visibility into their area. The review involves active participation from management, and the objective is to understand the current performance of the quality system, and to identify any potential improvements. There are specific ISO 9000:2000 requirements on what needs to be covered at the quality review. This includes the results of audits and customer satisfaction feedback, process performance and product conformity, and the status of corrective and preventive actions. Actions will be noted and the output of the review is a set of actions to be completed by the next review. A sample agenda for the quality review is provided in Figure 3.4.

ISO 9000 requires that records of the review be maintained and typically the agenda, presentations, and action plans are stored either electronically or physically. The quality review is usually chaired by the quality manager, and attended by management in the organization. The output of the review consists of actions and the quality manager verifies that the actions are completed at the next quality review. The actions yield further improvements of the quality management system.

3.4.3 Resource Management Clause

This clause includes requirements to ensure that appropriate resources are in place to deliver high quality software, and includes both the human resources, i.e., people, and the physical infrastructure. It includes requirements on training, as people need sufficient training and education in order to fulfill their role effectively. It also includes the work environment and physical infrastructure. It consists of the following sub-clauses:

Provision of Resources

The implementation of this clause requires that the organization determines the resources needed to implement the quality management system and provides the resources to meet current and future needs. The performance of the quality management system is considered at the management review, and resources needed to enhance the performance of the quality system are discussed. The resources include people, buildings, computers, etc. The organization needs to plan for future resource needs, and to enhance the competence of people by education and training, and to develop leadership skills for future managers. The organization needs a process for identifying the resource needs and its provision.

Human Resources

The human resource function plays a strategic role in the organization. It is responsible for staff recruitment and retention, career planning for employees, employee appraisals, health and safety, training in the organization, and a pleasant working environment in the organization. The implementation of this clause requires processes for employee appraisal and career planning, mentoring, education and training, employee leave, health and safety, code of ethics, etc. The HR function can play a key role in promoting a positive and pleasant work environment in the organization, and in facilitating two-way communication between management and employees. The HR function will usually investigate the reasons why people leave the organization, and will act on any relevant feedback.

The responsibilities and skills required for the various roles in the organization need to be defined, and training identified to address any gaps in the current qualification, skills and experience of the employees and the roles which they are performing. An annual organization training plan is usually produced, and the plan is updated throughout the year. There will normally be mandatory training for employees on key areas, for example, on quality. The objectives for individuals and teams are usually defined on an annual basis.

The training needs of the organization may change throughout the year owing to changes in tools and processes, or to a change in the strategic direction of the organization.

Infrastructure

The implementation of this clause requires that the organization have a process for defining the infrastructure for achieving effective and efficient product realization. The infrastructure includes buildings, furniture, office equipment, technologies, and tools, etc. The infrastructure may be planned one year in advance with budget allocated to the planned infrastructure needs for the year ahead. The infrastructure plan is then updated in a controlled manner throughout the year in response to medium and short-term needs. The infrastructure is there to support the organization in achieving its strategic goals and customer satisfaction. The infrastructure needs to be maintained to ensure that it continues to meet the needs of the organization, and the process for identifying the infrastructure includes maintenance. The infrastructure for a software organization includes computer hardware and software, and to be legally compliant the organization will need to ensure that there is a license for the software installed on each computer.

The organization will need a risk management plan to identify preventive measures to prevent disasters from happening, and a disaster recovery procedure to ensure disruption is kept to a minimum in the case of an actual disaster occurring. The disaster prevention and recovery procedure is a risk management strategy that identifies disaster threats to the infrastructure in the organization from accidents or the environment itself, and includes a recovery procedure to respond effectively to a disaster. The appropriate recovery procedure depends on the scale of damage, and the important thing is that recovery is planned with clearly defined roles and responsibilities. The damage assessment team and damage recovery team will work together to formulate the appropriate response to a disaster. The disaster recovery plan should be tested to ensure that it will be effective in the case of a real disaster. The individuals with responsibility for disaster prevention and recovery need to be trained in their roles.

Work Environment

The implementation of this clause requires the organization to develop a work environment that will promote employee satisfaction, motivation and performance. This may include flexibility in work practices, for example, flexitime, a state of the art building in a nice location which satisfies all the human requirements on noise, humidity, air quality, and cleanliness. It may include a sports and social club.

3.4.4 Product or Service Realization

This clause is concerned with the provision of efficient processes for product or service realization to ensure that the organization has the capability of satisfying its customers. Management plays a key role in ensuring that best in class processes are defined and implemented. The implementation of this clause involves the implementation of the following sub-clauses.

Planning of Product realization

This clause includes requirements for the organization to plan and define the processes needed for product realization. This requires a project management process to oversee the implementation of the project, and the project plan will typically include the scope of work for the project, the activities involved, the schedule and key milestones, the resources to implement the project, and any risks or dependencies.

A good software development process is needed to identify the customer requirements and efficiently implement the requirements through design, the software code and testing to ensure the correctness of the software product. The software development process may follow the waterfall model or may be a RAD lifecycle or whatever lifecycle that is appropriate to the business domain of the organization. The formality of the software process is dependent on the type of organization, as the safety critical requirements of an organization like NASA or the European Space Agency (ESA) are very stringent compared to an organization that produces computer games. Consequently, a very formal software development process is appropriate in safety-critical software development.

Customer related processes

The implementation of this clause requires a process for eliciting customer requirements, reviewing the requirements to ensure that the requirements are actually those desired by the customer, and an effective communication mechanism with the customer to ensure that customer enquiries and feedback are efficiently dealt with.

The task of identifying the correct customer requirements is [Ryn:00] is nontrivial, and changing requirements are a feature of many projects. In the standard waterfall lifecycle model it is assumed that each phase is completed prior to commencing the next phase. However, if requirements change, then there is a need to go through the lifecycle steps and the lifecycle is in effect an iterative waterfall model.

The requirements process will include a template to assist in the definition of the requirements, and the template will typically include sections similar to the following:

Table 3.12: Template for Requirements

Template for Requirements
Scope
Business context
Functional areas
System pre-requisites (performance, security, etc.)
List of requirements identified during requirements gathering
List of assumptions

The requirements are then documented and a review of the requirements is then scheduled with the customer. The objective of the review is to verify that the requirements specified are correct and correspond to what the customer needs. The assumptions made are critically examined to ensure their validity and any questions to be resolved are identified, and the answers are examined to ensure that there is sufficient information to complete the definition of the requirements.

The contract will detail the work to be carried out by the subcontractor, and this includes the requirements to be implemented, the schedule for implementation, the standards to be followed, and the acceptance criteria. The review of the contract ensures that both parties understand the commitments which they are making to one another, and the responsibilities of both parties throughout the project. A contract will usually include a penalty clause to address the situation where the supplier delivers the software later than the agreed schedule, or if the software is of poor quality.

There is an ISO 9000 requirement to maintain records of the review of requirements, and this protects both parties, as the review records will demonstrate that the review happened, and document any follow-up action from the review. The review record also enables independent verification to be performed by an auditor to ensure that the agreed changes have been implemented in the next revision of the requirements document. The organization needs to have a defined review process to ensure that reviews are consistently performed.

Ryan and Stevens [Ryn:00] have identified six best practice themes for requirements management: allowing sufficient time to the requirements process, choosing the right requirements elicitation approach, communicating the requirements, prioritizing the requirements, reusing the requirements, and tracking the requirements across the lifecycle. The ISO 9000 standard does not provide specific details to guide the implementation of a sound requirements management process, but does provide details of what the requirements process must satisfy.

There is an ISO 9000 requirement to implement an effective mechanism for communicating with customers in relation to enquiries, customer feedback, etc. Good communication channels are essential to delivering high-quality software to the customer.

Design and Development

The implementation of this clause requires that the organization has implemented a design and development process which is capable of delivering high-quality software on time to its customers. This clause includes sub-clauses to address design and development planning, design and development input and output, a review of design and verification, verification of design and development, validation of design and development, and control of changes to design and development.

The organization needs a planning process to ensure that all of the activities for design and development are planned, and that there are resources to carry out the activities. This will normally include project scheduling, estimation, etc. The project schedule needs to be agreed by all affected parties, communicated to all affected parties, and tracked throughout the project. A risk management strategy needs to be in place to identify potential risks and to have contingency plans to deal with the risk if it actually materializes.

The project management process will usually include a template for project planning. The project planning template will include sections similar to the following:

Table 3.13: Template for Project Planning

Template for Project Planning
Project deliverables
Project milestones
Project schedule
Risks and dependencies
Contingency plans
Staffing
Training needs
Travel
Standards to be followed
Testing
Configuration management
Quality audits
Release control
Post release support

The implementation of design and development input and output requires the software process to be documented, with each phase having inputs and then producing outputs. The inputs to design and development include the approved requirements document and the approved project plan for the project. The output typically includes the approved high-level and low-level design, the software code, the test plan and results, and inspection records. The software development process will detail the inputs and outputs.

Table 3.14 includes a release checklist which may be applied at the handover of the software to the system test group, or as criteria to be satisfied prior to the release the software to the customer. Tables 3.14 and Table 3.15 act as a control check for verification to demonstrate that the system requirements have been implemented correctly.

Table 3.14: Sample Handover Checklist

Project __ABC_ Milestone __Release__Date__22.06.2001_		
Project Handover Checklist		**Comments**
1.	Project plan reviewed, released and approved	√	No review records maintained.
2.	Detailed requirements reviewed, released, and approved	√	
3.	High level design reviewed, released, and approved	√	
4.	Low level design reviewed, released, and approved	√	
5.	Unit test plan reviewed, released, and approved	√	
6.	100% of source code reviewed	√	Informal code reviews
7.	Build complete and source code under source code management system	√	
8.	100% of unit testing run and passed	√	
9.	100% system test and acceptance test complete	√	Fixes complete
10.	100% of scheduled audit actions complete	√	No open audit actions @22/6/2001
11.	100% regression tests Run and 100% pass		99% run, 100%pass
12.	0 open showstoppers	√	All identified defects corrected.
13.	Release notes reviewed, released and approved	√	
14.	100% of known problems risk assessed and work-arounds	√	

The objective of the review of design and development is to ensure that quality has been built into the design and development deliverables, and that defects have been eliminated. The organization needs to employ a defined review process to ensure that reviews are consistently performed, and are effective. There is an ISO 9000 requirement to maintain records of the review.

The implementation of design and development verification requires checking to ensure that all of the inputs have been supplied, and that all of the outputs have been produced, and that the requirements have been implemented. The verification may take the form of an end of phase checklist to verify that all of the inputs and outputs of the phase are complete, or it may take the form of verification at key milestones in the project, for example, the handover to system testing, or to acceptance testing, etc. The handover checklist is usually in a form similar to Table 3.14 above. Table 3.15 demonstrates that all of the requirements are implemented and is the second part of the verification step.

The traceability matrix employs a one-to-many mapping where each requirement is mapped to several parts of the design document which demonstrates that the particular requirement has been implemented in the design. The trace matrix employs a one to many mapping of each requirement to several test cases, and this demonstrates that the implementation of the requirement has been effectively tested. This is clear from the following sample trace matrix.

Table 3.15: Sample Traceability Matrix

Requirement Section (or Number)	Corresponding Sections in Design	Corresponding Sections in Test Plan	Comments/ Risks
R1.1	D1.4, D1.5, D3.2	T1.2, T1.7	
R1.2	D1.8, D8.3	T1.4	
R1.3	D2.2	T1.3	
R 1.50	D20.1, D30.4	T20.1 T24.2	

The implementation of design and development validation is to ensure that the right system has been built and validation takes place during the lifecycle as well as at user acceptance testing. The requirements are validated during the customer review of the requirements, at user reviews of early versions of the software, especially where a prototype is produced and customer feedback provides invaluable information on whether the right system is being built. The essential difference between verification and validation is that verification is "building the system right" versus validation is "building the right system".

The implementation of control of design and development changes requires that the organization have a change-control approval body in place which is responsible for authorizing changes. The change approval body will usually consist of the project manager and other key players. The impact of the proposed change is considered, and a decision is made on whether to implement the change or not. There is an ISO 9000 requirement to maintain records of the review of changes and any necessary actions.

Purchasing Process

The implementation of this clause requires that the organization have an effective purchasing process in place for the procurement of high quality products.

The purchasing process will need to ensure that the purchased product conforms to the purchase requirements. The purchasing process includes the purchasing information to describe the requirements of the product being procured. The organization is required to ensure that the purchasing requirements are appropriate for its needs, and the purchasing information is then used to verify that the purchased product satisfies the desired requirements.

The verification of the purchased product may take the form of an inspection of the product to verify its suitability. The extent of control depends on the importance of the supplied product to the final end product. The organization is required to evaluate and select suppliers based on their ability to supply the product, and criteria for selection and evaluation will need to be established. There is an ISO 9000 requirement to maintain records of evaluations of suppliers and any actions arising from the evaluation of the supplier.

Software subcontracting is common in the software industry, and the software subcontractor may supply part or all of the software for a particular product to the prime contractor. Software organizations which employ software subcontractors will need a subcontractor process in place to manage the subcontractor effectively. This will usually include a statement of work which will detail the requirements to be implemented by the subcontractor, the key milestones, the schedule, the activities to be performed, the deliverables to be produced, the roles and responsibilities, the standards to be followed, the staff resources, and the acceptance criteria.

Production and Service Provision

The implementation of this clause involves planning and carrying out production and service provision under controlled conditions, validating production and service provision processes, establishing a process for identification and traceability, handling customer property correctly, and preserving the product. Efficient and reliable processes are essential to producing high-quality products in a manufacturing organization. The production of software involves the definition of the content of a release, performing a release build to produce the executables and associated files, and the storage of the released software on electronic media such as a CD or floppy disk, etc. These sub-clauses need to be interpreted to a software organization.

The control of production and service provision may be interpreted as the organization's having a sound configuration management system, and a sound release build process. The released software is usually accompanied by release notes and an installation guide. The validation of processes for production and service is addressed by audits of processes and products, and quantitative measurement of processes. The implementation of identification and traceability is interpreted as having a sound configuration management system in place which includes document change control, software source code control management, change control management, and release builds.

The versions of source files which make up a particular release should be clearly known, and the actual content of the release, including corrections to defects and enhancements, should be available. In a manufacturing environment a product is composed of many components, and the components are provided by various suppliers. It is important that the constituents of each product be fully known and traceable, as if it is discovered that a batch of components which has been used in the manufacture of a product contains defective items, it may be necessary to recall all products which have been manufactured with components from this particular batch. Consequently, the product must be clearly identified and traceable.

The customer property sub-clause requires the organization to exercise care with customer property while it is under the organization's control. This requires the organization to identify all customer property and to verify and protect it. This could potentially include confidential information, intellectual property, test data, etc. The software organization may have access to the customer computer network, and must handle the network with the utmost care and confidentiality.

The preservation of product clause requires the organization to have implemented processes for handling, storage, packaging, and delivery of the product. The implementation for a software organization usually requires that the software be stored on electronic media and packaged and delivered to the customer.

Control of Measuring and Monitoring devices

This clause is important in the manufacturing sector, and it requires the organization to ensure that regular calibration of the machines take place, and that machines be adjusted accordingly, to ensure the validity of the measurements recorded. The calibration status of each machine should be known. The interpretation of this clause to a software organization is related to the test tools and test scripts. Automated testing tools are typically used for regression testing and the objective is to run a suite of test cases to demonstrate that the core functionality remains in place following changes to the software. The test scripts may need to be updated from one major release of the software to the next, and the requirement is interpreted as ensuring that the test scripts are sufficient to test the software.

3.4.5 Measuring, Analysis, and Improvement

This clause is concerned with the measurement of processes to improve the performance of the quality management system. The sub-clauses include the measurement of customer satisfaction, internal audits, measurement and monitoring of processes, measuring and monitoring of products, control of non-conformity, analysis of data, and continual improvement. The measurements provide an objective indication of the current performance of the quality management system.

Analysis will be used to determine the improvement actions to prevent the re-occurrence of similar problems in the future. The objective is to continually improve the organization.

Customer Satisfaction and Audits

The measurement of customer satisfaction is fundamental, as the objective is to satisfy the customer requirements, and to achieve a high level of customer satisfaction.

The measurement of customer satisfaction will typically be via a customer satisfaction survey (Table 3.16), and monitoring of customer problems, complaints, etc. The customer satisfaction survey may be quite simple and will typically include a series of questions in which the customer rates the performance of the organization.

The feedback from the customer satisfaction survey is discussed, and a follow up meeting is scheduled with the customer. An action plan is produced to address any issues. The monitoring of customer satisfaction measurements will indicate the success of the organization in satisfying their customers. A sample customer satisfaction questionnaire is included in Table 3.16, and the objective of the questionnaire is to obtain feedback from the customer.

The implementation of internal audits requires the organization to establish an internal audit process. The objective of an audit is to provide visibility to management on the processes being used and the product being built. The audit is an independent examination, and is typically carried our by a trained auditor. The level of compliance to the defined process is considered, as is the effectiveness of the defined process. Improvement opportunities are identified and tracked to completion. The output from the audit is an audit report, and the audit report includes the findings of the audit and recommendations.

The audit of a group or project consists of an interview with the particular group and a review of documentation. The audit will need a clear purpose and scope to be effective, and usually the auditor will be examining the effectiveness of one particular area, for example, configuration management, project management, requirements management, development, or testing.

Table 3.16: Sample Customer Satisfaction Questionnaire

No	Criteria/ Question	Unacceptable	Poor	Fair	Satisfied	Excellent	N/A
1.	Quality of software	❑	❑	❑	❑	❑	❑
2.	Ability to meet committed dates	❑	❑	❑	❑	❑	❑
3.	Timeli-ness of projects	❑	❑	❑	❑	❑	❑
4.	Effective testing of software	❑	❑	❑	❑	❑	❑
5.	Expertise of staff	❑	❑	❑	❑	❑	❑
6.	Value for money	❑	❑	❑	❑	❑	❑
7.	Quality of support	❑	❑	❑	❑	❑	❑
8.	Ease of installa-tion of software	❑	❑	❑	❑	❑	❑
9.	Ease of use of software	❑	❑	❑	❑	❑	❑
10.	Timely resolution of prob-lems	❑	❑	❑	❑	❑	❑
11.	Accurate diagnos-tics	❑	❑	❑	❑	❑	❑
12.	Intention to recom-mend	❑	❑	❑	❑	❑	❑

The auditor will need excellent verbal and written communication, and will need to be tactful and diplomatic, as well as being thorough and forceful when required. The auditor may need to reassure the group being audited, and will usually explain that the purpose of the audit is to enable the organization to improve. A sample audit process is outlined in Figure 3.5:

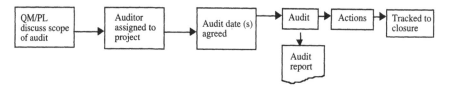

Figure 3.5: Sample Audit Process

Audit Planning

Step 1.	The quality manager produces an annual audit schedule
Step 2.	The quality manager and group leader discuss the scope of the audit
Step 3.	An auditor is assigned and a date for the audit agreed with the group
Step 4.	The auditor will interview the group and review appropriate documentation
Step 5.	The auditor will advise the attendees of documentation to be brought to the audit

Audit Meeting

Step 1.	The auditor will interview project team members and review documentation
Step 2.	The auditor will discuss preliminary findings at the end of the meeting

Audit Reporting

Step 1.	The auditor will publish the preliminary audit report and discuss with group leader.
Step 2.	The auditor makes agreed changes and publishes the final report.
Step 3.	The audit report will be sent to all affected parties.
Step 4.	The audit report will detail the actions to be addressed.

Audit Action Tracking

Step 1.	The auditor will monitor the closure of the actions.
Step 2.	The owner of the action will need to ensure closure by the due date, or agree new date.
Step 3.	Actions which are not resolved in a timely manner are escalated.

Audit Metrics

Step 1.	Audit metrics provide visibility into the audit program.
Step 2.	The audit metrics will be presented at the management review.

The implementation of measurement and monitoring of processes requires the organization to implement measurement to evaluate process performance. Process measurement is essential in a manufacturing environment, and process measurement in a software organization is concerned with the measurement of key software processes.

Measurement provides an objective indication of the performance of the processes, and quantitative goals will need to be set for process performance; actual results may be compared against the goals. The level 4 key process area maturity of the CMM includes a key process area for quantitative process management, and the objective of this KPA is to ensure that the organization processes are under control. This requires quantitative goals to be set for process performance and for quantitative process performance limits to be set for the key processes. The intention is that if process performance falls outside the control limits, then this will trigger corrective actions to adjust the performance of the process to ensure that it performs within the upper and lower control limits. This is best expressed via a process performance diagram:

The process performance diagram (Fig. 3.6) indicates the performance of the process over time, and whether it is performing within the lower and upper control limits. The example above indicates the presence of spikes in process performance, and these require investigation and adjustment to the process to ensure that it performs within the required control limits.

The implementation of measurement and monitoring of product requires the organization to monitor and measure the performance of the product to verify that the product requirements are fulfilled. The measurements enable an objective decision on whether it is appropriate to release the software to potential customers. One mechanism to implement this is to employ a product release checklist which stipulates the criteria to be satisfied before releasing software to potential customers. The checklist may be similar to the sample checklist described in the design and development clause. The quality function in the organization will usually play an independent role in approving the particular software release.

The level 4 key maturity level on the CMM includes the software quality management key process area, and the objective of this key process area is to provide a quantitative understanding of the quality of the product. The implementation of this key process area usually requires the projects to have an associated software quality management plan which includes quantitative goals and criteria to be satisfied prior to successful approval of the software.

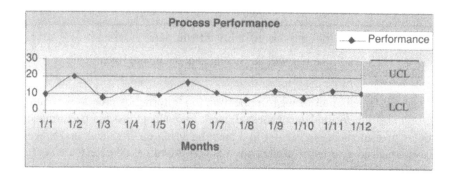

Figure 3.6: Process Performance

Control of Nonconformity

The control of nonconformity is concerned with the procedure for reporting defects, and the responsibilities for taking action to eliminate the defect. The defects are recorded either via a tool or a spreadsheet. The information recorded about the defect typically includes the severity of the defect, the date that it occurred, the originator of the defect, the technical person responsible for the correction of the defect, the type of defect, e.g., genuine defect, enhancement, or misunderstanding, the current status of the defect, etc. There are many tools available to record the defect data, and to show the current quality status of the project with respect to the reported defects. Negative trends in defects should be identified and improvement actions taken. The organization requires a procedure for handling nonconformity.

Analysis of Data

The implementation of the analysis of data sub-clause is that decision making should be based on the objective data obtained from the measurements, and that the organization should analyze the data to determine the appropriate actions for improvement. The organization will analyze customer satisfaction measurements, supplier data, etc.

Improvement

The objective of continual improvement is to improve the effectiveness of the quality management system through the use of the quality policy, quality objectives, audit results, customer satisfaction measurements, management review, analysis of data, and corrective and preventive actions.

The implementation of corrective action clause requires the organization to use corrective action for improvement. The objective is to learn from defects or issues to ensure that there is no reoccurrence. Corrective action is taken on customer complaints, defect reports, audit reports, etc., and the results of effective corrective action is a more effective quality management system. The implementation of this clause requires a procedure and includes a review of identified defects, a causal analysis of the defects, identifying actions to be taken, taking the actions, and reviewing the effectiveness of the actions. The management review is an effective forum for discussing corrective and preventive actions.

The objective of preventive action is to identify actions to prevent potential defects from occurring. This requires a documented procedure for determining potential defects and their causes, identifying actions to be taken, implementing the actions, and reviewing its effectiveness later.

3.5 ISO 9000 and Improvement

Many organizations aspire to excellence, and excellence may be achieved by continual improvements. An organization may assess its current level of excellence with respect to some standard or model, and use the feedback from the assessment to develop an improvement program. The ISO 9000 standard may be used by an organization to assess its current level of maturity. The findings from the assessment will indicate the areas which the organization needs to work on to improve. This section describes a simple self-assessment process, which has been adapted from ISO 9004:2000.

3.5.1 Self-Assessment Process

Table 3.17 is a sample self-assessment of an imaginary organization with respect to the ISO 9000 standard. The self-assessment yields a maturity profile for the organization. It is typically carried out by one or more people from the organization, and the objective is to rate the organization with respect to the various clauses and sub-clauses of the standard. The example presented here takes a small selection of the ISO 9000:2000 clauses and rates the maturity of the clauses in the organization.

Table 3.17: ISO 9000:2000 Maturity

ISO 9000 Clause	Not Qualified	Partially Qualified	Largely Qualified	Fully Qualified
4.2.4 Control of records				
5.3 Quality policy				
5.6 Management review				
6.2.2 Competence, training, and awareness.				
7.2.1 Customer requirements.				

Table 3.17 (*continued*): ISO 9000:2000 Maturity

ISO 9000 Clause	Not Qualified	Partially Qualified	Largely Qualified	Fully Qualified
7.2.2 Review of customer requirements				
7.3.4 Design and development review				
7.3.7 Control of changes				
7.4.1 Purchasing process				
8.2.1 Customer satisfaction				
8.2.2 Internal audit				
8.3 Control of nonconformity				
8.4 Analysis of data for improvement				
8.5.2 Corrective action				
8.5.3 Preventative action				

■ Requires major attention (0 – 15% satisfied)   ▨ Requires attention to satisfy (16 – 50% satisfied)   □ On track (51-85% satisfied)

The rating scheme employed here is to rate the clause as not qualified if it is less than 15% satisfied, to rate it partially satisfied if it is 16% to 50% satisfied, largely satisfied if it is 51% to 85% satisfied, and fully satisfied if it is 86% to 100% satisfied. The rating scheme is based on the ideas of SPICE which is discussed in chapter 5. The intention is to have an indication of the maturity, e.g., a rating of 15% indicates that 15% of the projects have implemented the clause, or it is approximately 15% satisfied at the organization level.

The approach suggested for rating the clauses in ISO 9004:2000 is to employ the following maturity levels: The reader is referred to the standard for more detailed information.

Table 3.18: Performance Maturity Level

Maturity	Performance Level	Guidance
1	No formal approach	No systematic approach evident; poor/ unpredictable results
2	Reactive approach	Problem or corrective based approach
3	Stable formal approach	Systematic, process-based approach
4	Continual improvement	Improvement process in use, good results and improvements
5	Best in class	Best in class benchmarked results.

3.5.2 Action Plans

The value of an assessment of an organization is that it presents a clear picture of where an organization is with respect to some model or standard. The output from the assessment typically yields the strengths of the organizations, and areas in which the organization would benefit from further improvement. There is little point in an organization undergoing an assessment unless the organization acts upon the findings. This typically involves an action plan (Table 3.19) to address the assessment findings over a period of time. Often, the organization produces a high-level plan of things to be done per quarter, and a detailed action plan for activities to be performed within six months.

Table 3.19: ISO 9000:2000 Action Plan

ISO 9000 Action Plan following Internal ISO 9000 self assessment				
Act No.	ISO Clause	Action	Actionee	Date Due / Status
1	4.2.4	Define a control of records procedure; communicate; monitor insitutionalization	Quality manager	28.02.01 Closed
2	5.3	Communicate the quality policy to all staff	Quality manager	31.03.01 Closed
3	5.6	Define a structure for the management review; work with other managers to introduce	Quality manager	30.06.01 Closed
4	6.2.2	Implement records of training and experience of all staff	HR manager	31.03.01 Closed
5	7.2.1.	Ensure requirements for post-delivery are considered as part of the requirements process	S/W manager	14.01.01 Closed

Act No.	ISO Clause	Action	Actionee	Date Due	Status
6	7.2.2	Record minutes and actions of the review of requirements and maintain records	Development	14.01.01	Open
7	7.3.4	Maintain records of design and development review	Development	14.01.01	Closed
9	7.3.7	Implement a change approval board to approve changes of design and development	Project manager	14.01.01	Closed
10	7.4.1	Define and document the purchasing process	Procurement	14.01.01	Open
11	8.2.1	Implement action plans from customer satisfaction feedback	Quality manager	30.04.01	Closed
12	8.2.2	Verify audit actions are completed in a timely manner	Quality manager	31.05.01	Open
13	8.3	Define the procedure for the control of non-conformity; communicate and institutionalise	Quality manager / Development	30.06.01. 01	Closed
14	8.4	Analyze the customer satisfaction data	Quality manager	30.06.01	Closed
15	8.5.2	Define the procedure for corrective action; communicate and institutionalise	Quality manager	31.10.01	Open
16	8.5.3	Define the procedure for preventive action; communicate and institutionalise.	Quality manager	30.09.01	Open

Table 3.19 (*continued*): ISO 9000:2000 Action Plan

3.6 ISO 9000 Certification Process

This certification process has been described earlier in the chapter as part of ISO 9000:2000 implementation; the typical steps in going for ISO 9000 certification include the following:.

Table 3.20: ISO 9000:2000 Action Plan

ISO 9000:2000 Certification Process
The company implements the quality management system as described in sections 3.4.1 through to 3.4.5.
A trial ISO 9000:2000 readiness audit is performed by an independent consultant.
Feedback is provided from the trial audit and corrective actions assigned.
The corrective actions from the trial audit are implemented.
A decision is then made to go for an official assessment.
The certification body / registrar is contacted.
An assessment date is agreed upon.
The participants are briefed and logistics organized.
The on-site assessment is conducted by the external assessment team.
The assessment team provide an evaluation report and findings
Any corrective actions are performed by the company.
Corrective actions are verified prior to registration.
The registration is granted.
The organization will need to maintain compliance with the ISO 9000 standard with on-going maintenance.
The feedback from the assessment is used to improve

3.7 Summary

ISO 9000 is an international quality standard which enables an organization to implement a sound quality system that is dedicated to customer satisfaction and continual improvement. The independent certification of ISO 9000 indicates that the company has a good quality management system in place, and that the company is committed to the core values of quality, customer satisfaction, and improvement.

The ISO 9000 standards may be applied to various types of organizations, including manufacturing, software, and service organizations. ISO 9000 is regarded as a minimal quality standard that an organization that takes quality seriously should satisfy. Many organizations require their subcontractors to be ISO 9000 certified, as this provides confidence in the subcontractor's quality system and in the ability of the subcontractor to produce high-quality software.

The latest revision of ISO 9000 is termed ISO 9000:2000, and it is a significant enhancement over the 1994 version of the standard. It places emphasis on customer satisfaction and continual improvement, and includes a process model. The older 1994 version of the standard placed emphasis on defining procedures for doing the work, whereas the new standard the emphasis is on processes. It is a simpler standard, and is effective from December 2000.

The standard includes ISO 9000, ISO 9001, and ISO 9004. The ISO 9004:2000 standard provides practical guidance on the implementation of ISO 9001:2000 and guidelines for performance improvement of the quality system.

The implementation of ISO 9000 is discussed and this involves setting up a steering group to manage the implementation and to provide the necessary resources for implementation. A self-assessment to indicate the current ISO 9000 status is generally performed and an action plan to address the weaker areas is defined. The implementation is managed and tracked like a normal project, and the implementation generally involves defining processes and procedures, maintaining records, and training. The quality group in the organization will play a key role in the implementation of the standard and in ensuring compliance with the ISO 9000:2000 requirements.

The award of ISO 9000 certification provides an indication that the company is focused on quality and customer satisfaction.

4
The Capability Maturity Model

4.1 Introduction

The Capability Maturity Model (CMM©) is a process maturity model which enables an organization to define and evolve its software processes. It is a premise in software engineering that there is a close relationship between the quality of the delivered software product and the quality and maturity of the underlying software processes. Consequently, it is important for a software organization to devote attention to the software processes as well as to the product. The CMM is a framework by which an organization may mature its software processes. It has been influenced by the ideas of some of the leading figures in the quality movement, such as Crosby, Deming, and Juran, etc.

Crosby's quality management maturity grip describes five evolutionary stages in adopting quality practices [Crs:80]. Crosby's ideas were adopted, refined, and applied to software organizations by Watt Humphrey in *Managing the Software Process* [Hum:89] and in early work done at the Software Engineering Institute. This lead to the development of a maturity model termed the Process Maturity Model (PMM) by the Software Engineering Institute [Hum:87]. The PMM is a questionnaire-based approach to process maturity, and subsequent work and refinement of the PMM lead to the Capability Maturity Model. The CMM is, in effect, the application of the process management concepts of total quality management (TQM) to software. The main rationale for the development of the CMM was the need of the Department of Defense (DOD) to develop a mechanism to evaluate the Capability of software contractors.

The CMM v1.0 was released in 1991, and following pilots it was revised and released in 1993 as v1.1. The Software Engineering Institute has been working on the CMMI^{SM} project, and the objective of this project is to merge the software CMM and the Systems CMM, and also to make the CMM compatible with SPICE (15504), the emerging international standard for software process assessment. The CMMI v1.0 was released in July 2000 and is expected to replace

---

the CMM in the future. SPICE is expected to be released as an international standard in the future, and it currently exists as an ISO technical report. It is termed a type 2 technical report, and this indicates that full agreement on its definition as a standard has not been achieved at this time but is expected to be achieved in the future.

The real benefit of the CMM is that it allows the organization to follow a logical path in improvement, and to evolve at its own pace, via the evolutionary path of satisfying the CMM maturity levels. Each maturity level provides a foundation for further improvements, and the maturity levels cannot be skipped. There is an increase in capability associated with greater maturity, and this enhanced capability is reflected in quality, timeliness of projects, reliability, etc. The result of a successful CMM improvement program is an evolution from an immature and poorly defined software process to a defined, measured, controlled, mature, and effective software process.

The maturity of an organization is a rating given to an organization following an external CMM assessment of the organization by a qualified external assessment team. The capability of the organization provides an indication of the expected results in its software projects. The expectation is that a highly mature organization will deliver the agreed functionality on time, within budget, with high quality, and reliability.

A mature organization is expected to have sound project management, configuration management, requirements management, and quality management practices in place. The process performance represents the actual results achieved by following the software process, and is contrasted with the expected results or software process capability. The immature organization has no objective mechanism to assess the quality of the product and little understanding of the importance of building quality into the product via peer reviews and testing. Immature organizations have little understanding as to how the steps in the software process may affect the quality of the product.

There are three key aspects of good software engineering, namely, people, technology and process (Fig. 4.1). Most problems are due to a defective process, and the focus is to fix the process rather than blaming people. This leads to a culture of openness in discussing problems, and identifying solutions.

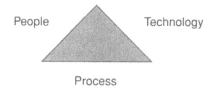

Figure 4.1: Process Triangle

There are other maturity models apart from the software CMM. The People Capability Maturity Model (P-CMM) is a maturity model that is focused on maturing the people in the organization to become a world class workforce. It is dedicated to improving the capability of individuals within the organization. The CMM is a model for software process maturity and the objective is to understand and mature the software process to improve the capability of the organization. The software process is defined as "*a set of activities, methods, practices and transformations that people use to develop and maintain software and the associated work products*". The process is the glue that binds people, tools and methods together, and as a process matures it is better defined with clearly defined entry and exit criteria, inputs and outputs, and an explicit description of the tasks, verification of process, and consistent implementation throughout the organization.

4.1.1 Motivation for CMM

This section includes justification as to why a company should consider implementing the CMM. Some benefits include:

Table 4.1: Motivation for CMM Implementation

Motivation for CMM Implementation
Enhances the credibility of the company
Marketing benefit of CMM maturity level
A framework to implement best practices in software engineering; the KPAs contain very valuable guidance
A logical path to improvement
Increased capability and maturity of organization
Increased capability of subcontractors
Improved technical and management practices
Increased quality of software
Increased timeliness of projects
Reduced cost of maintenance and incidence of defects
Measurement of processes and products
Projects/products may be quantitatively managed
Exploiting innovative technologies to enhance performance
Improved customer satisfaction
Fire prevention culture rather than a fire fighting culture
Culture of improvement
Higher morale in company

4.1.2 CMM and the Quality Group

The CMM model places responsibilities on management and staff in the company. The impact of the model on the Quality (SQA) group is considered in this section. The typical responsibilities of the quality group in a CMM environment are considered. The quality group will generally play a key role in the implementation of the model and the responsibilities of SQA include:

Table 4.2: Responsibilities of SQA in CMM implementation

Responsibilities of the Quality Group (SQA)
Perform audits of projects, subcontractors, and departments
Provide visibility into processes/products
Report results to management and affected groups
Act as a partner in quality with the projects
Evaluate extent to which quality is built into the project
Evaluate effectiveness of the defined processes
Work with groups to facilitate improvements to processes
Verify implementation and institutionalization of key process areas
Set quantitative goals for project quality
Participate in process improvement activities (on SEPG)
Participate in evaluation of capability of subcontractor.
Support/champion implementation of CMM
Facilitate internal and external CMM assessments
Champion SQA and SQM key process areas on CMM
Promote awareness and a culture of quality
Facilitate definition of metrics for groups including project management, requirements, development, testing, etc.
Implement a regular management quality review
Participate as a member of the project team
Review project plan
Participate in post-implementation reviews of the projects to learn lessons
Facilitate evaluation of new / innovative technologies
Implement a test process

The responsibilities of SQA change depending on the maturity of the organization: for example, the focus will be on ensuring compliance to processes at the early stages of maturity. Some of the responsibilities for the quality group are listed above. The role works most effectively when the SQA group is seen as a partner and facilitator for improvement rather than in a police-like role. The role is people focused, and the SQA group will meet with people at all levels in the organization, including managers, team leaders, developers, and testers.

4.2 Overview of CMM

The CMM describes an evolutionary path for an organization to evolve from an immature or *ad hoc* software process to a mature and disciplined software process. It is a five-level maturity model, where a move from one level to a higher level indicates increased process maturity and an enhanced capability of the organization. The five levels in the model are the initial level, the repeatable level, the defined level, the managed level, and the optimizing level. The organization moves from one maturity level to the next, with the current maturity level providing the foundation for improvement for the next level, and therefore maturity levels are not skipped. The maturity levels are described in the following diagram.

Initial Level

The first level is termed the *initial level* and a characteristic feature of a level 1 organizations is that processes are *ad hoc*, or poorly defined, or inconsistently implemented. Software development is like a black art in a level 1 organization with requirements flowing in and the product flowing out with little visibility into the process. Often, level 1 organizations are reactionary and engaged in fire fighting, and often there is an element of the *"hero culture"*, i.e., where the organization depends on the heroic efforts of its staff to resolve its latest crises, for example, a super programmer, or hero, resolves the latest crisis.

A level 1 organization may have many processes defined, but in a level organization the processes are neither enforced or consistently followed. Many software organizations in the world are believed to be at level 1 on the CMM scale. However, the fact that an organization is at level 1 does not mean that it is necessarily unsuccessful in delivering high quality software. Clearly, as many organizations are at level 1, and yet remain in business, they must be successful to some degree. The main argument against level 1 organizations is that whereas

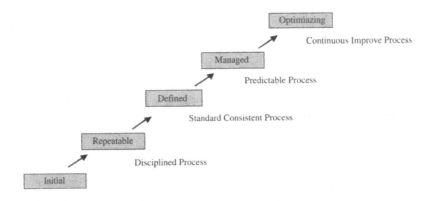

Figure 4.2: CMM Maturity Levels

they may be successful in one particular project, the success of the present or previous project is no guarantee of success in future projects. That is, a level 1 organization may lack the infrastructure to ensure repeatability of previous successes. Further, there is a dependency on key players or "heroes" to ensure the success of a particular project.

Repeatable Level

The second CMM level is termed the *"repeatable leve"* and organizations at level 2 on the CMM model have policies and procedures defined for implementing software projects. The characteristic feature of level 2 organizations is the emphasis on management processes. The software development is a series of black boxes with defined milestones. The planning and management of projects is based on the experience gained in managing previous projects.

The intention is that the organization is capable of repeating the success of previous projects, and to continue to use practices that have been proven to be successful in previous projects. Project commitments are made based on experience gained in managing previous similar projects. The project manager tracks the schedule, functionality, quality, milestones, deliverables, and manages risk. Subcontractors are managed by careful selection, agreeing to commitments, and tracking the agreed upon deliverables to completion. Requirements management and configuration management practices are in place, and there is independent visibility into the software project provided by the quality assurance group. It is not required that projects be managed in the same way, and different projects may do things differently.

Defined Level

The third level is termed the *"defined level"* and organizations at level 3 have defined a standard organizational software process (OSSP) for developing and maintaining software. The organization standard software process is tailored to individual projects. There is a group which is responsible for defining the organization's software process, and in managing improvements and changes to the organization process. This group is typically termed the software engineering process group (SEPG) in CMM terminology; however, the essential point is that there is a group which is responsible for the organization software process and is actively improving it.

There is an emphasis on training at this level, as all staff are required to know the software process and need the appropriate expertise to perform their roles effectively. Projects tailor the OSSP to yield the project's defined software process, which is the software process employed for the particular project. The tailoring means that projects do not need to do things exactly the same way, and the tailoring will indicate how the project's defined software process is obtained from the organization software process. The software engineering and management activities for level 3 organizations are stable. This maturity level also addresses organization communication and building quality into the software project via peer reviews.

There is a paradigm shift in a level 3 organization and the focus changes from emphasis on product management to emphasis on both product management and process management. There is a greater understanding of the software development process in a level 3 organization, and increased visibility into the tasks of the process. Processes are well defined with clearly defined entry and exit criteria, inputs and outputs, tasks and verification.

Managed Level

Level 4 is termed the *managed level* and it is characterized by processes and product performing within defined quantitative control limits. Quality goals are set for both products and processes, and performance is monitored with corrective action taken to ensure that the goals are met. It is required that projects maintain measurements of quality and performance of the various processes to satisfy this level. Control limits are set for the performance of the various processes, and the performance of the processes is monitored, with corrective action taken should the performance of a process fall outside of its control limits. The corrective actions triggered act to adjust process performance accordingly to ensure that it behaves within the defined control limits. The causes of process variation are identified and the problem in the process is corrected. New project targets are based on quantified measurements of past performance.

The paradigm shift of a level 4 organization is the change from a focus on the process definition to a focus on process measurement and analysis of measurement. The fundamental premise is that product performance is linked with process quality, and thus the emphasis is on improving the quality of the process. A high-quality and mature process has low variability from its mean process performance. The intention in quantitative process management is to narrow the control limits via process improvements and measurement, thereby leading to highly predictable processes with a corresponding effect on project quality. Decision making in a level 4 organization is based upon objective measurements.

The level 4 organization requires that an effective data gathering and measurement program be set up and institutionalized within the organization. This requires that there is already an organization standard software process defined.

Optimizing Level

Level 5 is termed the *optimizing level* and its focus is on continuous process improvement. Defects are analyzed to determine their root cause and known defects are eliminated from software processes. New processes and technologies are evaluated and piloted and data gathered to measure the effectiveness of the technologies or process. This enables an informed decision to be made as to whether the technology or process should become part of the process. There is an emphasis on a periodic examination of the software process for continuous improvement. A level 5 organization will objectively measure to determine if the changes to the software process have yielded quantitative improvements in performance.

New technology is piloted to determine its benefits and there is a transfer of innovations in software engineering to the organization in a controlled manner. The emphasis at all stages is in increasing process capability, and measurement is employed to verify that there actually is an improvement in process performance from the new technologies or processes.

The paradigm shift at the optimizing level is continuous improvement, and the objective is to eliminate waste and inefficiencies and thereby enhance process performance. It builds on the foundation of measurement and analysis in level 4 of the maturity model.

4.3 CMM Architecture

The CMM architecture is described in Figure 4.3. Each CMM maturity level with the exception of level 1 is composed of several key process areas (KPAs). Each KPA includes a set of activities to be performed and various goals to be satisfied to effectively implement and institutionalize the particular KPA. The KPAs are major building blocks in establishing the maturity level and the associated capability of the organization. There are 18 key process areas in the CMM, and each KPA is a building block for further improvement. The responsibilities for the implementation of the KPA are either the organization or the project, and where the organization is responsible it is required to ensure that the KPA goals are satisfied across the projects. The implementation of the KPA requires a sound infrastructure to ensure its sustainability.

The infrastructure includes organization policies, training, resources, people, tools, measurement, verification, etc., and these support the continuing performance of the activities of the KPA.

Organization policies for software engineering are defined at the organization level, and these policies must then be satisfied at the project level. The organization policy may be a high level statement or a detailed statement, and will include the core values and standards that the organization has in key areas including, for example, project management, requirements management, etc. The projects are required to satisfy the organization policy but are not required to have the same implementation.

The CMM is not a prescriptive model in that it does not state precisely how an organization should satisfy a particular KPA or maturity level. Instead, the CMM provides practical guidance to assist in implementing and tailoring the KPA to meet the needs of the organization. A maturity level is a well-defined evolutionary plateau and each maturity level represents an important milestone for an organization on its journey to mature its software process.

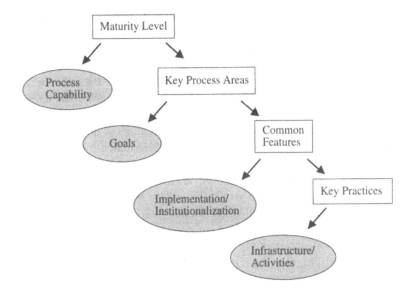

Figure 4.3: CMM Architecture

Each KPA includes a set of goals which must be satisfied in order for the KPA to be satisfied. The KPAs are organized by common features and these are responsible for the implementation and institutionalization of the KPA. They include the key practices such as the commitment to perform, the ability to perform, the activities performed, measurement and analysis, and verification. The successful implementation of the key practices means that the KPA goals and therefore the KPA are satisfied. There is a difference between the implementation and the institutionalization of the KPA. The KPA is implemented via the activities defined in the KPA, and this indicates that the KPA is being performed. The KPA is institutionalized via the policies, definition, and documentation of the process, training, resources, verification, and measurement. The institutionalization requires that the KPA becomes in effect part of the organization's and project's way of doing business, and this requires training, monitoring, and enforcement of the process.

The assessment of an organization yields a maturity rating for the organization. The award of a rating at a particular level indicates that the organization satisfies all of the goals for the key process areas at that maturity level, and the goals for all key process areas at any lower levels. The CMM model is evolutionary and it specifies a logical order or roadmap in which the organization may mature its software processes, and the approach to organizational maturity is step wise from one CMM level to the next. Each maturity level provides a firm foundation by which the processes for the next level may be implemented, and maturity levels are not skipped. The result is an organization with well defined and implemented processes which are institutionalized throughout the organization. The processes in a level 4 organization are measured, analyzed, and controlled, with corrective action taken whenever the process falls outside the defined control limits. The emphasis is continuous improvement of the process.

The CMM is a model, and a model is a simplification of the real world. The model is judged useful if it is a good representation of the world. The *adequacy* or otherwise of the model is of key importance as inadequate models are replaced, and adequate models are chosen as representations of the real world. The adequacy or otherwise of the particular model is determined by model exploration, and this includes asking questions. The ability of the model to explain or predict behavior is an important factor in evaluating its adequacy. The adequacy of the CMM has been determined via its review by hundreds of software engineering professionals, and its deployment in hundreds of software organizations worldwide. The CMM model enables an organization to plan and prioritize process improvement, and improvement generally takes the form of small steps. The maturity level provides a roadmap of the improvements to build a sound software process infrastructure in the organization.

The implementation of the CMM requires a thorough knowledge of the model, in-depth software engineering experience, and good judgment to apply it to the particular software engineering domain.

4.3.1 KPA Architecture

Each maturity level consists of several key process areas, where each KPA has a set of process goals to be satisfied. The architecture of a KPA is described in Figure 4.4.

The satisfaction of the process goals for the KPA is via the key practices and these detail the activities and infrastructure to address implementation and institutionalization. The key practices detail *what is to be done,* but not *how it is to be done.* They are organized by *common features* and these indicate whether the implementation and institutionalization of the key process area is effective. There are five common features (see Table 4.3)

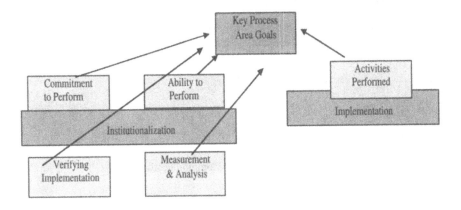

Figure 4.4: KPA Architecture

Table 4.3: Common Features

Common Feature	Description
Commitment to perform	This describes the action the organization must take to ensure that the process is established and will endure. It typically involves organizational policies, senior management sponsorship, and the responsibility of roles for particular activities
Ability to Perform	This describes any preconditions to implement the software process. It typically requires sufficient resources, training, and organizational structures to be in place, e.g., that a group exists, or that there are tools to support various activities, or that particular roles receive training.
Activities Performed	This describes the activities required to implement a key process area. It typically involves planning the work, performing the work, tracking the work, and taking corrective action. A plan is developed according to a documented procedure and the activities are performed according to the plan.
Measurement and Analysis	Measurements are used to control and improve the process. The measurements determine the effectiveness of the activities performed and the status of the activities. Good measurement requires a data collection program to be in place.
Verifying Implementation	This typically involves reviews and audits to verify that the activities performed are in compliance with the defined process and the effectiveness of the process. The reviews involve SQA, project management, and senior management.

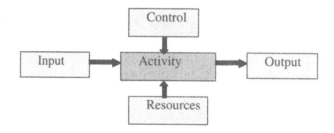

Figure 4.5: Activity and Common Features

Figure 4.5 summarizes how the common features apply to a process. An activity may be an engineering stage, a management task, or the measurement or verification of an activity.

The inputs to the activity are from prior steps in the process and the input and output process execution artifacts provide evidence that the process has been performed. The resources include trained staff, hardware and software, tools, etc., and are evidence of ability to perform. Controls include policies, procedures, standards, reviews, measurements, audits, etc., and are evidence of the commitment to perform.

The diagram is applied to the activities in the individual key process areas, for example, the project planning activity in the subcontractor management key process area. The inputs to this key process area include the statement of work and allocated requirements; the resources include the project manager, the tools, training, and schedule; the controls include the organization planning policy and the planning procedures for a project and the standards for planning at the project level; and the output includes the estimates and the plan.

4.4 CMM Maturity Levels

The maturity level of an organization indicates the capability and predictability of its software process. Each maturity level consists of several key process areas. The various maturity levels and their constituent key process areas are described in detail in this section.

4.4.1 Initial Level

The initial level (Fig. 4.6) is quite distinct from the four other maturity levels in that it has no key areas. Software development is like a black art in a

Figure 4.6: CMM Level 1 Software Development

level 1 organization; requirements flow in and the product flows out, and hopefully, the product works.

A level 1 organization often lacks a stable environment for developing and maintaining software. Often, there are problems with over-commitment, and the effort to deliver what has been committed often results in a crisis, with the realization that functionality committed to cannot be delivered on time. Quality may be compromised in an effort to deliver the commitments. Such organizations often lack a sound basis to know what they are capable of delivering, and often decisions are made more on intuition rather than by quantitative objective facts. However, level 1 organizations may be successful, even though their success and performance is often due to the heroic efforts of their staff. The success of a particular project is no guarantee that a subsequent project will be successful. The desire for repeatability of success brings us to the next maturity level.

4.4.2 Repeatable Level

The repeatable level differs from the initial level in that organization policies for managing a software project are defined, and procedures for implementing these policies are defined. The organization sets its expectations via policies. Level 2 organizations have developed project management controls for various projects although project management may vary from project to project. Project commitments are realistic and are made based on what was achieved with previous similar projects, and the allocated requirements of the current project.

Project management tracks the schedule, cost, and functionality in the project. Configuration management practices are in place and the requirements and associated work products have a baseline, and any changes to the configuration items are made in a controlled manner. Subcontractors are evaluated, selected, and managed. A software assurance group is established, and this group plays a key role in verifying that the defined process for the project is followed and in identifying any issues that may adversely project or product quality and the timeliness of delivery of the project. The level 2 organization is described as "disciplined" as planning and tracking is stabilized and earlier success can be repeated. The software for a project is delivered as a series of black boxes with defined milestones (Fig. 4.7).

Figure 4.7: CMM Level 2

The key features of a level 2organization are:

- Effective software project management system established
- Project management process is documented and followed
- Subcontractors are managed
- Success is dependent on managing similar projects
- Organization sets expectations via policies
- Disciplined and repeatable process
- Focus is on projects rather than the organization
- Projects are under control although each may do things in a different way

Management will need to balance between immediate business needs and future needs (which requires the right software engineering infrastructure to be in place). The individual key process areas in a level 2 organization are:

Table 4.4: CMM Level 2 KPAs

KPA	Description
RM	Requirements Management
PP	Project Planning
PT	Project Tracking
SSM	Subcontractor Management
SCM	Configuration Management
SQA	Software Quality Assurance

Requirements Management

The purpose of requirements management is to ensure that the customer and the project team share a common understanding of the requirements. The requirements is the foundation for the planning and management of the software project. The requirements will be documented and reviewed, and the plans, work products, and activities are kept up to date and consistent with the requirements. The requirements will have a baseline, and any changes made to the baseline will take place in a controlled manner and generally involve changes to the associated work products also to ensure consistency. Requirements management is difficult as customers may not wish to document the requirements, and changes to the requirements may occur during the project.

Project Planning

The customer's requirements are the basis for planning the software project. Realistic plans are made based on the requirements and experience from similar projects. The project plan documents the commitments made, the estimates of the work to be performed, the schedule, and the resources required to implement the project. It is the foundation for tracking the progress of the project against estimates. The estimation is based on historical data if available and is otherwise based on the judgment of the estimator. The plan includes risks that may affect the quality or timeliness of the project and details how these risks will be managed. The planning is based on commitments which various groups and individuals make, and changes to commitments can only take place with negotiation with the project manager as such changes generally affect the cost, quality, or timeliness of the project.

The project plan will usually include sub-plans such as the development plan, quality assurance plan, configuration management plan, test plan, and training plan. These sub-plans may be separate documents or there may be one master plan.

Project Tracking

Project tracking provides visibility into the actual progress of the software project. This involves reviewing the performance of the project against the project plan and taking corrective action when performance deviates significantly from the plan. The various milestones are tracked and the plans adjusted based on the actual results achieved. The original and adjusted plans are kept to enable lessons to be learned from the project. The tracking of progress may involve internal and customer reviews of progress; and effort, cost, schedule, deliverables, key milestones, risks, and size of deliverables are generally tracked.

Subcontractor Management

The purpose of subcontractor management is to assess and select a software subcontractor, to agree on the commitments with the subcontractor, and to track and review the results and performance of the subcontractor effectively. The selection of the subcontractor involves considering the available subcontractors, and generally the best qualified subcontractor capable of performing the work is selected; however, other factors such as the knowledge of the particular domain, strategic alliances, or agreements among subsidiaries of multinational corporations may influence the selection of the subcontractor. The software capability evaluation of a subcontractor is described in [Byr:96].

The prime contractor is the organization responsible for building the system and the prime contractor may decide to outsource part of the work to another contractor, i.e., the subcontractor. The management of the subcontractor includes specifying the work to be performed and the standards and procedures to be followed. This will usually include a statement of work, the requirements, products to be delivered, and the procedures to be followed. The prime contractor will track the work of the subcontractor via regular reviews throughout the project.

Configuration Management

The purpose of configuration management is to manage the configuration items of the project. Configuration management involves identifying the configuration items and systematically controlling change to maintain integrity and traceability of the configuration throughout the lifecycle. There is a need for an infrastructure to manage and control changes to documents and for source code change control management. The configuration items include the project plan, the requirements, design, code, and test plans.

A key concept in configuration management is a "baseline", and this is a work product that has been formally reviewed and agreed upon, and serves as the foundation for future work. It is changed by a formal change control procedure which leads to a new baseline. A change to the baseline may involve changes to several deliverables; for example, a change to the baseline of the software requirements will generally require controlled changes to the design, code, and test plans. Change control is formal and approval is via a change control board.

The organization is required to identify the configuration items that need to be placed under formal change control as some work products (for example, SQA plan) do not require a formal change control mechanism. Configuration management also provides a history of the changes made to the baseline.

Software Quality Assurance

The purpose of software quality assurance is to provide independent visibility to management on the processes being used in a software project, and compliance to the defined processes. software quality assurance is performed via audits of the various activities to ensure that they comply with the applicable procedures and standards. The software quality assurance group is independent of the group that it is auditing as the independence of an audit increases its objectivity and effectiveness.

The audits may identify various compliance issues, which may adversely affect the quality of the project or product. The results of the audits are communicated to the project and corrective actions are assigned to address any noncompliance issues, and the actions are resolved by the project team. In rare cases, issues may be escalated to senior management. Most key process areas include a contribution from SQA in verifying implementation of the KPA.

4.4.3 Defined Level

The main difference between a level 2 and a level 3 organization is that the focus of the former is on projects, whereas the emphasis shifts to the organization for a level 3 organization. The organization supports the projects by gathering best practices, employing common processes and common measurements, and providing tailoring guidelines and training to the projects. A level 3 organization has a standard process for developing and maintaining software. This process is termed the *"organization software standard process" (OSSP)* in CMM terminology, and it is documented and communicated throughout the organization. It includes software engineering and management processes. Projects tailor the organization's standard process, and the tailored process is termed the *"project's defined software process"*.

A level 3 organization includes a group that is responsible for the organization's software process. This is termed the *"software engineering process group" (SEPG)* in CMM terminology. The group is responsible for changes and improvements to the software process. There is a training program in place to ensure that all new staff receive appropriate training on the software processes, and that existing staff receive appropriate training on new processes and adequate training to perform their roles effectively. The level 3 organization is described as standard and consistent as software engineering and management practices are stable and repeatable.

The fact that there are common processes at the organization level does not mean that all projects do things exactly the same. The best practices in the organization are identified and used to define the common processes at the organization level. It means that the projects may use the best practices available in the organization, and tailor the common processes to their specific project needs to yield the project's software process. Thus a project in a level 3 organization is using the best that is available within the organization. The responsibilities are divided between the organization and the project.

The level 3 organization has increased visibility into the tasks and activities in the software process, as the engineering processes are defined.

Figure 4.8: CMM – Level Three CMM

The individual key process areas in a level three organization are described as follows:

Table 4.5: CMM – Level Three KPAs

KPA	Description
OPF	Organization process focus
OPD	Organization process definition
TP	Training program
IC	Intergroup coordination
ISM	Integrated software management
SPE	Software product engineering
PR	Peer reviews

Organization Process Focus

The objective of organization process focus is to ensure that there is sufficient emphasis on process in the organization. There is a group responsible for software process development and improvement, and this group will co-ordinate activities to assess, develop, maintain and improve the software process capability of the organization. New staff receive appropriate training and orientation on the software process.

Organization Process Definition

The objective of organization process definition is to develop, maintain and improve the organization's standard software process. The OSSP is a collection of the process assets of the organization. The process elements include project planning, estimation, design, coding, test, and peer review processes. Process elements are described in terms of standards, procedures, and templates and are hooked together to form a process. The order in which the process elements are connected is the software process architecture.

The OSSP may support more than one lifecycle, e.g., waterfall model or spiral model, as one lifecycle may not be appropriate for all projects. It includes guidelines to tailor the organization standard software process to the project's software process. The guidelines will indicate what can be tailored out and what cannot, and the extent to which a process element may be modified. Historical data and measurements are recorded from actual projects and are maintained in the organization's software process database. Numeric information is collected on the software processes and software work products and is used for future planning.

Training

The objective of training is to ensure that staff receive appropriate training to perform their roles effectively, and familiarization on the software process. The training needs of the organization, the projects, and individuals need to be identified and training provided to address these needs. There will usually be a training group or individual in the organization responsible for coordinating training.

Training may take several forms, including workshops, classroom, a mentor program, conferences, the internet, self-directed learning, or the library. The participants provide feedback on the effectiveness of the training courses.

Integrated Software Management

The purpose of integrated software management is to define the project's software process by tailoring the organization's software process. The project's software engineering and management activities are tailored from the organization's software process assets. The project is managed according to the project's defined software process, and the project plan is based on the project's software process. Projects can use and share process data and lessons learned and use the organization process database for assistance to determine estimates for cost, schedule, and resources.

Software Product Engineering

The purpose of software product engineering is to perform the software engineering activities consistently to produce correct software products. It involves performing the engineering tasks to build and maintain the software using appropriate methods and tools using the project's defined software process. It describes the technical activities of the project and the corresponding software work products. These include requirement documents, design documents, source code, and test documents.

The documents are required to be consistent with one another, e.g., the requirements need to be consistent with design and the system test plan. Traceability is employed to verify consistency. Product measures are maintained, e.g., the number of defects and defect categories and the size and cost of implementing change.

Intergroup Coordination

The purpose of intergroup coordination is to ensure that all engineering groups participate effectively together. This requires that the groups communicate effectively. All groups should be aware of the status and plans of the other groups. Communication is a major issue for large projects, as there are several groups involved, and good communication is essential for the success of the project. Commitments between groups are documented and agreed to by all groups and tracked to completion. Any changes to the commitments need to be communicated to and agreed with all the affected groups.

Peer Reviews

The purpose of peer reviews is to remove defects from software work products as early as possible, and to understand and learn lessons from the defects to prevent reoccurrence. One well-known implementation of peer reviews is the "*Fagan Inspection*" methodology, and software inspections were discussed in chapter 2.

A peer review involves a methodical examination of the work products by the author's peers to identify defects. The process involves identifying which work products require a peer review, planning and scheduling, training inspection leaders and participants, assigning inspection roles, and distributing the inspection material to the participants. Corrective action items are identified and tracked to closure. Effective software inspections can find 50% to 90% of defects prior to testing and as the cost of correction of a defect increases the later the defect is identified, there is a strong economic case for inspections.

4.4.4 Managed Level

The main difference between a level 3 and a level 4 organization is that the performance of a level 4 organization (Fig. 4.9) is within strict quantitative limits, i.e., the behavior is predictable. Measurements are defined and collected and decision making is based upon quantitative data. The variation in process performance is limited, as the process performance is between lower and upper control limits. Quantitative quality goals are set for the projects to obtain, and the project's software process is adjusted to ensure that the goals are achieved. Consequently, software products in a level 4 organization are of a predictably high quality. Decisions in a level 4 organization are based on the data collected, and projects set control limits.

Figure 4.9: CMM Level 4

There are two level 4 key process areas:

Table 4.6: CMM Level 4 KPAs

KPA	Description
SQM	Software Quality Management
QPM	Quantitative Process Management

Software Quality Management

The purpose of software quality management is to obtain a quantitative understanding of the quality of a project or product. Quantitative quality goals are set for the project, and these goals are related to the goals of the organization. The quantitative quality goals are tracked during the project, and the project's defined software process is adjusted accordingly to meet the quantitative goals. The status of the quantitative goals are used to make an informed decision as to whether the product has the desired quality to be released to potential customers. The product is judged to have the desired quality once the quantitative goals are satisfied. Plans are established to achieve the goals, and the quantitative goals are monitored.

Quantitative Process Management

The purpose of quantitative process management is to control the project's process performance quantitatively. Goals are set for process performance and performance is expected to be within the defined capability limits. The actual process performance is measured and corrective action is taken to adjust the process (i.e., to fix the process) if its performance is outside of these control limits. Quantitative process management makes sense only when the processes are stable within the organization. Control limits can be narrowed as a process becomes mature, and variance decreases with increased process capability.

Statistical techniques play an important role, as goals and control limits are set for the performance of the various processes (Fig. 4.10). The measurements are analyzed, variations in process performance are identified, the reasons for variation are identified, and adjustments are made to keep process performance within acceptable limits. The performance of the project is measured and various statistical quality control tools such as histograms, fishbone diagrams, trend graphs, and pareto charts are employed to analyze causes and trends. Measurement and problem solving are described in more detail in chapter 6.

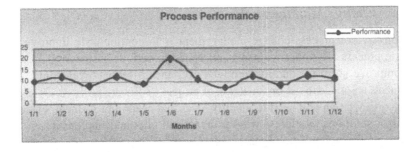

Figure 4.10: CMM Statistical Quality Control

4.4.5 Optimizing Level

The main difference between a level 4 and a level 5 organization is that while a level 4 has a quantitative understanding of the process, a level 5 organization is focused on continuous improvement using the quantitative data as a way of life to continually improve. The organization has a mechanism to identify opportunities for improvement to the software processes and to implement change in a controlled manner. Quantitative data is gathered to measure the improvements to the process in terms of productivity, quality, or cycle time. Innovations that exploit leading edge software engineering are identified, piloted, and deployed where appropriate in the organization.

Level 5 organizations place a strong emphasis on analyzing defects to learn from the defect and to take corrective action to prevent a reoccurrence. Level 5 organizations are described as continuously improving as the process capability and performance is continuously being enhanced.

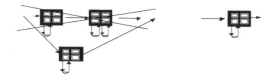

Figure 4.11: CMM – Level Five CMM

The level five KPAs include the following:

Table 4.7: CMM – Level Five KPAs

KPA	Description
PCM	Process Change Management
TCM	Technology Change Management
DP	Defect Prevention

Process Change Management

The objective of process change management is to continuously improve the software process. The improvements are related to various business goals such as to improve software quality, productivity, and to reduce cycle time. Improvements are made to the organization or project's software process.

The organization will need to identify areas that need improvement, evaluate options or solutions to address weaker areas, and pilot and implement the improvements throughout the organization. Improvement suggestions are evaluated, improvement teams are formed, procedures and processes updated and training provided on the new processes. There may be a productivity dip as people become familiar with the new process; however, the result of successful improvements is a process with enhanced capability.

Improvements tend to be incremental rather than revolutionary steps. The focus is on fire prevention rather than fire fighting. Process improvement is planned and managed.

Technology Change Management

The purpose of technology change management is to identify beneficial tools and methodologies and to transfer these to the organization in a controlled manner. This involves selecting technologies that may be beneficial, evaluating the technologies to determine which best meets the requirements, piloting technologies to ensure that they are suitable for the organization, and incorporating the new technology into the organization.

Technology change management uses quantitative data to perform the evaluation and to determine the actual benefits to the organization of the new technology. This includes the impacts on productivity, quality, and cycle time. There is an interesting discussion of whether the process or the tool comes first in [Bow:00].

Defect Prevention

The purpose of defect prevention is to identify the causes of defects and prevent them from recurring. The defects are identified, classified, analyzed; the root causes identified; and corrective action taken to prevent a recurrence. The results of the actions taken will need to be reviewed to ensure that they have been effective. Defects may be due to a defect within the software process, and this will require a change to the software process to correct. The defect may alternately be due to a misexecution of the software process and may need training or enforcement to resolve.

4.5 Implementing the CMM

The successful implementation of the CMM by an organization requires strong commitment by senior management. It requires vision, planning, adequate resources, selection of teams and team leaders, training for teams, formulation of plans for teams, and tracking of progress by internal and external assessments.

The implementation plan will detail what is required for successful implementation and the associated responsibilities. The plan will be communicated to staff and training provided. The plan will include a timeline for implementation and progress will be reviewed regularly. The implementation requires teams to be in place to coordinate and implement the work; these teams could be combined into one team for a small organization.

Table 4.8: CMM Implementation Teams

Team	Description
Management Steering Group	The management steering group (MSG) has overall responsibility for CMM implementation. It plans, sets goals, and provides sufficient resources and training. The MSG provides regular progress reports to senior management. The status of the CMM implementation is determined by regular internal CMM assessments. The MSG is responsible for coordinating an external assessment, and in ensuring that the organization is sufficiently prepared for an external assessment.
KPA Coordination Team	There may be a separate KPA coordination team for large organizations or this role may be provided by the MSG. It is responsible for the day-to-day monitoring of the progress with the implementation of the key process areas. The KPA coordination team tracks the progress of the KPA team action plans, and will facilitate regular internal assessments. The results will be communicated to the MSG. The KPA coordination team identifies any barriers that may adversely affect the CMM program, and these barriers are reported to the MSG, and are subsequently resolved by the MSG.
KPA Teams	There are 18 key process areas on the CMM, and dedicated KPA teams perform the implementation. The team may be responsible for more than one KPA, and in a small organization there may be one team responsible for all of the KPAs to be implemented. The starting point is a self-assessment to identify the extent to which the KPA is currently satisfied. Each goal and each key practice is evaluated and an action plan defined to address the weak areas in the KPA. The actions may require resources, sponsorship from management, training, and enforcement. The implementation of the KPA must satisfy the KPA goals for the KPA to be judged satisfied.
Software Engineering Process Group (SEPG Team)	The SEPG is the group with overall responsibility for the organization's software process and for ensuring that changes and improvements to the organization's software process are carried out in a controlled manner. The SEPG may define a mechanism to allow staff to make improvement suggestions to improve the software process. The SEPG will consider each individual suggestion and determine whether it is appropriate, and if so will act on the suggestion. Often, the SEPG will forward the suggestion to a particular KPA team.

Management will define a steering group to oversee the implementation for a large organization; the group will ensure that adequate resources and time are provided, and will track and report progress. There will usually be dedicated KPA team(s) to implement the actual work to satisfy the KPA. The following are typical teams that may be in place for CMM implementation.

In a small organization there will typically be just one team with overall responsibility for overseeing and implementation of the CMM.

4.6 CMM Internal Assessments

The CMM is a framework for process improvement within an organization, and may be used to diagnose the current state of maturity of the organization processes. The assessments may be internal or external. The result of an assessment is a maturity profile of the organization and yields strengths and weaknesses of the organization. An action plan is then defined to address the weaker areas, and the next assessment generally yields higher maturity processes if the improvement actions are successful.

Each key process area team typically performs a self assessment, and reports the results and findings. Typically, the following is involved:

- Identify internal self-assessment team
- Identify the key process areas to be assessed
- Gather documentation relevant to the key process area
- Rate the key practices on a numeric scale
- Produce an action plan to address weak areas identified
- Provide a maturity profile of the organization

The following section illustrates a combined self-assessment and action plan for a sample key process area (software quality management).

4.6.1 Sample Internal Assessment

Table 4.9 presents a sample internal assessment of the software quality management KPA and the associated action plan. Each goal and key practice of the KPA is rated on a scale from 1 to 10, and the key practice is satisfied if a score of 7 or above is achieved. Actions are required to address areas that score less than 7.

Table 4.9: CMM Internal Assessment and Action Plan

Act	Ref	Score	Issue (<7)	Action	Owner	Due Date	Status
	G 1	7					
001	G 2	4	Limited measurable quality goals in place	Define quality goals to be achieved and deploy	Quality manager	31.12.01	Open
002	G3	4	Limited tracking of quality goals	Track quality goals at weekly project meeting	Quality manager	31.10.01	Closed
	C 1	7					
	AB 1	7					
003	AB 2	4	Limited training provided in software quality management	Provide training on SQM to managers and engineers.	Training manager	31.12.01	Open
004	AB 3	4	Limited training in SQM	As in Action 003.	Training manager	31.12.01	Open
	AC 1	7					
	AC 2	7					
005	AC 3	4	Monitoring quality goals	Monitor goals at project meetings	Quality manager	31.12.01	Open
006	AC 4	4	Projects / products quality goals	As in action 005	Quality manager	31.12.01	Open
	AC 5		N/A				
	M 1	7					
007	V 1	5	No management review of SQM activities	Implement a quality review	Quality manager	31.12.01	Open
008	V2	5		As in action 007	Quality manager	31.12.01	

The overall score for the KPA is calculated as the average of the individual scores achieved, and the following formula is used:

$$\text{KPA score} = \frac{\Sigma G_i + \Sigma C_i + \Sigma Ab_i + \Sigma Ac_i + \Sigma M_i + \Sigma V_i}{(\text{Rated Items})} = \frac{76}{14} = 5.4$$

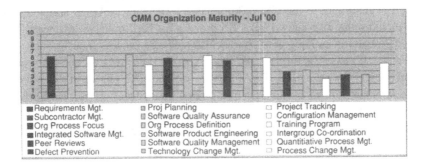

Figure 4.12: CMM Maturity in Organization

The score of the KPA is 5.4 (< 7) and this indicates that the KPA is not satisfied. The parts of the KPA that have recorded a score of less than 7 are identified and the corrective actions are identified. The symbols employed are to represent goals and key practices (G_i = Goal, C_i = Commitment, Ab_i = Ability, Ac_i = Activities, M_i = Measurement, and V_i = Verification).

Once the internal assessment of targeted KPAs is complete, the results are reported to the MSG. Figure 4.12 provides a simple mechanism to report the maturity profile of the organization, and it indicates the KPAs that the organization needs to address to achieve its CMM implementation goals.

Figure 4.12 provides a rating of 17 of the 18 KPAs, and generally only organizations which have a major improvement program in place would report on this number of KPAs. Typically, an organization would report on level two KPAs only or possibly level 2 and level 3 KPAs.

4.7 External CMM Assessments

The CMM is typically employed for the diagnosing phase of the IDEAL[SM] Model. The IDEAL model [Pet:95] acts as an overall framework for process improvement. The CMM is used to analyze the software process, establish its current maturity with respect to the model, and to identify strengths and opportunities for improvement. This allows the organization to set improvement priorities and to plan and act on improvement.

The assessment of an organization may be carried out in various ways, and internal self-assessments have been described in the previous section. External assessments are conducted by experts independent of the organization, and an objective CMM rating is provided to the organization.

The assessment of the organization requires planning and involves interviews with various managers and employees in the organization. An approach

---

[SM] Service Mark of Carnegie Mellon University

which is compliant to the CMM Appraisal Framework (CAF) is adopted, and this includes the well-known CBA IPI process for performing assessments. The IDEAL model is an integrated approach to software process improvement, and includes the phases, activities, and resources required for a successful process improvement program. The IDEAL model includes five phases in the software process improvement cycle. The five phases then repeat, as software process improvement is continuous. The five phases are *initiating, diagnosing, establishing, acting, and leveraging*. These are summarized as follows (Fig. 4.13):

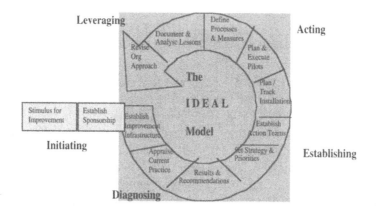

Figure 4.13: CMM – The IDEAL Model for Continuous Improvement

Table 4.10: Phases in IDEAL Model

Phase	Description
Initiating	This is concerned with initiating the improvement program. It involves aligning the software improvement goals with current and future business goals. SPI is based on business needs and requires management sponsorship and commitment to be successful.
Diagnosing	The diagnosing phase involves an appraisal of the current software practices in the organization, and its findings include strengths and recommendations. The SEI has defined an appraisal framework termed the CMM Appraisal Framework (CAF). Both the CMM Based Appraisal for Internal Process Improvement (CBA IPI) [Dun:96], and the software capability Evaluation (SCE) [Byr:96] are CAF compliant.
Establishing	The establishing phase involves planning and setting priorities following the CMM appraisal. This involves defining a medium and short term plan for improvement and setting up to address the findings and recommendations.

Table 4.10 (*continued*): Phases in IDEAL Model

Phase	Description
Acting	The acting phase involves performing the actions and this may involve defining new processes, piloting new processes or technologies, defining new measurements, and making the improvements part of the organization culture.
Leveraging	The leveraging stage involves documenting and analyzing the lessons learned during the process improvement cycle and revising the organizational approach for the next cycle as process improvement is continuous

The CMM appraisal framework (CAF) is used in the diagnosing phase. It details the requirements that an appraisal method needs to satisfy and includes requirements for planning and preparing for the appraisal, conducting the appraisal, and reporting the results. The CAF details the appraisal methods and its interface to the CMM, the appraisal components and the rating process. There are three main phases in the appraisal framework: planning the appraisal, conducting the appraisal, and reporting the findings. These are described in more detail below.

4.7.1 Assessment Planning

This phase involves planning and preparation for the assessment and includes identifying the KPAs that will be assessed; preparing an assessment plan; identifying and training the assessment team and assigning roles; identifying, briefing, and training the participants; administering a maturity questionnaire and examining the responses; and arranging logistics for the visit to the site, for example, interview rooms and laptops. A successful assessment requires a competent assessment team, good preparation and planning, and attention to detail.

4.7.2 Conducting the Assessment

This consists of an opening kick-off meeting which is attended by all the participants and the senior manager. The senior manager is the sponsor of the assessment and attends to demonstrate the importance of the assessment for organization improvement. The assessment consists of interviews with project leaders, managers, and functional area representatives (FARs), and a review of relevant documentation.

The assessment team will need to be able to meet all relevant people and groups to assess the KPAs within the scope of the assessment. The objective of an interview is to gather data, to discover first hand how work is performed and managed, and to identify strengths and opportunities. The assessment team records notes and observations during the interview and the information is consolidated after the interview. Documentation is reviewed to verify that the process is actually performed as described.

The assessment team will need to identify missing information which is required to rate the particular KPA, and to request missing information from the site coordinator. Often, the assessment team will use an assessment instrument or tool to assist in recording KPA findings, and sometimes a manual KPA wall chart is employed to record the KPA findings and to assist in identifying any missing information that is required to rate the KPA.

4.7.3 Assessment Reporting

The draft assessment findings are produced and presented by the assessment team leader to the participants, and feedback is used to produce the final set of findings. The final assessment findings include the CMM rating for the organization, and a rating of the individual key process areas. A KPA is satisfied if all of the goals for the KPA are satisfied. The assessment report will detail the KPAs which have been assessed and the strengths and weaknesses identified. The final findings are presented to the organization and to the sponsor. The organization formulates an action plan to address the findings and recommendations from the assessment. The process improvement strategy is re-launched and the process improvement cycle repeats.

4.8 CMM Worldwide Maturity

The Software Engineering Institute maintains data on worldwide CMM maturity of organizations. The data is provided to the SEI following a formal CMM assessment of the organization. The data presented here (Fig. 4.14) is based on a sample of 870 organizations: 39.3% of these organizations were assessed to be at the initial maturity level, 36.3% were assessed to be at the repeatable level, 17.7% at the defined level, 4.8% at the managed level, and 1.9% at the optimized level.

The majority of formal CMM assessments have taken place in the US, with about 30% of formal CMM assessments taking place outside the US. Figure 4.15 shows the maturity of US companies and companies based outside of the US. It includes subsidiaries of US companies based in Europe and Asia. The survey includes the results of assessments from 870 organizations 610 US based and 260 based outside the US.

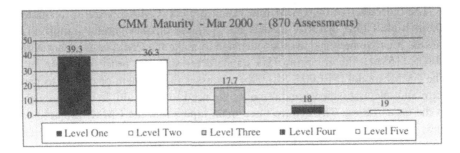

Figure 4.14: CMM Worldwide Maturity

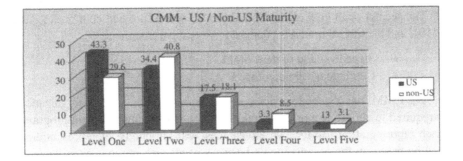

Figure 4.15: CMM Worldwide Maturity

The maturity of companies based outside of the US seem to be slightly higher than US companies with 8.5% of non-US companies assessed at level 4, and 3.9% of non-US companies assessed at Level 5. The figures for US companies are 3.3% and 1.9% respectively. This could be due to several factors: for example, subsidiaries of US companies based in Europe and Asia take the view that they have to prove their excellence to the parent company, in order to maintain and win business against competing subsidiaries.

4.9 CMMI Project

The objective of this section is to provide background to the CMMI[SM] project and to describe the model. The description provided here is brief and the objective here is to give a flavor of the new model: the interested reader is referred to the more detailed material published as SEI technical reports.

[SM] Service Mark of Carnegie Mellon University.

The objectives of the CMM Integration project (CMMI^{SM}) are to integrate the multiple CMM maturity models into a single model ,thereby simplifying process improvement and assessments, and to make the CMM conformant with SPICE (15504), the emerging ISO standard for software process assessment. The CMMI model [SEI:00a, SEI:00b] addresses the problem of having to perform multiple assessments and removes the need to use multiple CMM models in the organization. There were three main inputs into the CMMI project and these include:

- Draft CMM (v2.0) for SW-CMM.
- Electronic Industries Alliance / Interim Standard (EIA/IS) 731.
- Integrated Product Development Capability Maturity Model (IPD-CMM) v0.98.

The second main goal of the CMMI project was to provide conformance to 15504, and the CMMI model is published in two representations:

- Staged version of the CMM
- Continuous version of the CMM

The CMMI has a staged version and continuous version and the organization is required to choose one of these representations for its improvement program. Each representation has its own advantages, and the choice of representation will be based on the organization's business needs and previous experience in improvement programs.

The main advantage of the staged version is that it is quite familiar to organizations that have been using the CMM model, as it provides a well-known and proven roadmap for process improvement starting with basic management practices and progressing through the well-known path of successive maturity levels with each maturity level providing the foundation for improvements at the next level. The staged representation allows organizations to compare their maturity levels with similar organizations. There is an easy migration path from the software CMM to the CMMI model.

The continuous version allows the organization to focus on the improvements to processes that best meets the organization's business objectives. Comparisons between organizations are possible; however, the focus is in the comparison of process area by process area. The continuous model is similar to SPICE (15504).

There are two disciplines included in the CMMI model and these are systems engineering and software engineering. The systems engineering discipline covers the development of total systems which may or may not include software. The focus is to transform customer needs into a product solution that satisfies the requirements and to support the product solution. The software engineering discipline covers the development of software systems and the focus is to transform the software requirements into the software product via a disciplined software development and maintenance process. Both the systems engineering discipline and software engineering discipline are usually selected in the CMMI model, as the distinction between the two disciplines [SEI:00a] is "*at the level of amplification of practices within otherwise identical process areas*". The discipline amplifications appear in the individual process areas in the model and are essentially extra information specific to software engineering or to systems engineering.

The CMMI for systems/software engineering consists of the same process areas regardless of a staged or continuous representation. Each process area contains goals, practices, and typical work products. The goals consist of generic goals and specific goals, and the practices consist of generic practices or specific practices. Specific goals apply to only one process area and address the unique characteristics of the process area, whereas generic goals apply to all process areas and the achievement of the generic goals indicates whether the implementation and institutionalization of the process area is effective. The practices map onto the goals and the numbering scheme for goals and practices indicates which goal the practice maps on to; for example, SG1 indicates specific goal 1 in the staged model, and SP1.1 indicates that practice 1 maps onto to SG1. There are differences in the number scheme employed in the staged version and the continuous version of the CMMI model; for example, SP1.1-1 indicates that the practice is at capability level 1. The generic goals and practices are numbered in the form GG2 and GP2.1, respectively. The numbering scheme employed for each representation enables the corresponding practice in the staged or in the continuous representation to be easily located.

4.9.1 CMMI Staged Model

The staged model representation of the CMMI model (Fig. 4.16) is closer to the older software CMM [Pau:93]. It consists of maturity levels where each maturity level consists of a number of process areas (known as key process areas in the older software CMM), and specific and generic goals (known as just goals in the older SW-CMM), specific and generic practices (known as just practices in the older SW-CMM). The staged representation organizes processes into maturity levels to guide process improvement, and each maturity level is the foundation for improvements for the next level.

The specific goals and practices are listed first in the process area followed by generic goals and generic practices. The generic practices are organized by four common features, namely, commitment to perform, ability to perform, directing implementation, and verifying implementation. These are similar but not identical to the organization of key practices into five common features in the older software CMM.

There are five maturity levels in the CMMI model and each maturity level acts as a foundation for improvements in the next level. The maturity levels are numbered one through five as in the older software CMM; however, the naming of the levels is slightly different. The maturity levels are:

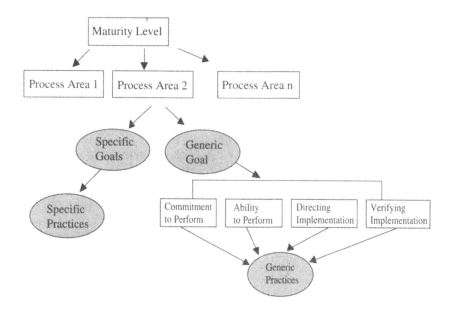

Figure 4.16: CMMI Staged Model

- Initial
- Managed
- Defined
- Quantitatively managed
- Optimizing

Organization process maturity is achieved when the organization attains the specific and generic goals for the process areas in a maturity level; organization maturity indicates the expected results likely to be achieved by an organization at that maturity level and is a means of predicting the most likely outcomes from the next project. Maturity levels are a foundation to the next level, and so maturity levels are rarely skipped as otherwise the foundation and stability for successful improvements is not in place.

The components of the CMMI model are grouped into three categories, namely, required, expected, and informative components. The required category is essential to achieving process improvement in a particular area and these include the specific and generic goals. The expected category includes specific and generic practices that an organization will typically implement and are intended to guide individuals or groups in implementing improvements or in performing assessments. The informative category includes information to understand the goals and practices and how they may be achieved and includes further elaboration to assist in implementation of the process area. The implementation of the process area will usually involve processes that carry out the specific or generic practices of the process area.

There are no process areas associated with the initial level and the process areas associated with maturity level 2 of the CMMI are similar to the key process areas on level 2 of the software CMM (except that measurement and analysis is a separate process area in the CMMI model) and include the following:

- Requirements management
- Project planning
- Project monitoring and control.
- Supplier agreement management
- Measurement and analysis
- Process and product quality assurance
- Configuration management

The process areas at maturity level 3 of the CMMI are quite different from level 3 of the software CMM and include the following:

- Requirements development
- Technical solutions
- Product integration
- Verification
- Validation
- Organization process focus
- Organization process definition
- Organization training
- Integrated product management
- Risk management
- Decision analysis and resolution

The process areas at maturity level 4 include:

- Organization process performance
- Quantitative project management

The process areas at maturity level 5 include:

- Organization innovation and deployment
- Causal analysis and resolution

4.9.2 CMMI–Continuous Model

The continuous model representation of the CMMI (Fig. 4.17) is closer to SPICE (15504). The continuous model uses capability levels, whereas the staged model uses maturity levels. Both representations use process areas, specific and generic goals, specific and generic practices, and the process areas are common to both representations. There are six capability levels in the continuous version and the capability levels are a maturity rating that apply to each process area. The six capability levels are numbered from 0 to 5. Each capability level consists of a set of specific and generic goals and practices, and the capability levels provide a path for process improvement within the process area. The organization will need to map its processes into the CMMI process areas as in SPICE (15504).

The capability levels focus on improving the organization's ability to perform and improve its performance in a particular process area. Each capability level indicates an increase in performance and capability of the process, and the six capability levels are:

- Incomplete
- Performed
- Managed
- Defined
- Quantitatively managed
- Optimized

The process is rated at a particular capability level if it satisfies all of the specific and generic goals of the capability level and if it satisfies all lower capability levels.

The judgment as to whether the goals of a particular capability level are satisfied is made by examining the extent of the implementation of the specific and generic practices of the particular capability level. The specific and generic practices are expected model components and are there to guide the implementation of the specific and generic goals of the capability level.

The capability levels are similar to SPICE (15504) and the following is a very brief description of each level, and in depth information is available in [SEI:00b] (Table 4.11).

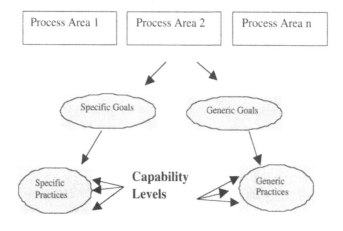

Figure 4.17: CMMI – Continuous Model

Table 4.11: CMMI Capability Levels

Capability Level	Description
Incomplete	The process does not implement all of the capability level 1 generic and specific practices.
Performed (1)	A process that performs all of the level 1 specific and generic practices. Performance may not be stable.
Managed (2)	A process at this level is managed, i.e., planned, performed, monitored, and controlled.
Defined (3)	A process at this level is defined process, i.e., a managed process that is tailored from the organization's set of standard processes.
Quantitatively Managed (4)	A process at this level is a quantitatively managed process, i.e., a defined process that is controlled by statistical techniques.
Optimizing (5)	A process at this level is an optimizing process, i.e., a quantitatively managed process that is continually improved through incremental and innovative improvements.

The CMMI assessment yields a maturity profile of the organization per process area. The process areas assessed are listed, and the associated capability level of each assessed process area provided.

There are four defined categories of CMMI process areas:

- Process management processes
- Project management processes
- Engineering processes
- Support processes

Each of these categories contain various process areas and these are described in detail in the continuous model. They are briefly summarized below:

Table 4.12: CMMI – Process Categories

Process Categorty	Process Areas
Process management processes	Organization process focus Organization process definition Organization training Organization process performance Organization innovation and deployment
Project management processes	Project planning Project monitoring and control Supplier agreement management Integrated project management Risk management Quantitative project management

Table 4.12 (*continued*): CMMI – Process Categories

Process Categorty	Process Areas
Engineering processes	Requirements development Requirements management Technical solution Product integration Verification Validation
Support processes	Configuration management Process and product quality assurance Measurement and analysis Decision analysis and resolution Causal analysis and resolution

4.10 Summary

This chapter provides an introduction to the CMM model, which is a process maturity model that enables an organization to define and evolve its software processes. Software engineering involves a multitude of software processes, and the delivery of high-quality software requires a focus on the quality and maturity of the underlying processes used to manage, develop, and test the software. The CMM is based on the premise that there is a close relationship between the quality of the delivered software product and the quality and maturity of the underlying software processes. It is therefore important for a software organization to devote attention to software process improvement as well as to the product, as the quality of the product will improve as processes become mature. The CMM is a vehicle or framework by which an organization may mature its software processes.

The CMM describes an evolutionary path for an organization to evolve from an immature or *ad hoc* software process, to a mature and disciplined software process. It is a five-level maturity model where a move from one level to a higher level indicates increased process maturity, and an enhanced capability of the organization. The five levels in the model are the initial level, the repeatable level, the defined level, the managed level, and the optimizing level. The organization moves from one maturity level to the next, with the current maturity level providing the foundation for improvement for the next level, and therefore maturity levels are not skipped. It allows the organization to follow a logical path in improvement, and to evolve at its own pace.

The implementation of the CMM was discussed and the implementation consists of defining a steering group for implementation and various dedicated teams. The implementation is tracked by internal CMM assessments and the steering group coordinates the external CMM assessment of the organization.

The IDEAL model includes the CMM in the diagnosing phase and assessments form one part of the improvement program.

The Software Engineering Institute has developed a new version of the CMM which merges the software and the system CMM and makes the CMM compatible with the SPICE standard. The CMMI model (v1.0) has been published in two representations namely the continuous CMMI and the staged CMMI model.

5
The SPICE (15504) Standard

5.1 Introduction

The ISO SPICE (Software Process Improvement and Capability Determination) is the emerging international standard for software process assessment. The need for an international standard arose out of the multiple models for software process assessment and improvement. These include the ISO 9000 standard, which was developed by the International Standards Organization [ISO:00]; Bootstrap [Kuv:93], which was developed in a EU ESPRIT research project; Trillium, a telecom specific assessment model developed in Canada; and the CMM [Pau:93], developed by the software Engineering Institute in the US. Both Bootstrap and the CMM models have been revised to be SPICE conformant.

The growth in the number of assessment approaches available was a key motivating factor in the development of the SPICE standard, and the objective is to provide an international standard for software process assessment. The standard is expected to allow comparability of results using different assessment models and methods. The initial work commenced in 1990, version 1 was released in 1995, version 2 was released in 1996, and the ISO 15504 type 2 technical report [ISO:98] was published in 1998. A type 2 technical report indicates a report which is close to acceptance by the standards body as an international standard, but that full agreement has not yet been reached on the final definition of the standard.

The early versions of the standard were piloted by organizations as part of the SPICE trials, and feedback provided to the ISO working group on SPICE. This lead to revisions in the definition of SPICE and the subsequent technical report in 1998. The changes in the design of SPICE to enable it to become an international standard for software assessment are described in [Rou:00]. This is likely to impact the contents of this chapter considerably, as it has been proposed to remove the reference model from the standard, and the reader is advised to follow the progress of the ISO standards body.

5.1.1 Motivation for SPICE

This section explains why a company should consider SPICE to assist its improvement program. The justification for CMM implementation was provided in chapter 4, and the reasons for SPICE implementation are similar and include the following:

Table 5.1: Motivation for SPICE

Motivation for SPICE Implementation
Reference model and exemplar model provide best practices in software engineering
Allows the company to focus on the key processes that will have the greatest impact on its business goals
Understand capability of its suppliers
Minimize risk in supplier selection
Set improvement targets for its suppliers
Understand its capability in software development
Understand capability of its key processes
Prioritize improvements based on capability
Confirm that improvements to the processes have been successful
Improved technical and management practices
Improved quality
Improved customer satisfaction
Fire prevention culture rather than fire-fighting culture
Culture of improvement
Higher morale in company

5.1.2 SPICE and the Quality Group

The SPICE standard places responsibilities on management and staff in the company. The impact of the standard on the quality (SQA) group is considered in this section, and this is similar to the discussion in chapter 4 on the impact in a CMM environment. The quality group will generally play a key role in the implementation of SPICE and the typical responsibilities of the group in a SPICE environment include the following:

Table 5.2: SPICE and the Quality Group

Responsibilities of the Quality Group (SQA)
Perform audits of projects, subcontractors, and departments
Provide visibility into processes/products
Report audit results to management and affected groups
Track audit actions to completion
Implement a quality management system
Champion the quality assurance process
Champion the audit process
Facilitate definition of metrics
Promote a culture of quality
Facilitate improvement
Champion/support the implementation of SPICE
Verify implementation of SPICE processes
Facilitate SPICE assessments of organization
Facilitate SPICE assessments of suppliers

5.2 Overview of SPICE

The standard provides a framework for the assessment of software processes and is designed to play a key role in software process capability determination and in software process improvement. It allows the organization to understand its key processes and their associated capabilities, and to prioritize further process improvements consistent with the business goals. It also allows the organization to assess the capability of a subcontractor's processes, and this enables an informed decision on subcontractor selection to be made. Process assessment is a disciplined evaluation of the organization's software processes. The process assessment may assess a specific process instance or multiple instances of the process. Each process instance is characterized by a set of five process capability ratings which indicate whether the process is *performed informally*, or whether it *is planned and tracked, well defined, quantitatively controlled,* or *continuously improving*. The terminology is similar to that employed in the CMM, and the main difference is that the CMM defines five maturity levels for a software organization, namely, *initial, repeatable, defined, managed,* and *optimizing*. Each maturity level (apart from level 1) contains several key process areas. However, the CMMI project has made the CMM compatible with SPICE, and this is described in [SEI:00a, SEI:00b].

The maturity level of an organization indicates its capability, and a CMM assessment yields the overall maturity rating for the organization, as well as providing feedback on the strengths and weaknesses of the key process areas, and whether the individual KPAs are satisfied. The SPICE assessment rates the maturity of each process within the scope of the assessment. The context of the process is taken into account. The assessment provides a clear indication of the extent to which the processes are meeting their goals.

There are nine parts in the SPICE standard, and these include guidance material and actual SPICE requirements. The standard includes a process model which acts as the basis against which software process assessment can be made. The process model includes a set of practices which are essential for good software engineering. The process model is generic and describes what is to be done rather than how it is to be done, and it is described in part 2 of the standard. It is known as the "reference model", and it describes the processes and a rating scheme to rate the capability of the software processes. Five process categories are distinguished in the SPICE model, and these include customer-supplier processes, engineering processes, management processes, support processes, and organization processes. The SPICE reference model has been influenced by the emergence of the ISO 12207 standard for software lifecycle processes (Table 5.3).

Table 5.3: ISO 12207 Lifecycle Processes

Processes		
Primary	**Supporting**	
Acquisition	Documentation	Joint review
Supply	Quality Assurance	Audit
Development	Verification /	Problem
Operation	Validation	
Maintenance	Configuration management	
Organization		
Management	Infrastructure	Improvement Training

The ISO 12207 standard has five primary processes, eight supporting processes, and four organization processes. The relationship between the SPICE processes and ISO 12207 is clear from Table 5.4 in which the five categories of SPICE processes are mapped to the ISO 12207 standard:

Table 5.4: ISO 12207 / SPICE Processes

Processes	
Primary	**Supporting**
Customer supplier	Support
Engineering	
Organization	
Management	Organization

The capability of an organization's or subcontractor's processes may be compared against a target process capability profile, i.e., a desired process capability level, to determine whether an organization is capable of undertaking a specific project. It is desirable that the target process capability profile required for a particular project should be within the actual process capability of the organization, or within the capability of targeted improvements to the organization's processes.

The standard is designed to provide assessment results that are repeatable, consistent, and objective. This ensures that the results are comparable within similar contexts. The requirements for performing an assessment are detailed in part 3 of the standard, and guidance for performing assessments is detailed in part 4 of the standard. The assessment process may be a user-defined process that satisfies the requirements for performing assessments, or it may be a third-party assessment method.

There is no specific SPICE method for performing an assessment, and the competent assessor is responsible for ensuring that the assessment process satisfies the requirements for performing the assessment. The assessment method could be self-assessment, third-party assessment, team-based assessments, or continuous assessments using a CASE tool. The SPICE standard does not provide a certification scheme for the assessment results, and instead requirements are placed on the process to preserve information to enable conformance to the assessment process to be demonstrated.

The SPICE standard refers to the competent assessor who is responsible for ensuring that the requirements for conducting an assessment are met. The non-functional requirements of an assessment include reliability, consistency, objectivity, and comparability of results. The competent assessor ensures that the assessors receive sufficient training and have sufficient expertise to perform the assessment correctly. The standard includes a framework for conducting assessments, rating processes, and presenting assessment results. An assessment includes assessment input, the compatible model, and yields assessment output. Currently, there is no certification or qualification scheme for assessors, although guidance on the competence of assessors is provided in the standard.

The reference model is generic and is not directly employed in the assessment. Instead, a model that is compatible with the reference model is employed. The compatible model is more detailed and is mapped onto the reference model, and it includes indicators to assist in the rating of the processes. The SPICE standard includes the "exemplar model" which is a compatible model of the reference model. There is a one-to-one mapping between the reference model and the exemplar model. Other compatible models have been developed, including the CMMI model developed by the Software Engineering Institute. The objectives of the CMMI project are described in chapter 4.

Process assessment (Fig. 5.1) is performed either as part of a process improvement initiative or to determine the capability of the organization's processes. There is a formal entry requirement for an assessment, and this includes defining the purpose and scope of the assessment and detailing any constraints

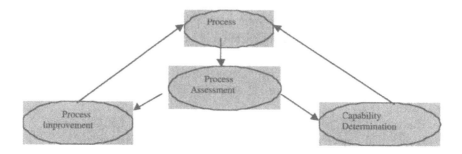

Figure 5.1: Process Assessment

on the assessment. Selected processes are assessed against the compatible model. The output of the assessment is the process capability level ratings. Process improvement priorities are identified from the assessment, and action is taken to change the organization's processes to meet organization needs and business goals more effectively. The effectiveness of the process improvement is measured by the improvement in process capability from the previous assessment.

A SPICE conformant assessment is an assessment which satisfies the following criteria:

- Based on a compatible model (e.g., Exemplar Model)
- Uses a comprehensive set of indicators
- Produces output using the defined rating scheme
- Retains objective evidence
- Process meets the assessment performance requirements

5.3 Process Management

A key premise of software process management is that the quality of a software system is highly influenced by the quality of the processes used to develop and maintain it. This implies focus on process as well as product. A *process* (IEEE) is a sequence of steps performed for a given purpose, and is the glue that ties the people, methods, tools, procedures, and standards together. The maturity of a process is measurable, and is an indication of process quality.

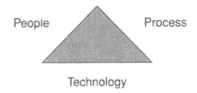

People   Process

Technology

Figure 5.2: Process Triangle

There are three important factors which influence the quality of a delivered software product: the expertise of the people employed by the organization, the technology employed in the development of the software, and the processes employed. The process triangle (Fig. 5.2) has been described previously in chapter 4. The SPICE standard is focused on process assessment and process improvement.

Processes may be immature or mature, and the extent of process maturity is an indication of capability and the expected results by rigorously following the process. Immature processes are *ad hoc*, rarely documented or defined, nor rigorously followed or enforced. Mature processes are consistent with the way in which work is done, and a mature process is defined, documented, well controlled via quality audits, measured, and continuously improving. The maturity of a process indicates its potential for further growth. The main characteristic of an institutionalized process is that it survives effectively long after the original author has departed from the organization.

The defects in a software product are typically due to defects with a particular process used to build the software, or due to a mis-execution of a process. The focus on fixing a defective process is a key part of a continuous improvement culture, and the philosophy of process improvement is to fix the software process and not the person. It is accepted that humans may occasionally err in the execution of the process, but often this is an indication of insufficient training to perform the particular process.

5.4 SPICE Reference Model

The role of a process model is to define the design, development, and production process for software unambiguously, and to provide guidance for all software personnel involved. A *process model* specifies the tasks and activities to be performed, and the sequence in which they are to be performed. It specifies the *actors* and *roles* involved in the production, and the *methods, tools, standards*, etc., used by the actors.

A process model has an associated life-cycle, for example, the *"waterfall model"* or *"V"* life-cycle model. The waterfall model is a traditional software development lifecycle model, and was developed by Royce [Roy:70]. One characteristic feature of the waterfall model is that requirements may be determined at project initiation or early in the lifecycle. The spiral model is applicable to situations where the requirements are not fully known at project initiation, and prototyping is employed to determine the appropriate requirements via an iterative process. The spiral model was developed by Boehm in [Boe:88].

The SPICE reference model includes key processes associated with software development, maintenance, acquisition, supply, and operation. The purpose of the reference model is to act as a common basis for software process assessment, and to facilitate the comparison of assessment results.

The architecture of the SPICE reference model is two dimensional: it comprises the *process dimension* and the *capability dimension*. The process dimension includes the processes to be assessed, and the capability dimension provides the scale on which to assess the processes (Fig. 5.3).

Figure 5.3: SPICE Process and capability Dimension

There are five categories of processes defined in the SPICE standard:

Table 5.5: SPICE Processes Categories

Category	Description
Engineering Processes	These processes are related to the engineering of the software and include requirements, design, implementation, and testing.
Customer-Supplier Processes	These are processes related to customer and supplier interface and include acquisition, supplier selection, and the requirements elicitation processes.
Management Processes	These processes are concerned with managing projects and include project management, quality management, and risk management.
Support Processes	These processes are there to support other processes and may be used by other processes (including other support processes) throughout the lifecycle. They include quality assurance and configuration management processes.
Organization Processes	These processes manage and improve the organization and processes in the organization. They include process improvement and assessment and human resources.

Each process includes a statement of its purpose and the outcome from executing the process. It includes a set of base practices that are essential for good software engineering. The capability dimension is organized by capability level, and there are six capability levels in the standard. The measure of capability for a particular level is based on a set of process attributes, and these measure a particular aspect of capability. There are nine process attributes and the capability levels and process attributes are described below:

Table 5.6: SPICE Capability Levels

Capability Level	Description
Level 0: Incomplete Process	The process is not implemented or fails to achieve its purpose. There are few work products and little evidence of the achievement of the defined attributes.
Level 1: Performed Process	The process achieves its process outcomes. The process may not be planned or tracked. Individuals within the organization recognize that an action is to be performed, and the action is performed. There are identifiable work products for the process. This capability level includes the process performance attribute, which is focused on the extent to which the process achieves the process outcomes, and indicators used include scope of work, input and output work products, base practices of the processes are performed, and expected outcome achieved.
Level 2: Managed Process	This capability level indicates that the process is performed in a managed fashion, i.e., planned, tracked, verified, and adjusted. It includes the performance management attribute and the work product management attribute. The performance of the process is planned, tracked, and verified to have followed standards and procedures for the project. The scope of work is clearly defined with the tasks and resources identified, planned, scheduled, and tracked to completion. Reviews or audits may be performed to verify and validate the work products. The work products are documented, are under version control, and changes to the work products are controlled. Quality is built into the work products.

Table 5.6 (*continued*): SPICE Capability Levels

Capability Level	Description
Level 3: Established Process	This capability level indicates that the process is now performed using a standard process. It includes the process definition attribute and the process resource attribute. Each implementation of a process uses approved process definitions tailored from standard documented processes. A defined process is one in which the inputs, outputs, entry and exit criteria, tasks, roles, and responsibilities are defined. A standard process is typically a library of different procedures, standards and controls with guidelines for tailoring them to meet the requirements for different process implementations. The process definition attribute indicates the extent to which the process definition is based upon a standard process. The process resource attribute indicates the extent to which the process draws upon suitable resources to deploy the defined process. This attribute recognizes that the effective implementation of a defined process, and institutionalization of the standard process requires planning and training.
Level 4: Predictable Process	This capability level indicates that the process performs consistently within defined limits to achieve its process outcomes. It includes the measurable attribute and the process control attribute. Measurements of process performance and work product quality are collected and analyzed. The performance of the process is quantitatively managed and the quality of the work products is quantitatively known. The process measurement attribute indicates the extent to which measurement is employed. Quantitative control limits for the process are defined and this indicates the extent to which the process is controlled through the collection, analysis and use of process measurements. Corrective action is taken from analysis and noting trends.
Level 5: Optimizing Process	This capability level indicates that the process dynamically changes to address current and predicted business goals. It includes the process change attribute and the continuous improvement attribute. The process is continually monitored against its quantitative process goals, and improvements made by analyzing the results, and by optimising the processes by piloting innovative ideas and technologies. Changes to the process are made in a controlled manner. The impact of the proposed changes is determined and quantitative analysis of the effectiveness of the process change is employed. The organization sets targets for process effectiveness and identifies opportunities for improvement. The process is continuously improving.

Each capability level is a significant enhancement over the previous level.
The capability levels include a set of process attributes which indicate the extent
to which the capability level is satisfied. The rating of the capability level is
based on the rating of the component process attributes. The process attribute is
rated as either not satisfied, partially satisfied, largely satisfied, or fully satisfied.
The ratings are on a scale from 0% to 100% satisfied:

Table 5.7: SPICE Ratings of Process Attributes

Rating	Description
Not satisfied (0–15%)	There is little evidence of achievement of the process attribute.
Partially satisfied (16% to 50%)	There is a systematic approach to achievement of the process attribute, but process performance may vary in some areas.
Largely satisfied (51% to 85%)	There is a sound systematic approach and significant achievement of the process attribute.
Fully satisfied (86% to 100%)	There is a complete and systematic approach and full achievement of the process attribute.

The process profile is obtained by grouping the nine process attributes together with the rating for each process attribute (Table 5.8). The process profile
for an assessed process is described in a format similar to the following where
each process attribute is rated as either not satisfied, partially satisfied, largely
satisfied, or fully satisfied.

Table 5.8: SPICE Process Attributes Ratings

Capability Level	Process Attribute	Description	Process Rating
L5	5.2	Process improvement	N
L5	5.1	Process change	N
L4	4.2	Process control	P
L4	4.1	Process measurement	P
L3	3.2	Process resource	F
L3	3.1	Process definition	L
L2	2.2	Work product management	L
L2	2.1	Performance management	F
L1	1.1	Process performance	F

The process is assessed at a particular capability level if it fully satisfies all
lower capability levels, and at least largely satisfies the process attributes at the
assessed capability level. For example, in the table above, the process is assessed to be at level 2, as it fully satisfies level 1, and the level 2 attributes are

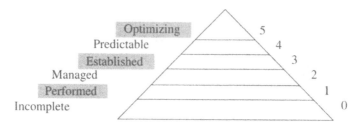

Figure 5.4: SPICE Capability Levels

largely or fully satisfied. The first letter of the rating is employed for brevity, e.g., "L" indicates largely satisfied.

The capability levels (Fig. 5.4) provide a structured path for the improvement of each process. This allows an organization to focus on improvements to those processes that are the key to its business success. The capability levels are summarized in the following diagram.

The reference model is generic and is not directly employed in the assessment. Instead, a model compatible with the reference model is employed. A compatible model includes a non-empty subset of the processes from the reference model, and a continuous subset of the capability levels (starting from level 1). The compatible model may include processes that do not map onto the reference model, and in such a case comparability with other assessments will not be possible.

The compatible model defines its scope against the reference model and includes a set of indicators for both dimensions in the reference model. It provides a mapping to the reference model and provides a mechanism to convert the data collected to ratings against the reference model. The exemplar model in part 5 of SPICE and the CMMI model are compatible models.

5.5 SPICE Processes

There are five process categories defined in the SPICE standard, namely, customer-supplier processes, engineering processes, management processes, support processes, and organization processes. The various process categories are described in more detail in the following sections.

5.5.1 Customer Supplier Process Category

This particular process category consists of processes that directly impact the customer and includes processes for acquiring software, requirements elicitation, supply of software, and operation and use of the software. The customer-supplier processes include:

Table 5.9: Customer Supplier Process Category

Process	Description
Acquisition	This includes acquisition preparation, supplier selection, supplier monitoring, customer acceptance.
Supply	This involves supplying the agreed product to the customer.
Requirements Elicitation	This involves gathering and tracking customer needs throughout the life of the product.
Operation	This includes operational use and customer support

The purpose of the acquisition base practice is to obtain the product or service that satisfies the needs expressed by the customer. This typically involves a contract between the customer and the supplier and acceptance criteria. The acquisition is monitored to ensure it meets schedule, cost and quality constraints. The acquirer may be different from the customer, for example, when the acquirer performs the purchasing for a third party that will be the final user of the product.

The purpose of the *supplier selection process* is to select an organization to implement the project. Supplier monitoring involves monitoring the technical progress of the supplier regularly to ensure that cost, schedule and quality constraints are met. The purpose of the *customer acceptance process* is to specify criteria to validate and accept the deliverables provided by the supplier, and to ensure that they are of the right quality and satisfy the requirements of the customer.

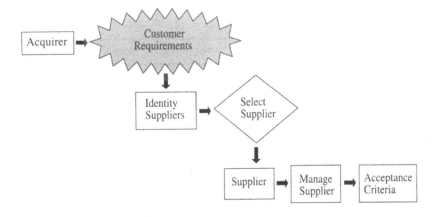

Figure 5.5: Customer Supplier Interaction

The purpose of the *supply process* is to provide software to the customer that meets the agreed requirements. It includes the preparation of a proposal in response to a customer request and includes a contract to implement the agreed customer requirements. The acquisition process and the supply process provide both sides of the customer supplier relationship. The software product delivered is installed in accordance with the agreed requirements.

The purpose of the *requirements elicitation process* is to gather and track the evolving customer needs and requirements throughout the life of the software product. A requirements baseline is established and this serves as a basis for defining the software work products. The changes to the baseline are controlled, and a formal mechanism is available for introducing new requirements into the baseline.

The purpose of the *operation process* is to operate the software product in its intended environment and to provide support to the customers of the software product. The product must be tested in the operational environment prior to its deployment. The purpose of the *customer support process* is to maintain an acceptable level of service to the customer and to ensure effective use of the software. The supplier corrects any identified defects in the software product.

5.5.2 Engineering Process Category

The engineering process category is concerned with processes that directly specify, design, implement, or maintain a software product. It includes a *development process* to transform a set of requirements into a software system that satisfies the customer's stated needs. It requires a software development process, the identification of the intermediate work products, and a mechanism for tracing requirements through the work products, ensuring consistency between requirements and design, and verifying that the end product meets the requirements. It includes the following processes:

Table 5.10: Engineering Process Category

Process	Description
System Requirements Analysis and Design	The purpose of system requirements analysis and design process is to establish the system requirements (functional and nonfunctional) and architecture, and to identify which system requirements should be allocated to which elements of the system. The system requirements need to be approved by the customer
Software Requirements Analysis	The system requirements specific to software form the basis of the software engineering activities. There is consistency between software requirements and designs, and the software requirements are communicated to affected parties and approved.

Table 5.10 (*continued*): Engineering Process Category

Process	Description
Software Design	The purpose of software design is to provide a design for the software that implements the requirements and can be tested against them. The structure of software is defined into modules and interfaces between the modules are defined. Data structures and algorithms to be used by the software are defined.
Software Construction	The purpose of software construction is to provide executable software units and to verify that they reflect the software design.
Software Integration	The purpose of the software integration process is to combine the software units producing integrated software, and to verify that the integrated software reflects the design.
Software Testing	The purpose of the software testing process is to test the integrated software product to verify that it satisfies the software requirements. This involves defining criteria to test against, recording test results, defining and performing regression testing as appropriate, and recording results.
System Integration and Testing	The purpose of system integration and testing is to integrate the software component with the other components, producing a complete system that will satisfy the customer's expectations as expressed in the system requirements. This involves defining criteria to test against, and testing against the criteria, and recording results. Regression testing is carried out as appropriate.
System and software maintenance	The purpose of system and software maintenance process is to modify the system, i.e., the hardware, network, software and associated documentation in response to customer requests while preserving the integrity of the system design. This includes the management of modification, migration and retirement of system components in response to customer requests. It involves updating specifications, designs and test criteria and performing testing to verify requirements are satisfied.

5.5.3 Management Process Category

The management process category is concerned with processes that contain generic practices that may be used in the management of projects or processes in a software lifecycle. It includes the following processes:

Table 5.11: Management Process Category

Process	Description
Management	The purpose of the *management process* is to manage performance of processes or functions within the organization to achieve their business goals. This process supports performance management and work product management attributes for level 2 capability. It includes effort estimation, tasks, resources, assignment of responsibilities, work products to be generated, quality control measures, and schedules.
Project Management	The purpose of the *project management process* is to identify, coordinate and monitor activities, tasks, and resources necessary for the project. It supports the performance management attribute for level 2 capability and defines the scope of work, estimating size and costs for the various project tasks, defining the project plan and tracking the plan. Corrective actions are taken to address deviations from the plan.
Quality Management	The purpose of *quality management process* is to monitor the quality of the project and to ensure that it satisfies the customer. It involves setting quality goals for the project and a strategy to achieve the goals. Quality control and assurance activities will be performed, and the actual performance against the quality goals is tracked, and corrective action taken when quality goals are not achieved. It is closely related to the process control attribute for level 4.
Risk Management	The purpose of *risk management process* is to identify and mitigate risks throughout the lifecycle. There will be a baseline of risks identified at project initiation. Further reviews take place during the project to identify new risks. A risk is characterized by the probability of its occurrence, and its impact upon schedule, cost, or quality. Once a risk is identified, a suitable mitigation strategy is defined, and this may involve actions to reduce the likelihood of the risk occurring, actions to reduce the impact if it should occur, or finding an alternate solution that bypasses the risk.

5.5.4 Support Process Category

The support process category consists of processes that may be used by any of the other processes, including other support processes. They include processes for documentation, configuration management, quality assurance, audit, verification, validation, joint review, and problem resolution. These are described below.

Table 5.12: Support Process Category

Process	Description
Documentation	The purpose of the documentation process is to develop and maintain documents that record information produced by a process. Documents needed by engineers, managers, users, and customers are developed and maintained. The documents to be produced during the lifecycle are identified, and standards for the development of the documents are available.
Configuration Management	The purpose of the configuration management process is to establish and maintain the integrity of the work products of a process or project. It is employed to control and manage all products of the lifecycle, including the tools used to develop the software. All items generated by the process or project will be identified, defined and baselined. Modifications and releases of the items will be controlled, and completeness and consistency of items will be ensured.
Quality Assurance	The purpose of the quality assurance process is to ensure that work products and activities comply with their specified requirements and adhere to their established plans. It provides confidence that the software conforms to requirements and is related to verification, validation, joint reviews, audits, and problem resolution processes. In larger organizations there is usually an independent quality assurance group. The result is software work products that adhere to the applicable procedures and standards.
Verification	The purpose of the verification process is to confirm that each software work product of a process properly reflects the specified requirements.
Validation	The purpose of the validation process is to confirm that the requirements specified for the intended use of the software work product are fulfilled. This typically takes the form of testing. Criteria for the validation of all required work products is identified, the validation takes place, and any problems resolved.
Joint review	The purpose of the joint review process is to maintain a common understanding between the supplier and the customer on progress against the objectives. The reviews ensure that the product is being built according to the specified requirements, and that it is technically correct and consistent. The review results are made known to all affected parties, and any action items are tracked to closure.

Table 5.12 (*continued*): Support Process Category

Process	Description
Audit	The purpose of the audit process is to provide independent confirmation that selected products and processes comply with the requirements, plans and contract. The auditor gives an objective and independent account of the level of compliance to the defined process. Any detected audit issues are detailed in the audit report and actions are assigned to affected groups to correct, and tracked to completion.
Problem Resolution	The purpose of the problem resolution process is to ensure that any discovered problems are promptly reported, analyzed, and removed.

The support processes are closely related to the performance management attribute and the work product management attribute at level 2 capability for a managed process, and the support processes play a key role in implementing the behavior for a managed process.

5.5.5 Organization Process Category

The organization process category consists of processes that help to establish the business goals of the organization. This process category is concerned with building organization infrastructure, and the emphasis is on organization improvement. It includes organization alignment and improvement, process assessment and improvement, human resource management, infrastructure and reuse. These processes are described are described in more detail below:

Table 5.13: Organization Process Category

Process	Description
Organization Alignment	The purpose of organization alignment is to ensure that the individuals in the organization share a common vision, culture, and business goals to function effectively in achieving the goals of the business. This requires the definition of the vision, mission, and goals of the organization, and communicating these to everyone in the organization.
Improvement	The purpose of the organization improvement process is to establish, assess and measure, control, and improve a software lifecycle process. The improvement process is typically part of a software process improvement project, and improvement is accomplished as a series of specific improvement actions. A set of organizational process assets will be developed, and the organization's processes will be assessed periodically to determine their effectiveness and efficiency in achieving business goals.
Process Establishment	The purpose of the process establishment process is to establish a suite of organizational processes which may then be used as the basis for defining processes within the software projects. This process is related to the process definition attribute at level three capability. The output from this process is a set of defined set of processes including the tasks and associated work products and expected performance characteristics.
Process Assessment	The purpose of the process assessment process is to determine the extent to which the organization's standard software process contribute to the achievement of its business goals. The use of process assessment encourages a culture of improvement and the establishment of a proper infrastructure for improvement. The output of the process assessment yields the strengths and weaknesses of the processes.
Process Improvement	The process improvement process is to improve the effectiveness and efficiency of the processes used by the organization in line with its business needs. Changes to the defined processes will be made in a controlled way with predictable results.

Table 5.13 (*continued*): Organization Process Category

Process	Description
Human Resource Management	The purpose of human resource management process is to provide the organization and projects with the individuals who possess skills and knowledge to perform their roles effectively. The necessary roles and skills for operation will be identified, and training identified and provided to ensure the individuals have the skill to perform their roles effectively.
Infrastructure	The purpose of the infrastructure process is to maintain a stable and reliable infrastructure that is needed to support the performance of any other process. The infrastructure will need to meet functionality, safety, performance, security, and availability requirements.
Measurement	The purpose of the measurement process is collect and analyze data relating to processes and products. The objective is to support the effective management of processes and to objectively measure the quality of the product. Measurements will be used to support decisions and to provide an objective basis for communication. This process is closely related to the process measurement attribute at level 4 capability.
Reuse	The purpose of the reuse process is to promote and facilitate reuse within the organization. Reusability yields software elements that can be re-used in many different applications, and supports a software development process relying on preexisting software components.

5.6 The Exemplar Model

The exemplar model is described in part 5 of SPICE and is compatible with the reference model in part 2 of the standard. The exemplar model contains a set of best practices in software engineering which may be used by the organization to assist its improvement program. The exemplar model supports the performance of process assessment, and provides guidance on the use of process indicators in the assessments. An assessment indicator is an objective attribute or characteristic associated with the process that supports the assessor's judgment of the performance or capability of the process. The indicators provide extra confidence in the reliability of the assessment. Indicators may be base practices, work products, or the characteristics of these work products.

, The base practices are a minimal set of practices necessary to achieve the process purpose. If the assessor notes that the base practices are all followed, then there is strong justification for concluding that the process purpose is satisfied. The work products are associated with the execution of a process or base practice, and the existence of work products that exhibit the expected work product characteristics is evidence of process implementation. Indicators are recorded as part of the records of the assessment (Fig. 5.6) and the presence or absence of characteristics will help the assessor in forming a judgment, and the assessor will take the context in which the process is being used into account.

The indicators for the attributes at levels 2 to level 5 are the management practices that are indicators of process capability, and the indicators for the attribute at level 1 consists of the process performance attribute and the base practices, work products, and work product characteristics. The output of the assessment consists of process attribute ratings for each process assessed, and the ratings are based on the indicators included in the exemplar model or the chosen compatible model.

The assessor takes the organization environment into account when forming a judgment on the rating of process capability. The absence of some indicators may not be significant, as indicators are there to guide the assessor in making a judgment.

The compatible model is required to define its scope against the reference model; it is required to contain a non-empty set of processes from the reference model and a continuous set of capability levels starting from level 0. There is a one-to-one correspondence between the processes in the exemplar model and the reference model and also between the set of capability levels of both models.

There is a requirement to define a mechanism to convert the data collected against the indicators in the compatible model to the attribute ratings against the processes in the reference model.

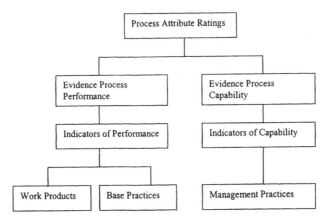

Figure 5.6: SPICE Process Attribute Indicators

5.7 SPICE Assessment

CMM assessments were discussed in chapter 4, and the steps in an assessment method such as CBA IPI were discussed. The steps in a SPICE conformant assessment (Fig. 5.7) are similar to CBA IPI. The objective of a SPICE conformant assessment is to determine the maturity and capability of the organization's or supplier's processes. This enables the organization to prioritize further process improvement or to determine the capability of a supplier. A SPICE conformant assessment is carried out by a competent assessor, and the requirements for performing a SPICE conformant assessment are detailed in part 3 of the standard. Guidance for the performance of assessments is available in part 4, and the role and preparation of the competent assessor is detailed in part 6. The objective of the standard is to define minimum requirements for performing an assessment to ensure consistency and repeatability of the ratings. Evidence is maintained to substantiate the ratings. The assessors and team members are required to have the necessary skills and competence to apply the rules consistently.

A SPICE assessment may be performed by an external assessment team, or it may be an internal self-assessment, or a continuous assessment performed by a CASE tool. There are several phases in an assessment. These include planning the assessment, determining its scope, preparing for the assessment, selecting the assessors and assessees, selecting an assessment approach and assessment instruments, gathering data, determining actual ratings and validating the ratings, presenting the assessment findings and writing an assessment report.

The scope of the assessment details the processes to be assessed, and the levels to which they are to be assessed. The scope includes the number of process instances of the process, and the rating of the process is determined from the rating of the individual process instances. The number of process instances chosen depends on the size of the assessment team, the duration of the assessment, and the organization size. The assessor will examine each process instance to determine its maturity, and use this to determine the overall rating for the process.

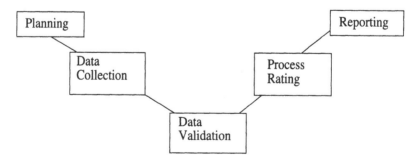

Figure 5.7: SPICE Conformant Assessment

The assessment is performed according to the assessment plan, which is a documented process that is capable of meeting the assessment purpose. The plan will include the schedule of activities, the assessors, the assessees, the preparation of the assessment team, briefing the organization unit on how the assessment will be run, and providing information on confidentiality and assessment output.

5.7.1 Planning for the Assessment

A good assessment requires planning and preparation, and good planning ensures that everything will go smoothly. The assessment team is chosen with care and includes a competent assessor who has the right skills for performing the assessment. The competent assessor will verify that the other assessors have the appropriate background and will ensure that the appropriate participants take part in the assessment.

The assessment plan is produced and communicated to the assessment sponsor. The sponsor is responsible for approving the assessment plan and committing the resources, time and people to undertake the assessment. The sponsor is required to ensure that the lead assessor has the required competence. A competent assessor is knowledgeable regarding software engineering and SPICE and has the desired personal attributes to perform effectively at the assessment. These personal attributes include judgment, leadership, diplomacy, good communication skills, and resistance handling ability.

The activities planning and preparation include the following:

Table 5.14: Assessment Planning

Planning Activity	Responsibility
Agree purpose, scope, and constraints of the assessment	Sponsor/competent assessor
Identify processes and capability levels to assess to	Sponsor/competent assessor
Identify the compatible model to be used	Competent assessor
Choose assessors, assign assessment roles and responsibilities, prepare assessment team	Competent assessor
Document assessment plan, identify risks and constraints, communicate plan and schedule	Competent assessor
Map organization processes to compatible model	Competent assessor/ Site coordinator
Select projects to be examined	Site coordinator
Prepare participants in organization	Site coordinator
Arrange logistics and infrastructure	Site coordinator
Include timing and participants for each meeting	Competent assessor

Table 5.14 (*continued*): Assessment Planning

Planning Activity	Responsibility
Select assessment techniques (individual or group interviews, presentations, questionnaires, observation, document reviews)	Competent assessor
Select assessment instruments (tools to collect, record, process, and present assessment data)	Competent assessor
Plan feedback sessions	Competent assessor
Document the confidentiality agreements	Competent assessor
Include output of assessment (reporting of results)	Competent assessor

The schedule of activities for an on site assessment includes a format similar to the following (Table 5.15):

Table 5.15: Assessment Schedule

	Day 1	Day 2	Day 3	Day 4	Day 5
9–10	Opening session	Project 1	Organization reps	Closed session	Complete final findings
10–11	Interview PM	Project 1	Organization reps	Follow-up meetings	Present final findings
11–12	Interview PM	Documentation review	Documentation review	Prepare preliminary findings	
12–1	Closed session	Closed Session	Follow-up meetings	Prepare preliminary findings	Executive briefing
1–2	Lunch	Lunch	Lunch	Lunch	Lunch
2–3	Interview PM	Project 2	Organization reps	Present preliminary findings	
3–4	Interview PM	Project 2	Organization reps	Follow up	
4–5	Consolidate	Consolidate	Consolidate	Prepare final findings	

5.7.2 Data Collection and Validation

Various techniques may be employed to gather the required information, and these may include interviews, documentation reviews, presentations from the organization, and group discussions. The objective is to gather all the information required to judge whether a process is performed or not, and the extent to which the process attributes are achieved. The accuracy of the rating of the processes is dependent on the accuracy and consistency of the data gathering, as the data collected is used to rate the process. Tools may be employed to perform the data collection effectively. The minimal requirements for the data collection process are defined in part 3 of the SPICE standard. It requires the identification of the data collection techniques to be used in the assessment, and that a mapping is defined between the processes in the organization unit and the processes of the compatible model, and a mapping between the compatible model and the reference model.

The mapping between the organization processes and the processes of the compatible model is useful, as this will help the assessment team's understanding of the software process in the organization, and thereby ensure more effective data collection.

Assessment instruments or tools are used to support the evaluation of the existence or adequacy of the practices within the scope of the assessment. The tools may be used to collect, record, analyze, store, retrieve, and present information of an assessment. The assessment instrument may be paper-based or (semi-) automated computer-based tools. The main purpose of the assessment instrument is to support the assessor to perform the assessment in an objective manner, and to enable an objective rating to be made based on the recorded information.

The assessment team needs to ensure that the set of information collected is sufficient, and that the observations recorded accurately reflect the practices of the organization for each process. The validity of the data may be confirmed in different ways, e.g., using different information sources for the same purpose, using information gathered in previous assessments, having feedback sessions to discuss findings, and obtaining first-hand information from the process practitioners.

5.7.3 Process Ratings

Once sufficient data has been gathered and validated, the processes within the scope of the assessment are assigned a rating for each process attribute, and a process profile is formed. The assessor's judgment is based on the indicators of the compatible model. It is a SPICE requirement to record the decision-making process to derive the rating judgments, and the decision process may be consensus of the assessment team, majority voting, or an alternate mechanism.

The derivation of the ratings is non-trivial as the judgment of the adequacy of performance and capability of a process depends on the context of the process in the organization. Sufficient data must be available to enable the process to be rated accurately, and in the case of an absence of information, the assessor makes an informed judgment. The implementation of configuration management for a small project may be totally inadequate for a larger project. Therefore, good judgment is required from the assessors. If conflicting opinions exist within the assessment team, a decision-making process to determine the actual rating is required.

Records are preserved to be used in post-assessment activities. The assessment plan, detailed findings, and report may be used in planning a future assessment, or in generating detailed action plans.

5.7.4 Assessment Reporting

The results of the assessment are shared with the assessment sponsor and the participants in the assessment. The records of the assessment are preserved, and confidentiality of the assessment data is preserved. The assessment report will detail the scope of the assessment, the activities carried out, and the activities to be carried out post-assessment. Information is preserved on the set of process profiles for each process assessed in the scope of the assessment.

The assessment records include the date of the assessment; the names of the assessors; the assessment input; the assessment approach which details how the assessment was carried out; and the set of process profiles and any additional information. This will be analyzed in detail by the organization, and used to produce an action plan for improvement.

5.8 Process Capability Determination

One of the key advantages of SPICE is that it allows the capability of key processes to be determined. This enables an organization to determine whether it or a subcontractor is capable of delivering what is required. That is, before the actual software development takes place, it is important that the organization knows whether it is capable of performing the work successfully. SPICE provides guidance to enable the organization to determine its capability or the capability of a subcontractor. The information on capability may be used in decision making to determine whether to award work to a subcontractor, to select an alternate subcontractor, or to do the work itself. This is described in part 8 of the SPICE standard.

Capability determination is useful for risk management, as it provides a mechanism to evaluate the risk of a particular subcontractor or organization in carrying out the software activities (Fig. 5.8). It is based on a comparison of capability needs versus capability available, and the gap between capability needs versus availability indicates the degree of risk in proceeding with the software activities, and techniques to reduce risk are typically employed.

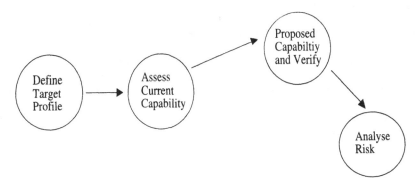

Figure 5.8: SPICE Capability Risk Analysis

The gaps in capability may be due to missing practices, and the supplier will generally be required to implement improvements to narrow the gap between the desired capability rating and the actual capability rating. The target capability is expressed as a process profile of the key processes. The assessed capability is determined, and where a gap exists a proposed capability is agreed on between the supplier and prime contractor, and the supplier is required to implement an improvement plan to achieve the proposed capability.

The target profile is expressed in table format (Table 5.16) and consists of the key processes and the target capability of each process.

Table 5.16: SPICE Target Capability Profile

Process	Performed PP	Managed PM WPM	Estab- lished PD PR	Predict- able PM PC	Opti- mizing CI PC
ENG 1.1	F	F F	F F		
ENG 1.2	F	F F	L L		
MAN .1	F	F F			
CUS .2	F	F F	F L		

The ratings of fully (F), largely (L), partially (P), and not satisfied (NS) have been discussed previously. The target profile is dependent on the type of work that the prime contractor wishes the subcontractor to perform.

An assessment of the key processes takes place to determine the capability of the supplier, the actual ratings are then compared to the target ratings, and a proposed profile will be agreed upon.

Table 5.17: SPICE Actual Assessed Capability Profile

Process	Performed PP	Managed PM WPM	Estab- lished PD PR	Predict- able PM PC	Opti- mizing CI PC
ENG 1.1	F	L L	L P		
ENG 1.2	F	F L	L P		
MAN .1	F	F L			
CUS .2	F	F L	L L		

The subcontractor is required to perform process improvement activities to achieve the proposed process capability ratings. An internal self-assessment or an independent or joint assessment may be employed to determine the actual capability profile of the organization (Table 5.17). There may also be verification via an assessment to confirm that the proposed capability profile has been achieved.

The next task is to assess the risk by examining the gaps between the target capability profile and the actual capability profile. The gap between the target and actual rating for each attribute is rated as none, minor, or major, and is determined from the following table.

Table 5.18: SPICE Gap Analysis per Process Attribute

Capability Level	Target Rating	Assessed Rating	Gap
PA 1.1	F	F	None
PA 2.1	F	L	Minor
PA 2.2	F	L	Minor
PA 3.1	F	P	Major
PA 3.2	F	NS	Major
PA 4.1	L	F	None
PA 4.2	L	L	None
PA 5.1	L	P	Major
PA 5.2	L	NS	Major

The number of process gaps at each capability level is calculated (Table 5.18), and the risk per capability level is determined. Three is only a slight risk if there are minor gaps, and a significant or substantial risk for the capability level if there are major gaps. The overall risk is then calculated and may be low, medium, or high.

A report of the capability determination is then produced and includes a statement of confidence in the proposed capability, and the gap between the target capability and the proposed capability, and the risk analysis. There are no gaps at level 1 capability for the example above, and there are minor gaps at level 2 capability, and two major gaps at level 3 capability. A gap of two majors is considered substantial and indicates a medium risk. The mechanism for calculating risks is described in part 8 of the SPICE standard.

5.9 SPICE and Process Improvement

Studies by Caper Jones [CJ:96] have indicated that approximately 50% of small or medium projects are delayed or over budget by 20%;that over 75% of large systems either do not work correctly or are never used; and almost all large projects exceed their budget or complete late. Consequently, organizations need to focus on improvements to assist with on-time delivery and quality of the delivered software. Software process improvement using the CMM and the IDEAL model has been discussed in chapter 4, and SPICE also plays a key role in software process improvement. Software process improvement is a cyclical activity in which the current status of the organization with respect to some improvement model or standard is made, areas for improvement are then identified and improvements made, and then the effect of the improvements checked before repeating the cycle.

There is a guide to software process improvement in part 7 of the SPICE standard, and the guide describes how software process assessment may be applied to process improvement. The feedback from a SPICE assessment may be used to prioritize improvements to the organization's processes so that they better meet the organization's business needs, and to achieve the business goals more effectively. The software process capability is determined via an assessment, and areas for improvements are identified. The targeted improvements are made and checked via pilots to ensure that they have the right effects.

Data is gathered to verify that the improvements have been successful. The improvements are then fully implemented and the cycle repeats, with a new assessment providing confirmation of progress. The SPICE standard has defined an eight-step model for improving the software processes and it forms a continuous improvement cycle that is similar to the IDEAL model.

The eight step continuous improvement cycle is summarized in Figure 5.9.

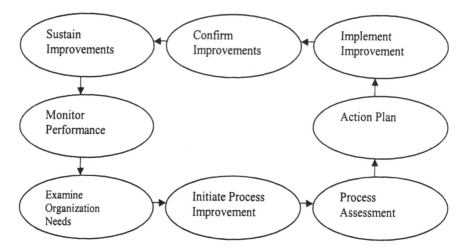

Figure 5.9: SPICE Improvement Process

The steps in process improvement include the following:

Table 5.19: SPICE Gap Analysis per Process Attribute

Step	Description
Business Needs	Customer satisfaction, greater competitiveness, profitability.
Initiate Process Improvement	SPI requires senior management sponsorship to succeed. Business goals may include improving software quality, reducing maintenance, providing on-time delivery, staying within budget, etc.
Prepare/conduct assessment	The assessment of key processes in the organization is performed against the SPICE standard. The output is analyzed and an action plan prepared.
Analyze results/ action plan	Software process improvement requires a considerable investment in time and people, and a plan of improvement actions for the changes is made.
Implement improvements	Involve staff in the improvement effort as changes affect staff, and buy in for changes is achieved by staff participating in the definition and implementation of the change.
Confirm improvements	Evaluate whether the improvement has achieved the desired target. Improvements may be piloted in restricted areas and this requires planning and control. Measurements may be employed to verify the results or the confirmation may be via an assessment.

Table 5.19 (*continued*): SPICE Gap Analysis per Process Attribute

Step	Description
Sustain improvements	The deployment of change needs to be considered, and for the changes to be effective, a planned and controlled implementation of the change is required. Any lessons learned should be identified and acted upon.
Monitor performance	The improvement process is monitored and new areas for improvement are selected. The deployment of improvements is tracked and corrective action taken to address any issues. Goals are set for the next improvement cycle.

The CMM recommends a specific group for the organization processes and for process improvement within the organization namely, the software engineering process group (SEPG). An organization-wide process improvement suggestion database is set up within the organization to enable the software engineering community to submit ideas on process improvement. The SEPG team then meets regularly to discuss and implement valid improvement suggestions. New or altered processes are introduced in a controlled manner and older processes retired in a controlled manner.

The SPICE process model may be employed to identify practices to improve the capability of the process. Software process assessment is used to verify that the improvements are successful. The organization category in the SPICE reference model includes processes concerned with improvement activities. The assessment may be limited to several processes as the organization may wish to focus on a small number of key processes, and an assessment of a small number of processes requires less effort by the assessment team. The assessment will yield strengths and weaknesses, for example, processes with very high capability ratings, or processes with very low capability ratings, or processes with missing or incomplete base practices. A profile of the assessed processes will be included in the assessment report, and the process ratings and capability level ratings are analyzed to derive the improvement plan.

The success of a software process improvement initiative is dependent on the following:

- Driven by organization's business needs
- Needs senior management commitment
- Needs to focus
- Needs clear goals
- Requires investment of time
- Team effort
- Continuous activity
- Quantitative measurement

Process improvement requires the support and leadership from senior and middle management within the organization. The sponsorship of senior management is essential for success, as unless the improvement program is seen to be a priority of senior management it is likely to fail. Senior management needs to ensure that there is sufficient time available for staff to participate in improvement activities. The goals of process improvement are related to the needs of the organization and the organization sets goals for improvement.

The improvement activities require staff to be available to work on process improvement projects as distinct from their normal project work. Process improvement projects vary in size and complexity. A large process improvement project will require a detailed plan with a work breakdown and schedule. It will require teamwork and this may consist of a cross-functional team formed within the organization. The values of the benefits of process improvement will need to be instilled in the organization culture. This may be facilitated by implementing a reward and recognition mechanism to reward staff who make outstanding contributions to process improvement.

The owners of the processes, process improvement projects, etc., will need to be identified. The effectiveness of the process improvement program will need to be measured, for example, increased capability levels or process effectiveness measurements. Progress will need to be monitored and reviewed with respect to the goals and time scales of the program and corrective action taken as appropriate. software process assessments are conducted at the appropriate time.

One key factor in the success of an improvement program in an organization is the mindset or attitude of management and staff in the organization. The attitude of management and staff may require change before a successful improvement program can take place.

Changing the mindset of an organization may be difficult, and typically requires training of staff on the new core values of the organization, and motivating the importance of change and continuous improvement in the organization. The change facilitator may face resistance to change within the organization, and this may take various forms for example, staff apathy. This may be overcome by several techniques including an open discussion to justify the necessity for change, the benefits of the new approach, and the implementation plan for the new approach.

5.10 The Implementation of SPICE

The implementation of SPICE in the organization requires that a roadmap for implementation be defined. The implementation of SPICE is closely related to the section on process improvement as discussed previously in this chapter, and there are many valid implementations of SPICE. The main challenges are to identify the key processes that are closely related to the business goals of the organization, and to target implementation and improvements to these processes. The set of processes that the organization will initially target will be from the various process categories in 15504, for example, requirements gathering from

CUS.3, software development from ENG.1, project management from MAN.2, configuration management from SUP.2, quality assurance from SUP.3, and risk management from MAN.4.

The first step is usually to set up a steering group, and the steering group will then need to identify the targeted capability level for these processes. There is a relationship between the targeted capability and processes belonging to the management, support and organization process categories, and therefore there may be a need to consider and include further processes to achieve the targeted capability level. There is then a need to put the right structures in place and to provide the resources to do the actual work to implement or improve the targeted processes. The steps involved in a typical implementation of SPICE include the following:

- Form steering group
- Set goals and objectives for implementation
- Identify processes to be implemented
- Identify targeted capability of processes
- Form process teams
- Provide resources and time
- Analyze current maturity of each targeted process
- Form improvement plan for each process
- Track improvement status of each process per quarter
- Communicate progress to steering group
- Provide any required additional resources
- Organize formal assessment to verify targeted capability level
- Set new implementation goals and objectives

Each organization is different, and the initial set of processes will differ from one organization to another. The implementation of a SPICE process (e.g., CUS.3) to the managed capability level will usually involve the examining the process indicators and the capability process indicators in the compatible model as these will provide information on the typical work products expected and the characteristics of the work products expected, and any other pertinent information.

5.11 SPICE A Critical Analysis

The work on SPICE has had a significant influence on the process improvement field, and the software Engineering Institute has worked to make the CMM model compatible with SPICE. The objectives of the CMMI project were described in chapter 4. The original CMM was a staged model with five maturity levels, and the new CMMI model is published in two representations, namely, the staged representation that is familiar to the CMM community, and the continuous representation that is familiar to the SPICE community. The fact that the

SEI has made the CMM SPICE compatible indicates the importance that is attached to SPICE by one of the leading organizations for process improvement in the world.

The SPICE standard has been applied or extended to many diverse fields; for example, an ISO 15504-conformant method (S4S) for software process assessment has been developed for the European space agency [Cas:00]. This includes an assessment model based on the exemplar model, four new processes, and 50 new base practices to incorporate space software practices, including, safety and dependability requirements. The ability to employ SPICE in many diverse fields and to extend SPICE to reflect the domain to which it is being applied is a very useful feature of the standard. The SPICE standard is also useful in that it allows comparability of results and thus enables organizations to benchmark themselves and their processes against one another.

SPICE is a model-based approach and is subject to the limitations of models in that models are simplifications of the real world and do not reflect all of the attributes of the real world. There is the well known quotation that *"All models are wrong, but, some are useful"* and pragmatism is needed with models; a model is judged useful if it assists in more effective software development.

The use of a model such as SPICE can be quite difficult initially as the terminology is alien to people unfamiliar with the field. Also, its current definition with 9 parts makes it a very large document, and this poses difficulties with its usability. The CMM provides a clear roadmap as to how organizations may improve; however, SPICE was designed to give the organization freedom in choosing improvements to yield the greatest business benefit, but it requires that the organization defines its own improvement roadmap.

SPICE currently exists as a technical report (type 2) and agreement on the final definition of the standard is likely in the future. This will affect the contents of this chapter.

5.12 Summary

SPICE (15504) is the emerging international standard for software process assessment that arose owing to the multiple models for software process assessment and improvement such as CMM, Trillium, Bootstrap, and ISO 9000. The objective is to have an international standard to allow effective assessments to take place and allow compatibility of results between different assessment methods. A SPICE-conformant assessment provides the capability rating of key processes within the scope of the assessment and this may be used in software process improvement.

The SPICE standard includes the reference model, which includes a process dimension and a capability dimension. There are five categories of SPICE processes: customer supplier, engineering, organization, management, and support processes. The SPICE processes map on to the ISO 12207 standard for software processes and contain key practices essential to good software engineering. The model is applicable to software organizations and does not presume a particular organization structure or software development or management philosophy.

The model offers a framework to develop sound software engineering processes and enables an organization to assess and prioritize improvements to its processes. It enables an organization to understand its own capability and the capability of third-party software suppliers, and to thereby determine if a particular project is within its own capability or within the capability of a proposed third-party supplier, and the associated risks of awarding a contract to a third-party supplier.

The standard is useful for internal process improvement and one of the advantages of the standard is that it allows the organization to focus on improvements to selected processes related to its business goals rather than the step-wise evolution approach of the standard CMM. The importance of the standard is evident from the work of the CMMI project in which the continuous representation of the CMM is now SPICE compatible.

6
Metrics and Problem Solving

6.1 Introduction

Measurement is an essential part of mathematics and the physical sciences, and has been successfully applied in recent years to the software engineering discipline. The purpose of a measurement program is to establish and use quantitative measurements to manage the software development environment in the organization, to assist the organization in understanding its current software capability, and to provide an objective indication that improvements have been successful. Measurements provide visibility into the various functional areas in the organization, and the actual quantitative data allow trends to be seen over time. The analysis of the trends and quantitative data allow action plans to be derived for continuous improvement. Measurements may be employed to track the quality, timeliness, cost, schedule, and effort of software projects. The term "metric" and "measurement" are used interchangeably in this book. The formal definition of measurement given by Fenton [Fen:95] is the following:

> "Measurement is the process by which numbers or symbols are assigned to attributes or entities in the real world in such a way as to describe them according to clearly defined rules."

Measurement has played a key role in the physical sciences and everyday life, for example, the distance to the planets and stars, the mass of objects, the speed of mechanical vehicles, the electric current flowing through a wire, the rate of inflation, the unemployment rate, and many more. These measurements provide a more precise understanding of the entity under study. Often several measurements are used to provide a detailed understanding of the entity, for example, the cockpit of an aeroplane contains measurements of altitude, speed, temperature, fuel, latitude, longitude, and various devices essential to modern navigation and flight, and clearly an airline offering to fly passengers using just the altitude measurement would not be taken seriously.

Metrics also play a key role in problem solving. Various problem-solving techniques were discussed earlier in chapter 1, and good data is essential for obtaining a precise objective understanding of the extent of a particular problem.

For example, an outage is measured as the elapsed time between down -time and subsequent up-time. For many organizations, e.g., telecommunications companies it is essential to minimize outages and the impact of an outage should one occur. Measurements provide this data, and the measurement data is used to enable effective analysis to take place to enable the root cause of a particular problem, e.g., an outage, to be identified, and to verify that the actions taken to correct the problem have been effective.

Metrics may provide an internal view of the quality of the software product, and care is needed before deducing the behavior that a product will exhibit externally from the various internal measurements of the product. A leading measure is a software measure that usually precedes the attribute that is under examination; for example, the arrival rate of software problems is a leading indicator of the maintenance effort. Leading measures provide an indication of the likely behavior of the product in the field and need to be examined closely. A lagging indicator is a software measure that is likely to follow the attribute being studied; for example, escaped customer defects is an indicator of the quality and reliability of the software. It is important to learn from lagging indicators even if the data can have little impact on the current project.

6.2 The Goal Question Metric Paradigm

The Goal Question Metric (GQM) paradigm was developed by Victor Basili of the University of Maryland and is described in detail in [Bas:88]. It is a rigorous goal oriented approach to measurement in which goals, questions, and measurements are closely integrated. The business goals are first identified, and then questions that relate to the achievement of the goal are identified, and for each question a metric that gives an objective answer to the particular question is identified. The statement of the goal is very precise and the goal is related to individuals or groups. Many software metrics programs have failed because they had poorly defined, or even non-existent goals and objectives. The GQM concept is a simple one, and managers and engineers proceed according to the following three stages:

- Set goals specific to needs in terms of purpose, perspective and environment
- Refine the goals into quantifiable questions
- Deduce the metrics and data to be collected (and the means for collecting them) to answer the questions

The GQM approach (Fig. 6.1) may be applied to many domains, and as this book is primarily concerned with software quality, it is appropriate to consider an example from the software field. Consider the following example whose goal is to identify the effectiveness of a new programming language *L:* There are several valid questions which may be asked at this stage, including who are the

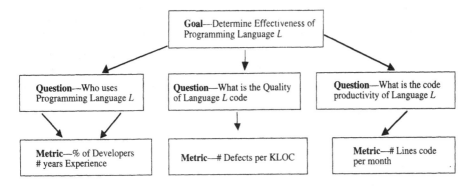

Figure 6.1: GQM Example

programmers that use *L* and what is their level of experience? what is the quality of software code produced with language *L*? and what is the productivity of language *L*? This leads naturally to the quality and productivity metrics below.

Goal

The focus on improvements in an organization should be closely related to the business goals, and the first step is to identify the business goals the improvement program is to address. The business goals are related to the strategic direction of the organization and particular problems that the organization is currently facing. There is little sense in directing improvement activities to areas which do not require improvement, or for which there is no business need to improve, or from which there will be minimal return to the organization.

Question

These are the key questions which require answers to determine the extent to which the goal is being satisfied, and for each business goal the set of pertinent questions need to be identified. The questions are identified by a detailed examination of the goal and determining what information needs to be available to determine the current status of the business goal and to help the business goal to be achieved. Each question is then analyzed to determine the best approach to obtain an objective answer to the question and to identify which metrics are needed, and the data that needs to be gathered to answer the question objectively.

Metrics

These are the objective measurements to give a quantitative answer to the particular question. The questions and measurements are thereby closely related to the achievement of the goals, and provide an objective picture of the extent to which the goal is currently being satisfied. The objective of measurement is to improve the understanding of a specific process or product, and the GQM approach leads to focused measurements which are closely related to the goal, rather than measurement for the sake of measurement. This approach helps to ensure that the measurements will be used by the organizations to improve and to satisfy the business goals more effectively. The successful improvement of software development is impossible without knowing what the improvement goals are and how they are related with the business goals.

The GQM methodology is a rigorous approach to focused software measurement, and the measures may be from various viewpoints, e.g., manager viewpoint, project team viewpoint, etc. The idea is always first to identify the goals, and once the goals have been decided common-sense questions and measurement are employed. There are two key approaches to software process improvement: top-down or bottom-up improvement. Top-down approaches to software process improvement are based on assessment methods and benchmarking, for example, the CMM, SPICE, and ISO 9000:2000, whereas GQM is a bottom-up approach to software process improvement, where the focus is to target improvements related to certain specific goals. The two approaches are often combined in practice.

6.3 The Balanced Scorecard

The balanced scorecard (BSC) (Fig. 6.2) is a management tool to clarify and translate the organization vision and strategy into action. It was developed by Kaplan and Norton [KpN:96] and has been applied to many organizations.

The balanced scorecard assists in selecting appropriate measurements to indicate the success or failure of the organization's strategy. There are four perspectives in the scorecard: customer, financial, internal process, and learning and growth. Each perspective includes objectives to be accomplished for the strategy to succeed, measures to indicate the extent to which the objectives are being met, targets to be achieved in the perspective, and initiatives to achieve the targets. The balanced scorecard includes financial and non-financial measures.

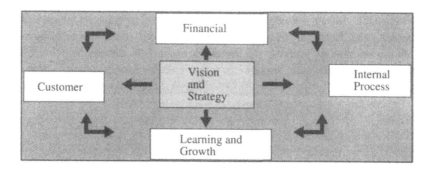

Figure 6.2: The Balanced Scorecard

The balanced scorecard is useful in selecting the key processes which the organization should focus its process improvement efforts on in order to achieve its strategy (Fig. 6.3). Traditional improvement is based on improving quality, reducing costs and improving productivity, whereas the balanced scorecard takes the future needs of the organization into account and identifies the processes that the organization needs to excel at in the future to achieve its strategy. This results in focused process improvement, and the intention is to yield the greatest business benefit from the improvement program.

The starting point is for the organization to identify its vision and strategy for the future. This often involves clarifying the vision and gaining consensus among the senior management team. The vision and strategy are translated into objectives for the organization or business unit. The next step is communication, and the vision and strategy and objectives are communicated to all employees. The critical objectives must be achieved for the strategy to succeed. All employees will need to determine their own local objectives to support the organization strategy. Goals are set and rewards are linked to performance measures.

The financial and customer objectives are first identified from the strategy and the key business processes to be improved are then identified. These are the key processes that will lead to a breakthrough in performance for customers and shareholders of the company. It may require new processes and this may require re-training of employees on the new processes. The balanced scorecard is very effective in driving organization change. The financial objectives require targets to be set for customer, internal business process, and the learning and growth perspective. The learning and growth perspective will examine competencies and capabilities of employees and the level of employee satisfaction.

The organization metrics presented in the next section have been influenced by the ideas in the balanced scorecard.

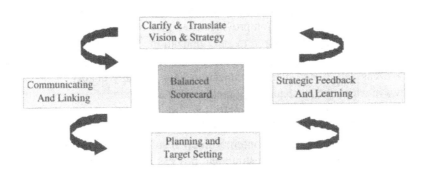

Figure 6.3: BSC as Framework for Action

Table 6.1: BSC Objectives and Measures for IT service organization

Financial	Customer
Cost of provision of services Cost of hardware/software Increase revenue Reduce costs	Quality service Accurate information Reliability of solution Rapid response time Timeliness of Solution 99.999% network availability 24x7 customer support
Internal Business Process	**Learning and Growth**
Requirements elicitation Software design Implementation Testing process Compliance to lifecycle Maintenance Problem resolution Project / risk management Help desk expertise Customer support and training Hardware and network provision E-Mail and monitoring Security / proprietary information Disaster prevention and recovery Legal issues (IT)	Expertise of staff • S/W development • Project management • Customer support Staff development Career structure Objectives for staff Employee satisfaction Leadership

6.4 Metrics for an Organization

The objective of defining a metrics set for an organization is to provide visibility into the various areas in the organization, and to facilitate further improvements in the organization. This section provides examples of various metrics that may potentially be applied or tailored to an organization. The objective is to give an overview of how metrics may potentially be employed for effective management in the organization, and many organization have monthly quality or operation reviews in which the presentation of metrics play a key part.

This section includes sample metrics for the various functional areas in a software organization, including the human resources area, the customer satisfaction area, supplier quality, internal audit results, project management, requirements and development, testing, and process improvement. These metrics would typically be presented at a monthly management review and trends observed. The main output from a management review is a series of actions to be completed by the following review.

6.4.1 Customer Satisfaction Measurements

Figure 6.4 indicates the survey arrival rate per customer per month, and it indicates that there is a customer satisfaction process in place in the organization, that the customers are surveyed, and the extent to which they are surveyed. It does not provide any information as to whether the customers are satisfied, whether any follow-up activity from the survey is required, or whether the frequency of surveys is sufficient for the organization.

Figure 6.5 gives the overall customer satisfaction figures in 20 categories including the overall satisfaction, ability of the company to meet committed dates and to deliver the agreed content, the ease of use of the software, the quality of documentation, and value for money. Examples of the kind of feedback that Figure 6.5 provides are as follows: a score of 2.1 for reliability indicates that the customers perceive the software to be unreliable, and a score of 2.5 for problem

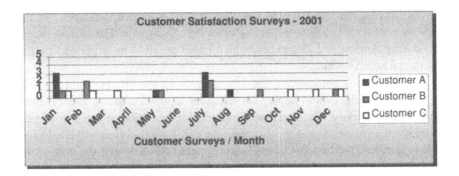

Figure 6.4: Customer Survey Arrivals

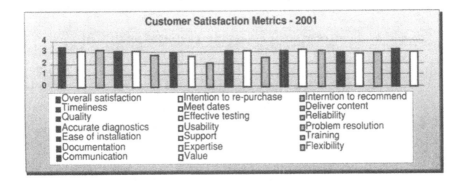

Figure 6.5: Customer Satisfaction Measurements

resolution indicates that the customers perceive the problem resolution effectiveness to be less than satisfactory.

The chart is interpreted as follows:

    4 = Exceeds expectations
    3 = Meets Expectations
    2 = Fair
    1 = Below Expectations

6.4.2 Process Improvement Metrics

Many organizations have a continuous improvement program in place, and the objective of process improvement metrics is to provide visibility into the improvement program.

Figure 6.6 shows the arrival rate of improvement suggestions from the software community. The chart indicates that initially the arrival rate is high and the closure rate low, which is consistent with the commencement of a process improvement program. The arrival rate then improves, which indicates that the improvement team is active and acting upon the suggestions. The closure rate is low during August and December, which could possibly be explained by the traditional holiday period.

The chart does not indicate the effectiveness of the process improvement suggestions and the overall impact the particular suggestion has on quality, cycle time, or productivity. There are no measurements included of the cost of performing improvements, and this is important as the organization will need to be able to compare the benefits of the improvement activities with the cost of the improvements.

Figure 6.7 provides visibility into the status of the improvement suggestions, and the number of raised, open, and closed suggestions per month. The chart indicates that gradual progress has been made in the improvement program with a gradual increase in the number of suggestions that are closed.

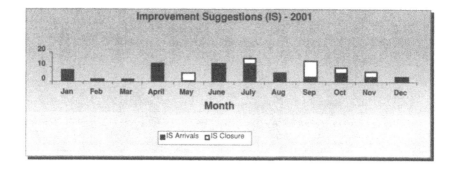

Figure 6.6: Process Improvement Measurements

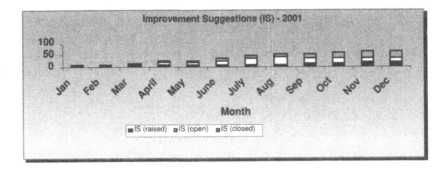

Figure 6.7: Process Improvement Status

Figure 6.8 provides visibility into the age of the improvement suggestions, and indicates the effectiveness of the organization in acting on the improvement suggestions. It is a measure of the productivity of the improvement team and its ability to do its assigned work.

Figure 6.9 gives an indication of the productivity of the improvement program, and shows how often the team meets to discuss the improvement suggestions and to act upon them. This chart is slightly naive as it just tracks the number of improvement meetings which have taken place during the year, and contains no information on the actual productivity of the meeting. The chart could be considered with Figure 6.6 to get a more accurate idea of productivity as the number of closed improvement suggestions per month.

There will usually be other charts associated with an improvement program, for example, a metric to indicate the status of the CMM program is provided in section 6.4.8. It includes a maturity rating per key process area, and it is shared with management to ensure that sufficient resources are provided to remove any roadblocks. Similarly, a measure of the current status of the ISO 9000 implementation in the organization could be derived from the number of actions

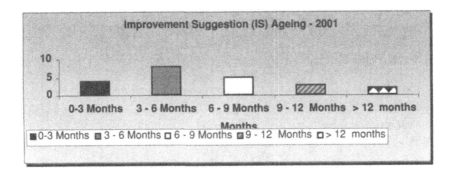

Figure 6.8: Process Improvement Status Measurements

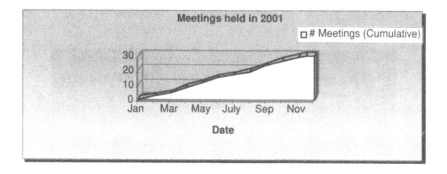

Figure 6.9: Process Improvement Productivity

which are required to implement ISO 9000, the number implemented, and the number outstanding.

6.4.3 Human Resources and Training Metrics

These charts give visibility into the human resources and training areas of a company. They provide visibility into the current headcount (Fig. 6.10) of the organization per calendar month and the turnover of staff in the organization (Table 6.2). The human resources department will typically maintain measurements of the number of job openings to be filled per month, the arrival rate of resumes per month, the average number of interviews to fill one position, the percentage of employees that have received their annual appraisal, etc.

The key goals of the HR department are defined and the questions and metrics are associated with the key goals. For example, one of the key goals of the HR department is to attract and retain the best employees, and this breaks down into the two obvious sub-goals of attracting the best employees and retaining them.

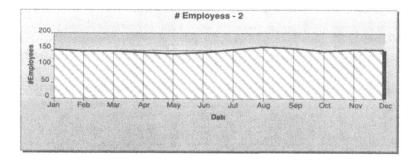

Figure 6.10: Employee Headcount in Current Year

The key goals of the HR department are defined and the questions and metrics are associated with the key goals. For example, one of the key goals of the HR department is to attract and retain the best employees, and this breaks down into the two obvious sub-goals of attracting the best employees and retaining them.

The next chart gives visibility into the turnover of staff per calendar year and enables the organization to benchmark itself against the industry average. It indicates the effectiveness of staff retention in the organization.

Table 6.2: Employee Turnover per Year

Year	Turnover	Turnover (%)
1999	10	10%
2000	12	11
2001	15	10

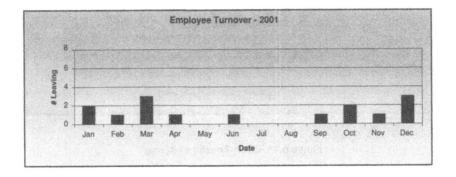

Figure 6.11: Employee Turnover in Current Year

6.4.4 Project Management Metrics

The objective of the project management metrics is to assist in determining the effectiveness of project management in the organization. The goal of successful project management is to deliver a high-quality product that satisfies the agreed requirements within time and budget. Consequently, the project management metrics provide visibility into the effectiveness of key attributes of the software project with respect to timeliness, quality, cost, and the agreed content. The first metric presented here is a timeliness metric and provides visibility into whether the project has been delivered on time (Fig. 6.12), and the number of months over or under schedule per project in the organization. The schedule timeliness metric is a lagging measure, as it indicates that the project has been delivered on

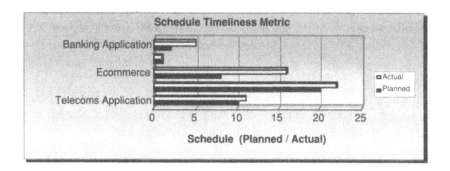

Figure 6.12: Schedule Timeliness Metric

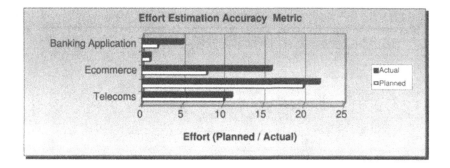

Figure 6.13: Effort Timeliness Metric

time or within schedule or has been late after the event. It is advisable that time-liness issues be considered during the project post-mortem.

The on-time delivery of a project requires that the various milestones in the project be carefully tracked and corrective actions taken to address slippage in milestones during the project. Modern risk management practices help to mini-mize the risks of schedule slippage and to achieve or improve upon the expecta-tions of the agreed schedule.

The second metric provides visibility into the effort estimation accuracy of a project (Fig. 6.13). Effort estimation is a key component in calculating the cost of a project and in devising the agreed schedule, and accuracy is essential.

The effort estimation chart is similar to the schedule estimation chart, except that the schedule metric is referring to time as recorded in elapsed calendar months, whereas the effort estimation chart refers to the human effort estimated to carry out the work, and the actual human effort which was employed to carry out the work. Projects are required to have an estimation methodology to enable them to be successful in project management, and historical data will usually be employed.

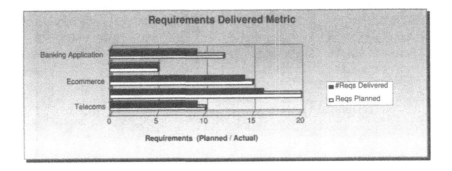

Figure 6.14: Requirements Delivered

The next metric is related to the commitments which are made to the customer with respect to the content of a particular release, and indicates the effectiveness of the projects in delivering the agreed requirements to the customer (Fig. 6.14). This chart could be adapted to include enhancements or fixes promised to a customer for a particular release of a software product.

6.4.5 Development Quality Metrics

These charts give visibility into development and testing of the software product. Testing metrics have been presented previously in chapter 2. The first chart presented here (Fig. 6.15) provides an indication of the quality of the software produced and the stability of the requirements. It gives the total number of defects identified and the total number of change requests and provides details on the severities of the defects or change requests. If the number of change requests is quite high, this suggests that there is room for improvement in the requirements management process.

Figure 6.16 gives the status of open issues with the project which gives an indication of the current quality of the project and the effort required to achieve the desired quality in the software. This chart is not used in isolation, as the project manager will need to know the arrival rate of problems to determine the stability of the software product.

The organization may intend to release a software product containing problems which have not yet been corrected, and it is therefore important to perform a risk assessment of these problems to ensure that the product may operate effectively. A work-around for each problem is typically included in a set of release notes for the product.

The project manager will also need to know the age of the particular problems which have been raised, as this will indicate the effectiveness of the team in resolving problems in a timely manner. Figure 6.17 presents the age of the open problems in a particular project, and includes the severities. The chart be-

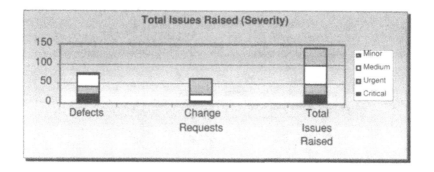

Figure 6.15: Total Number of Issues in Project

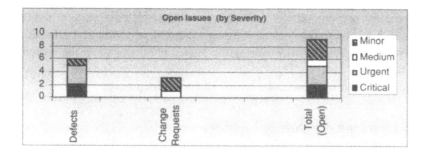

Figure 6.16: Open Issues in Project

low indicates that there is one urgent problem that has been open for over one year, and a project manager would typically prevent this situation from arising, as critical and urgent problems need to be addressed in a prompt and efficient manner.

The problem arrival rate (Fig. 6.18) is a key metric for the project manager to enable the stability of the project to be determined, and to enable an objective decision as to whether the product should be released to be made. A sample problem arrival chart is included here, and a preliminary analysis of the chart indicates that the trend is positive, with the arrival rate of problems falling. The project manager will need to do analysis to determine if there are other causes that could contribute to the fall in the arrival rate; for example, it may be the case that testing was completed in September, which would mean, in effect, that no testing has been performed since then, with an inevitable fall in the number of problems reported. The important point is not to jump to a conclusion based on a particular chart, as the circumstances behind the chart must be fully known and taken into account in order to draw valid inferences.

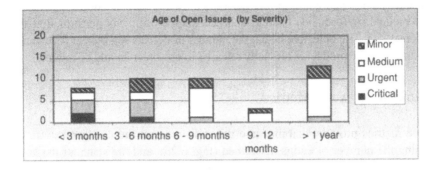

Figure 6.17: Age of Open Issues in Project

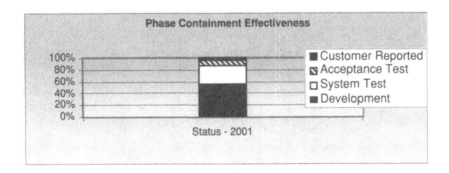

Figure 6.18: Problem Arrivals per month

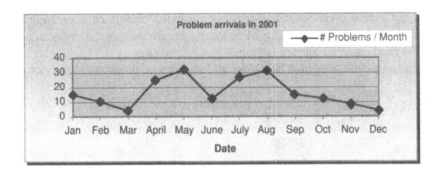

Figure 6.19: Phase Containment Effectiveness

The next metric measures the effectiveness of the project in identifying defects in the development phase (Fig. 6.19), and the effectiveness of the test
groups in detecting defects which are present in the software. The development
portion typically includes defects reported on inspection forms and in unit test-

ing; the system testing is typically performed by an independent test group and may include performance testing; and acceptance testing is performed at the customer site. The objective is that the number of defects reported at acceptance test and after the product is officially released to customer should be minimal.

6.4.6 Quality Audit Metrics

These metrics provide visibility into the audit program in an organization, including the number of audits performed (Fig. 6.20), and the status of the audit actions (Fig. 6.21). The first chart presents visibility into the number of audits performed in the organization and the number of audits which remain to be done. It shows that the organization has an audit program, and provides information on the number of audits performed in a particular time period. The chart does not give a breakdown into the type of audits performed, e.g., supplier audits, project audits, and audits of particular departments in the organization, but the chart could be adapted to provide this information.

The next chart presented here gives an indication of the status of the various

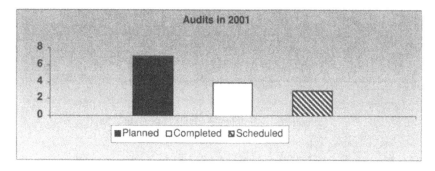

Figure 6.20: Annual Audit Schedule

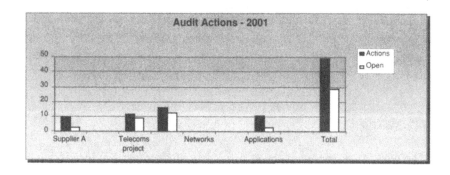

Figure 6.21: Status of Audit Actions

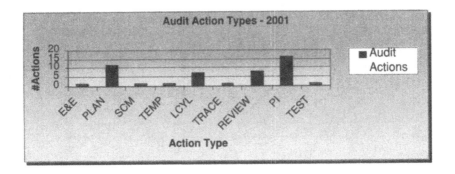

Figure 6.22: Audit Action Types

audits performed. An audit is performed by an auditor and the results of an audit include an audit report and audit actions to be completed by the group which has been audited. The status of the audit actions assigned to the affected groups is detailed in the chart. Audit actions need to be resolved in a timely manner in an effective audit program, and the chart below provides an objective status of the extent to which the actions have been addressed by the affected groups.

Figure 6.22 gives visibility into the type of actions raised during the quality audit of the particular area. The audit categories need to be defined by the organization but could potentially include entry and exit criteria, planning issues, configuration management issues, issues with compliance to the lifecycle or templates, traceability to the requirements, issues with the review of various deliverables, issues with testing, or process improvement suggestions.

6.4.7 Customer Care Metrics

The goals of the customer care group in an organization include responding efficiently and effectively to customer problems, ensuring that their customers receive the highest standards of service from the company, and ensuring that the company's products function reliably at the customer's site. The organization will need to know its efficiency in resolving customer queries, the number of customer queries, the availability of its software systems at the customer site, and the age of open queries. A customer query may result in a defect report in the case of a problem with the software.

Figure 6.23 could be developed further to include a severity attribute for the query, and various goals would normally be set for the resolution of queries. The organization will usually maintain a chart for the age of open queries in a format similar to the development chart of open problems (Fig. 6.17) presented earlier, and it is not presented here. The organization will need to know the status of the backlog of open queries per month, and a simple trend graph would provide this. The chart shows the arrivals and closures of queries: in the early part of the year

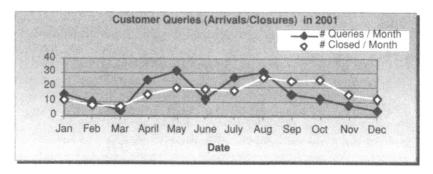

Figure 6.23: Customer Queries (Arrivals/Closures)

the arrival rate exceeds the closure rate of queries per month. This indicates an increasing backlog which needs to be addressed.

The customer care department responds to any outages which occur and ensures that the outage time is kept to a minimum. Many of the top companies in the world set ambitious goals on network availability, e.g., the "five nines" initiative on availability at Motorola in which the objective is to develop systems which are available 99.999% of the time, i.e., approximately five minutes of down time per year. The calculation of availability is from the formula:

$$\text{Availability} = \frac{\text{MTBF}}{\text{MTBF} + \text{MTTR}}$$

where the mean time between failure (MTBF) is the average length of time between outages.

$$\text{MTBF} = \frac{\text{Sample Interval Time}}{\text{\# Outages}}$$

The formula for MTBF above is for a single system only, and the formula is adjusted when there are multiple systems.

$$\text{MTBF} = \frac{\text{Sample Interval Time}}{\text{\# Outages}} * \text{\# Systems}$$

The mean time to repair (MTTR) is the average length of time that it takes to correct the outage, i.e., the average duration of the outages that have occurred, and it is calculated from the following formula:

$$\text{MTTR} = \frac{\text{Total Outage Time}}{\text{\# Outages}}$$

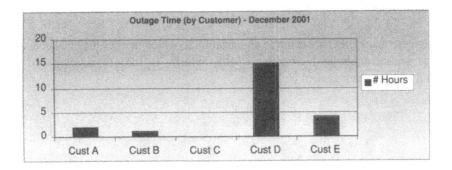

Figure 6.24: Outage Time per customer

Figure 6.24 presented on outages provides information on the customers impacted by the outage during the particular month, and the extent of the impact on the customer.

An effective customer care department will ensure that a post-mortem of the outages is performed to ensure that lessons are learned to prevent a reoccurrence. This causal analysis information can be presented in chart form to give visibility into the root causes of the outages and the actions to be taken to prevent a reoccurrence. Metrics to record the amount of outage time per month will typically be maintained by the customer care group in the form of a trend graph.

Figure 6.25 provides visibility of the availability of the system at the customer sites as derived by the availability formula as described earlier. Ambitious organizations such as Motorola are designing systems to be available 99.999% of the time.

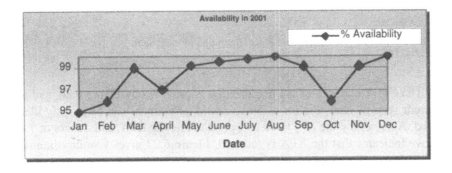

Figure 6.25: Availability of System per Month

6.4.8 Miscellaneous Metrics

There are many other areas in the organization to which metrics may be applied. This section includes metrics on CMM maturity in the organization and a configuration management build metric.

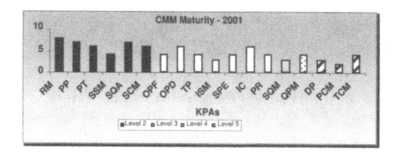

Figure 6.26: **CMM Maturity**

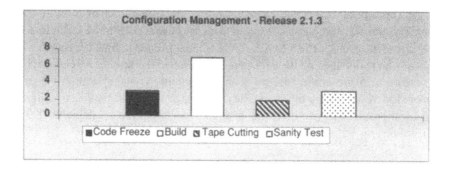

Figure 6.27: Configuration Management

The CMM maturity of the organization is provided by Figure 6.26, and its current state of readiness for a formal CMM assessment can be quickly identified. A numeric score of 1 to 10 is applied to rate the KPA, and a score of 7 or above indicates that the KPA is satisfied. Figure 6.27 gives visibility into the effectiveness of configuration management in the organization.

6.5 Implementing a Metrics Program

The charts which have been presented in this chapter may be adapted and tailored to meet the needs of other organizations. The metrics are only as good as

the underlying data, and good data gathering is essential. The following are typical steps in the implementation of a metrics program in an organization:

Table 6.3: Implementing Metrics

Implementing Metrics in Organization
Identify business goals
Identify questions
Identify metrics
Identify tools
Identify data
Identify and provide resources
Gather data
Identify reporting mechanism
Provide training

The business goals are the starting point in the implementation of a metrics
program as there is no sense in measurement for the sake of measurement, and
the objective is to define and use metrics that are closely related to the business
goals. Various questions to indicate the extent to which the business goal is being achieved and to provide visibility into the actual status of the goal need to be
identified, and metrics provide an objective answer to these key questions.

The organization identifies the goals that need to be satisfied, and each department develops its specific goals to meet the organization's goals. Measurement will indicate the extent to which specific goals are being met. Good data
are essential and this requires data to be recorded and gathered efficiently. First,
the organization will need to determine which data need to be gathered, and to
determine methods by which the data may be recorded. The analysis of what
information is needed to answer the questions related to the goals will assist in
determining the precise data to be recorded. A small organization may decide to
record the data manually, but usually automated or semi-automated tools will be
employed to assist in data recording and data extraction. Ultimately, unless an
efficient and usable mechanism is employed for data collection and extraction,
the metrics program is likely to fail. The data gathering is at the heart of the metrics program, and is described in more detail in section 6.5.1.

The roles and responsibilities of staff will need to be defined with respect to
the implementation and day-to-day operation of the metrics program. Training
will need to be provided to implement the roles effectively. Finally, a regular
management review will need to be implemented in the organization where the
metrics are presented and actions taken to ensure that the business goals are
achieved.

6.5.1 Data Gathering for Metrics

The metrics are only as good as the underlying data, and data gathering is therefore a key activity in the metrics program. The data to be recorded will be closely related to the questions, and the intention is that the data may be used to enable the question to be answered objectively. The following illustrates how the data to be gathered is identified in a top-down manner. The starting point is the business goal, and a good business goal will usually be quantitative for extra precision.

Table 6.4: Identifying Data to be gathered

Goal	Reduce escaped defects from each lifecycle phases by 10%.
Questions	How many faults are identified within each lifecycle phase?
	How many defects are identified after each lifecycle phase is exited?
	What % of defects escape from each lifecycle phase?

Table 6.5 is one implementation to determine the effectiveness of the software development process, and to enable the above questions to be answered. The table includes a column for inspection data which records the number of faults recorded at the various inspections. The defects include the phase where the defect originated; for example, a defect identified in the design phase may have originated in the requirements phase. The data is typically maintained in a spreadsheet, e.g., Excel, and it needs to be kept up to date. It enables the phase containment effectiveness to be calculated for the various phases.

Table 6.5: Phase Containment Effectiveness

	Phase Of Origin							
Phase	Inspect Faults	Reqs	De-sign	Code	Accept Test	Total Faults	Total Defects	% PCE
Reqs	4		1	1		4	6	40%
Design	3					3	4	42%
Code	20					20	15	57%
Unit Test		2	2	10			14	
Sys Test		2	2	5			9	
Acc Test								

A fault is a problem which is usually detected by an inspection, and it is detected in the phase in which it is created. A defect is a problem which is detected out of phase, for example, a fault with the requirements may be discovered in the design phase, which is out of the phase in which it was created.

In the example table above, the effectiveness of the requirements phase is judged by its success in identifying defects as early as possible, as the cost of correction of a requirements defect increases the later in the cycle that it is identified. For example, the requirements PCE is calculated to be 40%, i.e., the total number of faults identified in phase divided by the total number of faults and defects identified. There were four faults identified at the inspection of the requirements, and six defect were identified, one defect at the design phase, and one at the coding phase, two at the unit testing phase, and two at the system testing phase, i.e., 4/10 = 40%. Similarly, the code PCE is calculated to be 57%.

The overall PCE for the project is calculated to be the total number of faults detected in phase in the project divided by the total number of faults and defects, i.e., 27/52 = 52%. The table above is in effect a summary of collected data, and the data is collected in a format similar to the following:

- Maintain inspection data of requirements, design and code inspections
- Identify phase of origin of defects
- Record the number of defects and phase of origin

There is a responsibility for staff performing inspections to record the problems identified, and to record whether it is a fault or a defect, and the phase of origin of the defect. Staff will need to be trained and periodic enforcement performed to verify institutionalization.

The above is just one example of data gathering, and in practice the organization will need to collect various data to enable it to give an objective answer to the extent that the particular goal is being satisfied.

6.6 Problem-Solving Techniques

Problem solving is a key part of quality improvement, and the idea of a quality circle or problem-solving team, i.e., a group of employees who do similar work and volunteer to come together on company time to identify and analyze work-related problems was proposed by Ishikawa. Various tools that assist problem solving include trend charts, bar charts, scatter diagrams, fishbone diagrams, histograms, control charts, pareto analysis [BR:94]. These provide visibility into the particular problem and help to quantify the extent of the problem. The main features of a problem-solving team or quality circle include the following:

- Group of employees who do similar work
- Voluntarily meet regularly on company time
- Supervisor as leader
- Learn to identify and analyze work-related problems
- Recommend solutions to management

- Implement solution where possible

The facilitator of the quality circle coordinates the activities of the quality circle, ensures that the team leaders and teams members receive sufficient training, and obtains specialist help where required. The quality circle facilitator has the following responsibilities:

- Focal point of quality circle activities
- Train circle leaders / members
- Coordinate activities of all the circle groups
- Assist in inter circle investigations
- Obtain specialist help when required

The circle leaders receive training in problem-solving techniques, and are responsible for training the team members. The circle leader needs to keep the meeting focused and requires skills in team building. There are various steps in problem solving or starting a quality circle and these include the following:

- Select the problem
- State and restate the problem
- Collect the facts
- Brainstorm
- Choose course of action
- Present to management
- Measurement of success

There are benefits to a successful problem solving culture in the organization, and these include:

- Savings of time and money
- Increased productivity
- Reduced defects
- Fire prevention culture

The various problem-solving tools include trend charts, bar charts, scatter diagrams, fishbone diagrams, histograms, control charts, and pareto charts. These are discussed in the following sections and concrete examples are included.

6.6.1 Fishbone Diagram

This is a well-known tool in problem solving and consists of a cause and effect diagram that is in the shape of the backbone of a fish. The objective is to identify the various causes of some particular effect, and then these various causes are broken down into a number of sub-causes. The various causes and sub-causes are analyzed to determine the root cause of the particular effect, and actions to address the root cause are then identified to prevent a reoccurrence of the manifested effect. There are various categories of causes and these may include people, methods and tools, and training.

The great advantage of the fishbone diagram is that it offers a crisp mechanism to summarize the collective knowledge that a team has about a particular problem, as it focuses the team on the causes of the problem and facilitates the detailed exploration of the causes.

The construction of a fishbone diagram involves a clear statement of the particular effect and this is placed at the right-hand side of the diagram, the major categories are then drawn on the backbone of the fishbone diagram, brainstorming is used to identify causes, and these are then placed in the appropriate category. For each cause identified the various sub-causes may be identified by asking the question *why does this happen*? This leads to a more detailed understanding of the causes for a particular effect.

Example 1

An organization wishes to determine the causes for a high number of customer-reported defects.

There are various categories which may be employed in this example including people, training, methods, tools, and environment.

In practice, the fishbone diagram would be more detailed than that presented in Figure 6.28 as sub-causes would also be identified by a detailed examination of the identified causes. The root cause(s) are determined from detailed analysis.

This example indicates that the particular organization has significant work to do in several areas, and that a long-term change management program is required to implement the right improvements. Among the key areas to address in this example would be to implement a software development process and a software test process, to provide training to enable staff to do their jobs more effectively, and to implement better management practices to motivate staff and provide a supportive environment for software development.

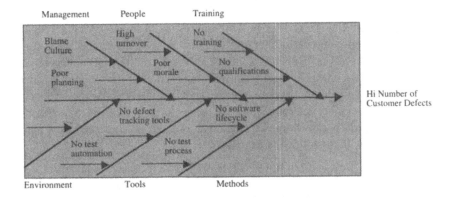

Figure 6.28: Fishbone Cause-and-Effect Diagram

The causes identified may be symptoms rather than actual root causes: for example, high staff turnover may be the result of poor morale and a "blame culture", rather than a cause in itself of poor quality software. The fishbone diagram provides a more detailed understanding of the collection of possible causes of the high number of customer defects; however, from the list of identified causes and discussion and analysis, a small subset of causes are identified as the root cause of the problem.

The organization then acts upon the identified root cause by defining an appropriate software development lifecycle and test process and providing training to all development staff on the lifecycle and test process. The management attitude and organization culture will need to be corrected to enable a supportive software development environment to be put in place.

6.6.2 Histograms

A histogram is a way of representing data in bar chart format and shows the relative frequency of various data values or ranges of data values. It is typically employed when there is a large number of data values, and its key use is that it gives a very crisp picture of the spread of the data values and the centering and variance from the mean. The histogram has an associated shape; for example, it may be a normal distribution, a bimodal or multi-modal distribution, or be positively or negatively skewed. The variation and centering refer to the variation of data and the relation of the center of the histogram to the customer requirements. The variation or spread of the data is important as it indicates whether the process is too variable or whether it is performing within the requirements. The histogram is termed process centered if its center coincides with the customer requirements; otherwise the process is too high or too low. A histogram enables predictions of future performance to be made, assuming that the future will reflect the past. The data is divided into a number of data buckets, where a bucket is a particular range of data values, and the relative frequency of each bucket is displayed in bar format.

The construction of a histogram first requires that a frequency table be constructed, and this requires that the range of data values be determined. The number of class intervals or buckets are then determined, and the class intervals are defined. The class intervals are mutually disjoint and span the range of the data values. Each data value belongs to exactly one class interval and the frequency of each class interval is determined.

The histogram is a well-known statistical tool and its construction is made more concrete with the following example:

Example 2

An organization wishes to characterize the behavior of the process for the resolution of customer queries in order to achieve its customer satisfaction goal.

Goal

Resolve all customer queries within 24 hours.

Question

How effective is the current customer query resolution process, and what action is required (if any) to achieve this goal?

The histogram below includes a data table where the data classes are of size 6 hours. In standard histograms the data classes are of the same size, although there are non-standard histograms that use data classes of unequal size. The sample mean is 19 hours in this example.

This histogram (Fig. 6.29) is based on query resolution data from 35 samples. The organization goal of customer resolution within 24 hours is not met for all queries, and the goal is satisfied in (25/35 = 71% for this particular sample).

Further analysis is needed to determine the reasons why 29% of the goals are outside the target 24-hour time period. It may prove to be impossible to meet the goal for all queries, and the organization may need to refine the goal to state that instead all critical and urgent queries will be resolved within 24 hours, or alternately, more resources may be required to provide the desired response.

6.6.3 Pareto Chart

The objective of a pareto chart is to help the problem-solving team focus on the problems of greatest impact, as often 20% of the causes are responsible for 80% of the problems. The pareto chart helps to identify the key problems, and the

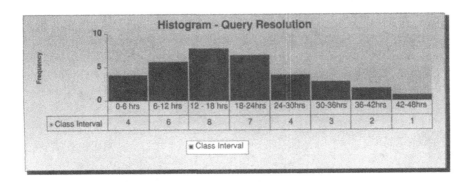

Figure 6.29: **Histogram**

focus may then be placed on these. The problems are classified into various cause categories, and the frequency of each category of problem is then determined. The chart is then displayed in a descending sequence of frequency, with the most significant cause detailed first, and the least significant cause detailed last.

The pareto chart is a key problem-solving tool, and a properly constructed pareto chart will allow the organization to focus its improvement efforts to resolve the key causes of problems, and to verify the resolution of key causes of problems. The progress and success of the improvement efforts can be determined at a later stage by analyzing the new problems and creating a new pareto chart. If the improvement efforts have been successful, then the profile of the pareto chart will indicate that the key cause categories have been significantly improved.

The construction of the pareto chart first requires the organization to decide on the problem to be investigated, then to identify the causes of the problem via brainstorming, analyze either historical or real data, compute the frequency of each cause, and finally display the frequency in descending order of each cause category.

Example 3

An organization wishes to minimize the occurrences of outages and wishes to understand the various causes of outages, and the relative importance of each cause.

The pareto chart (Fig. 6.30) below includes the data obtained following an analysis of historical data of outages and classifies the outages into various causes. There are six cause categories defined: hardware, software, operator error, power failure, an act of nature, and unknown cause of outage.

The pareto chart indicates that the three key causes of outages are hardware, software, and operator error. Further analysis is needed to identify the actions that are needed to address these three key causes.

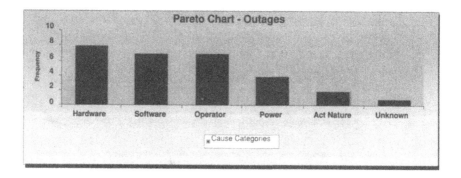

Figure 6.30: Pareto Chart Outages

The hardware category may indicate that the reliability of the hardware of the system is problematic, with some parts failing. The organization would need to investigate solutions for existing systems and new systems to be deployed. This may include discussions with other hardware vendors to alter the hardware specification for new systems to address availability and reliability concerns, or the replacement of existing hardware in existing systems to correct reliability issues.

The analysis of software faults may be due to the release of poor-quality software or to usability issues in the software, and this requires further investigation. Finally, operator issues may be due to lack of knowledge or training of operators.

6.6.4 Trend Graph

A trend graph monitors the performance of a variable over time, allows trends in performance to be identified, and enables predictions of future trends to be made. The first step to the construction of a trend graph is to decide on the process whose performance is to be measured, and then to gather the data points and to plot the data.

Example 4

> An organization wants to improve its estimation accuracy, has deployed an enhanced estimation process in the organization, and wishes to determine if estimation is actually improving.

The estimation accuracy is computed from the quotient of the actual effort by the estimated effort, and an estimation accuracy of 1.0 indicates that the estimated effort is equal to actual. The trend chart (Fig. 6.31) indicates that initially that estimation accuracy is very poor, but then there is a sudden improvement coinciding with the successful deployment of the new estimation

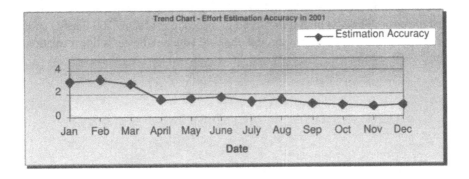

Figure 6.31: Trend Chart Estimation Accuracy

process, and performance in estimation has improved. The graph indicates that at the end of the year estimated effort is very close to the actual effort.

It is important, of course, to analyze the trend chart in detail; for example, the estimation accuracy for August (1.5 in the chart) would need to be investigated to determine the reasons why it occurred. It could potentially indicate that a project is using the old estimation process, or that the project manager received no training on the new process, etc. A trend graph is useful for noting positive or negative trends in performance; and negative trends are analyzed and actions are identified to correct performance.

6.6.5 Scatter Graphs

The scatter diagram is used to measure the relationship between variables and to determine whether there is a relationship or correlation between the variables. The results may be a positive correlation, negative correlation, or no correlation between the data. Correlation has a precise statistical definition and provides a mathematical understanding of the extent to which two variables are related or unrelated.

The scatter graph provides a visual means to test the extent that two particular variables are related, and may be useful to determine if there a connection between identified causes in a fishbone diagram and the effect.

The construction of a scatter diagram requires the collection of paired samples of data, and the drawing of one variable as the x-axis, and the other as the y-axis. The data is then plotted and interpreted.

Example 5

An organization wishes to determine if there is a relationship between the inspection rate and the error density of defects identified.

The scatter graph (Fig. 6.32) provides evidence for the hypothesis that there is a relationship between two variables, namely, lines of code inspected and the error density recorded (per KLOC). The graph suggests that the error density of defects identified during inspections is low if the speed of inspection is too fast, and the error density is high if the speed of inspection is below 300 lines of code per hour. A line can be drawn through the date which indicates a linear relationship.

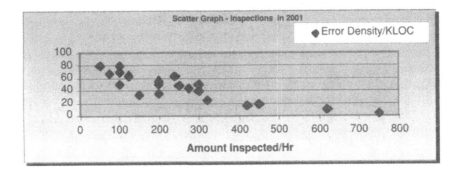

Figure 6.32: Scatter Graph Amount Inspected Rate / Error Density

6.6.6 Metrics and Statistical Process Control

The principles of statistical process control have been described in earlier chapters and form an important part of the achievement of level 4 of the CMM, i.e., having a process with predictable performance. Measurement plays a key role in achieving a process which is under statistical control, and the following example (Fig. 6.33) on achieving a break through in performance of the estimation process is adapted from [Kee:00].

The initial upper and lower control limits for estimation accuracy are set at ±50%, and the performance of the process is within the defined upper and control limits. However, the organization will wish to improve its estimation accuracy and this leads to the organization's revising the upper and lower control limits to ±25%. The organization will need to analyze the slippage data to determine the reasons for the wide variance in the estimation, and part of the solution will be the use of enhanced estimation guidelines in the organization. In this chart, the organization succeeds in performing within the revised control limit of ±25%, and the limit is revised again to ±15%. This requires further analysis to determine the causes for slippage and further improvement actions are needed to ensure that the organization performs within the ±15% control limit.

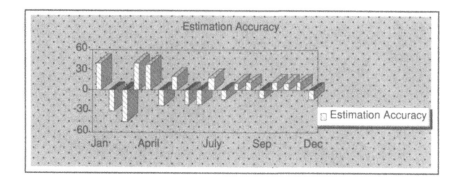

Figure 6.33: Estimation Accuracy and Control Charts

6.7 Summary

Measurement is an essential part of mathematics and the physical sciences, and has been successfully applied in recent years to the software engineering discipline. The purpose of a measurement program is to establish and use quantitative measurements to manage the software development environment in the organization, to assist the organization in understanding its current software capability, and to provide an objective indication that improvements have been successful. This chapter included comprehensive sample metrics to provide visibility into the various functional areas in the organization, including customer satisfaction metrics, process improvement metrics, project management metrics, HR metrics, development and quality metrics, and customer care metrics. The actual quantitative data allow trends to be seen over time. The analysis of the trends and quantitative data allow action plans to be derived for continuous improvement. Measurements may be employed to track the quality, timeliness, cost, schedule, and effort of software projects

The balanced scorecard assists the organization in selecting appropriate measurements to indicate the success or failure of the organization's strategy. Each of the four scorecard perspectives includes objectives to be accomplished for the strategy to succeed, and measurements to indicate the extent to which the objectives are being met.

The Goal, Question, Metric (GQM) paradigm is a rigorous, goal-oriented approach to measurement in which goals, questions, and measurements are closely integrated. The business goals are first identified, and then questions that relate to the achievement of the goal are identified, and for each question a metric that gives an objective answer to the particular question is identified. The statement of the goal is very precise and the goal is related to individuals or groups.

Metrics play a key role in problem solving, and various problem solving techniques have been discussed in this chapter. The measurement data are used to assist the analysis and determine the root cause of a particular problem, and to verify that the actions taken to correct the problem have been effective.

Metrics may provide an internal view of the quality of the software product, but care is needed before deducing the behavior that a product will exhibit externally from the various internal measurements of the product.

7

Formal Methods and Design

7.1 Introduction

This chapter discusses more advanced topics in the software quality field, including software configuration management, the unified modeling language, software usability, and formal methods.

Software configuration management is concerned with identifying the configuration of a system and controlling changes to the configuration, and maintaining integrity and traceability. The configuration items are generally documents in the early part of the development of the system, whereas the focus is on source code control management and software release management in the later parts of the system.

The consequences of poor configuration management are illustrated in the following, and it is clear that configuration management is a key part of the quality system.

Table 7.1: Poor configuration management

Symptoms of Poor Configuration Management
Bugs corrected suddenly begin to re-appear
Cannot find latest version of source code
Unable to match source code to object code
Wrong functionality sent to customer
Wrong code tested
Cannot replicate previously released code
Simultaneous changes to same source component by multiple developers with some changes lost

Configuration management involves identifying the configuration items and systematically controlling change to maintain integrity and traceability of the configuration throughout the lifecycle. There is a need to manage and control changes to documents and for source code change control management. The configuration items include the project plan, the requirements, design, code, and test plans.

A key concept is a "baseline": this is a work product that has been formally reviewed and agreed upon and serves as the foundation for future work. It is changed by a formal change control procedure which leads to a new baseline. The organization is required to identify the configuration items that need to be placed under formal change control. Configuration management also maintains a history of the changes made to the baseline.

The unified modeling language is a visual modeling language for software systems. The advantage of a visual modeling language is that it facilitates the understanding of the architecture of the system by visual means and assists in the management of the complexity of large systems. It was developed by Jim Rumbaugh, Grady Booch, and Ivar Jacobson [Rum:99] at Rational as a notation for modeling object oriented systems and was published as a standard by the Object Management Group (OMG) in 1997.

UML allows the same information to be presented in many different ways, and there are nine main diagrams with the standard. These provide different viewpoints of the system.

Table 7.2: UML Diagrams

Diagram	Description
Use Case Diagrams	Use cases describe scenarios or sequences of actions for the system from the user's viewpoint.
Class and Object Diagrams	These diagrams refer to classes and instances of classes.
Sequence and Collaboration Diagrams	These diagrams show the interactions between objects/classes in the system for each use case.
Activity Diagrams	These are used to show the sequence of activities in a use case and are similar to flow charts.
State Diagrams	State diagrams (state charts) are used to show the dynamic behavior of a class.
Component Diagrams	These are used to show the architecture of the code and associated dependencies.
Deployment Diagrams	These tend to be used in large/complex systems and show the distribution of software across the enterprise.

UML provides a standard notation for modeling a software system, however, at this time there is no standard methodology to use the notation for building software, although the unified process is being promoted by the Rational Corporation [CSE:00]. An organization is unlikely to use all of UML and instead will need to make a judgment as to which parts of the notation are suitable to employ.

Software usability is an important aspect of the quality of the software and has been discussed briefly in chapter 1. It is one of the characteristics of quality defined in the ISO 9126 standard for information technology [ISO:91] and is the user's perception of the ease of use of the software. It is essential to have guidelines for building a usable software product and to assess the usability of the software product. There have been several standards developed for software usability, and these include the product-oriented standards such as parts of ISO 9241 [ISO:98a] and the process-oriented standards such as ISO 13407 [ISO:99] and parts of ISO 9241 (Table 7.3).

The ISO 13407 standard provides guidance on the usability design of computer-based systems and is concerned with human-centered design processes. The ISO 9241 standard is large and consists of 17 parts. These include guidance on usability and requirements for workstation layout, keyboards, environment, presentation of information, dialogue principles, and ergonomic requirements.

Table 7.3: Usability Standards

Standard	Description	Purchase Info
ISO 9241	Ergonomic Requirements	www.iso.ch/(ISO)
	Visual display	
	Keyboard	
	Environmental	
	Human computer interface	
ISO 13407	Human centered design process	www.iso.ch/(ISO).
	Iterative design	
	Active user involvement	
	Multi disciplinary design	

Usability, like quality, needs to be built into the software product, and therefore usability needs to be considered from the earliest stages in the software development lifecycle. Usability requires an analysis of the user population and the tasks that they perform in the targeted environment. This will help produce a more precise user requirements specification. The objective is that the system should enable its users to perform their tasks more effectively and efficiently

It is important to understand and specify the context of use and to specify user and organizational requirements. There will often be a variety of different viewpoints from different individuals and roles in the organization, and this leads to multiple design solutions and an evaluation of designs against the requirements.

An iterative software lifecycle development lifecycle is generally employed and there is active user involvement during the development of the software and especially at the early stages. Prototyping is generally employed to give users a flavor of the proposed system, thereby allowing early user feedback to be received. User acceptance testing provides confidence that the software is correct and matches the usability, reliability, and quality expectations of users.

Usability may be assessed via structured questionnaires and one well-known questionnaire approach is the SUMI methodology. This was developed by Jurek Kirakowski at the Human Factors Research Group (HFRG) as part of a European funded research project [Kir:00]. The group has also developed the WAMMI web-based tool for assessing usability. The SUMI questionnaire may be completed on early prototypes of the software or on the completed software. A small sample size of 10 to 12 users is recommended to obtain precise and valid results.

Formal methods is a mathematical approach to the correctness of software. The objective is to specify the program in a mathematical language and to demonstrate that certain properties are satisfied by the specification using mathematical proof. The ultimate objective is to provide confidence that the implementation satisfies the requirements.

The mathematical techniques may also be applied to requirements validation, in effect to *"debug the requirements"*. This involves exploring the mathematical consequences of the stated requirements, and ensuring that the implications are considered and known and that the requirements are explicitly stated. Current software engineering is subject to the following limitations:

Table 7.4: Motivation for Formal Methods

Limitations of Current Software Engineering
No *proof* that the specification satisfies the requirements
No *proof* that the implementation satisfies the specification
No p*roof* of the absence of defects
Proof of correctness and termination is via inspections or testing.
No *proof* of correctness and termination on all valid inputs
Resources devoted to maintenance and testing is extensive
Danger of litigation for failure of safety critical software

It would be misleading to state that the use of formal methods will eliminate these problems. However, the mathematical techniques used in formal methods offers a precision and rigour which is not matched by the conventional approaches such as peer reviews and testing. The use of formal methods cannot provide an absolute guarantee of correctness, as they are applied by humans who are prone to error, although tool support should reduce the incidence of errors.

Consequently, formal methods will never eliminate the need for testing or for the various test departments in the organization.

The successful deployment of formal methods should lead to a shorter test cycle, as the quality of the software entering the testing phase should be higher as it has been subject to some degree of formal verification. The real benefits of formal methods are the increased confidence in the correctness of the software. Real-time testing may not be feasible or subject to limitations in several domains, and in such cases there is a need for an extra quality assurance step to provide additional confidence in the reliability and quality of the software; and formal methods is one way of achieving this. The safety-critical domain is one domain in which the use of formal methods is quite useful.

There are many examples of the applications of formal methods, including the collection from Mike Hinchey and Jonathan Bowen in [HB:95].

7.2 Software Configuration Management

Software configuration management is concerned with the controlled evolution of the software and involves identifying the configuration of a system and controlling changes to the configuration, and maintaining integrity and traceability. The configuration items are generally documents in the early part of the development of the system, whereas the focus is on source code control management and software release management in the later parts of the system. It involves identifying the configuration items and systematically controlling change throughout the lifecycle.

A work product that has been formally reviewed and agreed upon is a baseline, and this serves as the foundation for future work. It is subject to formal change control and this leads to a new baseline. There are four key parts to software configuration management.

Table 7.5: software Configuration Management

Area	Description
Configuration Identification	This requires planning in order to identify the configuration items, to define naming conventions for documents and a version numbering system, and baseline /release planning. The version and status of each configuration item should be known.
Configuration Control	This involves implementing effective controls for configuration management. It involves a controlled area/library where documents and source code are placed and access to the library/area is controlled. It includes a mechanism for releasing documents or code and the changes to work products are controlled and authorized by a change control board or similar mechanism. Problems or defects are reported by the test groups and the customer, and following analysis any changes to be implemented are subject to change control. The version of the work product is known and the constituents of a particular release are known and controlled. The previous versions of releases can be recovered as the source code constituents are fully known.
Status Accounting	This involves data collection and report generation. These reports include the software baseline status, the summary of changes to the software baseline, problem report summaries, and change request summaries.
Configuration Auditing	This includes audits of the baselines to verify integrity of the baseline and audits of the configuration management system itself and verification that standards and procedures are followed. The audit reports are distributed to affected groups and any actions are tracked to completion.

A typical software release, e.g., in the telecommunications domain, consists of incremental development where the software to be released consists of a number of release builds where each build initially consists of new functionality, and the later builds consists of fix releases. Software configuration management is planned for the project and each project will typically have a configuration management plan which will detail the planned delivery of functionality and fix release to the project (Table 7.6). The configuration management plan is then tracked as part of project management responsibility.

Table 7.6: Software Configuration Management Plan

Release Baseline	Contents
R 1.0.0.0	F_1, F_2, F_6,
R.1.0.0.1	F_4, F_5, F_7 + fixes
R.1.0.0.2	F_3 + fixes
R.1.0.0.3	F_8 + fixes (functionality freeze)
R.1.0.0.4	Fixes
R.1.0.0.5	Fixes
R.1.0.0.6	Official release

Each of the R.1.0.0.k are termed release builds and they consist of functionality and fixes to problems. The content of each release build is known; i.e., the project team and manager will target specific functionality and fixes for each build, and the actual contents of the particular release baseline is documented. Each release build can be replicated, as the version of source code to create the build is known and the source code is under control management.

There are various tools employed for software configuration management activities, and these include well-known tools such as clearcase, pvcs, continuity, source save for source code control management, and the pv tracker tool for tracking defects and change requests. A defect tracking tool will list all of the open defects against the software and a defect may require several change requests to correct the software, as a problem may affect different parts of the software product and a change request may be necessary for each part. The tool will generally link the change requests to the problem report. The current status of the problem report can be determined, and the targeted release build for the problem identified.

The CMM includes a level 2 key process area on software configuration management and this provides guidance of the activities to be performed to implement configuration management effectively. It includes four goals for the SCM key process area:

Table 7.7: CMM Goals for SCM

Goal	Description
Goal 1	Software configuration management activities are planned.
Goal 2	Selected software work products are identified, controlled, and available.
Goal 3	Changes to identified software work produces are controlled.
Goal 4	Affected groups and individuals are informed of the status and content of software baselines.

The symptoms of poor configuration management include corrected bugs that suddenly begin to reappear, difficulty in or failure to locate the latest version of source code, or failure to determine the source code that corresponds to a software release. Good configuration management is a necessary part of the infrastructure to deliver high-quality software, as the consequences of an inadequate configuration management practices are embarrassment at best and loss of credibility and reputation in a worse case scenario.

7.3 Unified Modeling Language

The unified modeling language is a visual modeling language for software systems and facilitates the understanding of the architecture of the system and in the management of the complexity of large systems. It was developed by Jim Rumbaugh, Grady Booch, and Ivar Jacobson [Rum:99] as a notation for modeling object-oriented systems.

UML allows the same information to be presented in many different ways, and there are nine main diagrams providing different viewpoints of the system. This section will give a flavor of UML by discussing a selection of the key UML diagrams. It is based on the UML technical briefing from the Centre for software Engineering (CSE) [CSE:00].

The first diagram considered here is a use-case diagram. Use cases describe scenarios or sequences of actions for the system from the user's viewpoint, and a very simple example of an ATM application is considered. The typical user operations at an ATM machine include the balance inquiry operation, the withdrawal of cash, and the transfer of funds from one account to another.

The behavior from the user's viewpoint is described in the following diagram and the use-cases include "withdraw cash", "check balance", "transfer" and "maintain/reports".

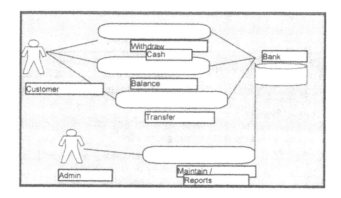

Figure 7.1: Simple Use-Case of ATM Machine

Next, class and object diagrams are considered and the object diagram is related to the class diagram in that the object is an instance of the class. There will generally be several objects associated with the class. The class diagram (Table 7.8) describes the data structure and the valid operations on the data structure are part of the definition. The concept of class and objects are taken from object-oriented design.

In the ATM example the two key classes are customers and accounts, and this includes the data structure for customers and accounts and also the operations on customers and accounts. These include operations to add or remove a customer and operations to debit or credit an account or to transfer from one account to another. There are several instances of customers and these are the actual customers of the bank.

Table 7.8: Simple Class Diagram

Customer	Account
Name: String	Balance:Real
Address: String	Type:String
Add	Debit()
Remove	Credit()
	CheckBal()
	Transfer()

The objects of the class are the actual customers and their corresponding accounts. Each customer can have several accounts. The names and addresses of the customers are detailed as well as the corresponding balance in the customer's accounts. There is one instance of the customer class below and two instances of the account class (Fig. 7.2).

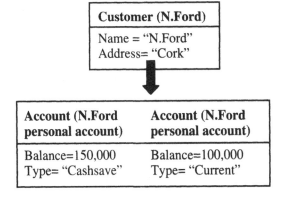

Figure 7.2: Simple Object Diagram

The next UML diagram (Fig. 7.3) considered is the sequence diagrams and these show the interaction between objects/classes in the system for each use case. The example as adapted from [CSE:00] considers the sequences of interactions between objects for the "check balance" use case. This sequence diagram is specific to the case of a valid inquiry, and there are generally sequence diagrams to handle exception cases also.

The behavior of the "check balance" operation is evident from the diagram. The customer inserts the card into the ATM machine and the PIN number is requested by the ATM machine. The customer then enters the number and the ATM machine contacts the bank for verification of the number. The bank confirms the validity of the number and the customer then selects the balance enquiry. The ATM contacts the bank to request the balance of the particular account and the bank sends the details to the ATM machine. The balance is displayed on the screen of the ATM machine. The customer then withdraws the card.

The actual sequence of interactions is evident from the sequence diagram.

The next UML diagram concerns activity diagrams (Fig. 7.4) and these are similar to flow charts. They are used to show the sequence of activities in a use case and include the specification of decision branches and parallel activities.

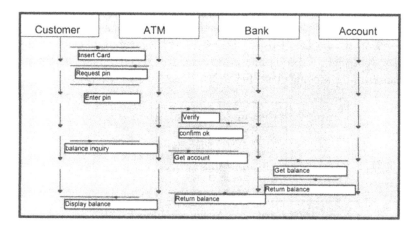

Figure 7.3: UML Sequence Diagram

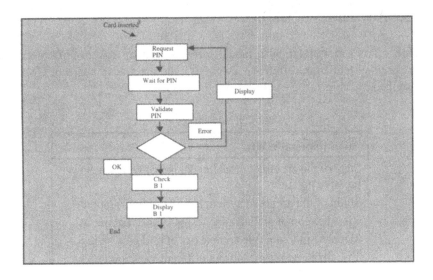

Figure 7.4: UML Activity Diagram

The final UML diagram (Fig. 7.5) that will be discussed here is state diagrams or state charts. These show the dynamic behavior of a class and how different operations result in a change of state. There is an initial state and a final state being and the different operations result in different states entered and exited from.

There are several other UML diagrams including the collaboration diagram which is similar to the sequence diagram except that the sequencing is shown via a number system. The reader is referred to [Rum:99].

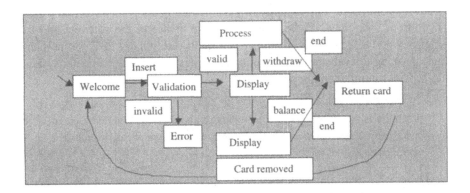

Figure 7.5: UML State Diagram

7.3.1 Advantages of UML

UML offers a rich notation to model software systems and to understand the proposed system from different viewpoints. The main advantages of UML are described in Table 7.9.

Table 7.9: Advantages of UML

Advantages of UML
State of the art visual modeling language with a rich expressive notation.
Study of the proposed system before implementation
Visualization of architecture design of the system.
Mechanism to manage complexity of a large system.
Visualization of system from different viewpoints. The different UML diagrams provide a different view of the system.
Enhanced understanding of implications of user behavior.
Use cases allow description of typical user behavior.
A mechanism to communicate the proposed behavior of the software system to describe what it will do and what to test against.

7.4 Software Usability

Usability is a specialized field in software engineering and has become important in recent years especially with the emergence of the world wide web and electronic commerce. The usability of the software is the perception that a user or group of users have of the quality and ease of use of the software and its efficiency and effectiveness. Usability is a multi-disciplinary field and psychological testing to evaluate the perception that users have of the computer system has become an important part of the field.

Usability is defined in part 11 of the ISO 9241 standard:

> Usability is the extent to which a product can be used by specified users to achieve specified goals with effectiveness, efficiency and satisfaction in a specified context of use.

There are several questionnaire based approaches to assessing the usability of the software, and one such usability questionnaire (SUMI) [Kir:00] developed by the Human Factors Research Group (HFRG) at University College Cork is discussed here. The SUMI methodology and the WAMMI web based tool are a questionnaire-based approach for assessing usability. Usability is a multi dimensional concept with several properties associated with each dimension of usability. The SUMI methodology lists five dimensions of usability to be measured and these dimensions are related to users' expectations and attitudes to the computer system being evaluated. They include the following:

Table 7.10: SUMI – Dimensions of Usability

Dimension	Description
Helpfulness	This measures the degree to which the software is self-explanatory as well as adequacy of help facilities and documentation.
Control	This measures the extent to which the user feels in control of the software as opposed to being controlled by the software.
Learnability	This measures the speed of learning and ease of mastering the software system or new features.
Efficiency	This measures the extent to which the users feel the software assists them in their work.
Affect	This measures the degree to which users like the computer system, i.e., likeability or the general emotional reaction to the software.

A questionnaire needs to be developed with care, as often the outcome of the questionnaire is influenced by the way in which the questions are phrased. The reliability and validity of the questionnaire is therefore essential and needs to be verified prior to its use.

The SUMI questionnaire consists of 50 questions and mapped onto the five dimensions of usability. The questions are similar to Table 7.11:

Table 7.11: Questions in SUMI Questionnaire

Item No	Item Wording
Item 1	This software responds too slowly to inputs.
Item 3	The instructions and prompts are helpful.
Item 22	I would not like to use this software every day.

There are three possible responses to the questions (Agree, Don't know, Disagree) and the questionnaire should be completed rapidly. The questionnaire is completed by a representative sample of users and the overall results are reported by usability dimension with an overall global usability factor determined for the computer system (Table 7.12). The global usability factor represents the perceived quality of use of the software.

Table 7.12: SUMI Output Sample Size = 25

Categorty	Mean
Global	22.1
Helpfulness	21.5
Control	21.6
Learnability	23.7
Efficiency	21.7
Affect	21.4

The SUMI methodology also allows a diagnosis to be made of usability problems in the software. This is achieved by generating a standard expected pattern of responses for each question and by comparing the actual responses to the expected responses. Further analysis identifies the areas to focus on to achieve improvements. There is more detailed information on human computer interaction in [Pre:94].

7.4.1 Usability Standards

The International Standards Organization have developed several usability standards, including ISO 9241 [ISO:98a] and ISO 13407 [ISO:99]. These may be purchased from the standards bodies in member countries, e.g., the British Standards Institute (BSI) in the UK, or may be ordered or purchased over the web (www.iso.ch) from ISO in Geneva, Switzerland.

These standards differ from the well-known ISO 9000 or ISO 14000 series of standards in that there is no official certification against the standard at this time. However, organizations dedicated to usability may wish to contact third-party bodies with expertise in usability to perform an assessment against these standards. These experts would then give an objective account of the extent of compliance with respect to the standards, and allow improvements to be identified. These assessments have no official recognition at this time and the assessment report reflects the judgment of the assessor of the extent of compliance and includes the rationale for the rating.

The advantage of the independent assessment is that it enables the organization to be ready for an official assessment when this becomes available. It also has a marketing benefit in that it allows the organization to state that it has been independently assessed to be 90% (or fully) compliant with respect to ISO 13407 and has an action plan to get to 100% compliance.

7.4.2 ISO 9241

The ISO 9241 standard is large and consists of 17 parts. It includes guidance and requirements for equipment, environment, and the human computer interface (HCI). The standard is summarized below:

Table 7.13: ISO 9241 Standard

Part	Part Name	Description
Part 1.	General Introduction:	Introduction and guidance material.
Part 2.	Guidance on Task Requirements:	This includes guidance with design of tasks and jobs for work with visual display terminals.
Part 3.	Visual Display Requirements:	This part specifies the ergonomic requirements for display screens to ensure they may be read safely and efficiently.
Part 4.	Keyboard Requirements:	This part specifies the ergonomic design characteristics of an alphabetic keyboard.
Part 5.	Workstation Layout and Postural Requirements:	This part specifies the ergonomic requirements for the visual display terminal workplace for comfortable and efficient posture.
Part 6.	Environmental Requirements:	This part specifies the ergonomic requirements for the visual display terminal working environment for comfortable and safe working conditions.
Part 7.	Display Requirements with Reflections:	This part specifies methods of measurement of glares and reflections from display screens.
Part 8.	Requirements for displayed colors:	This part specifies the requirements for multi-colored displays.
Part 9.	Requirements for non-keyboard input devices:	This part specifies the ergonomic requirements for non-keyboard input devices, e.g., mouse.
Part 10.	Dialogue Principles:	This part includes general ergonomic principles which apply to the design of dialogues between humans and information systems including suitability to the task, learning, conformance to user expectations, etc.
Part 11.	Guidance on Usability Specification and Measures:	This provides information to assist in specifying or evaluating usability in terms of measures of user performance and satisfaction.

Table 7.13 (*continued*): ISO 9241 Standard

Part	Part Name	Description
Part 12.	Presentation of Information:	This part includes specific recommendations on the presentation of information on visual displays.
Part 13.	User Guidance:	This part includes recommendations for the design and evaluation of user guidance attributes of software user interfaces including prompts, error management, etc.
Part 14.	Menu Dialogues:	This part includes recommendations for the ergonomic design of menus used in computer dialogues. It includes menu structure, navigation, and presentation.
Part 15.	Command Dialogues:	This part includes recommendations for the ergonomic design of command languages used in user computer dialogues.
Part 16.	Direct Manipulation Dialogues:	This part includes recommendations for the ergonomic design of direct manipulation dialogues, e.g., manipulation of objects via GUI.
Part 17.	Form-Filling Dialogues:	This part includes recommendations for the ergonomic design of form filling dialogues.

7.4.3 ISO 13407

The ISO 13407 provides guidance on human-centered design activities throughout the software development lifecycle. It provides information and guidance on usability design and recognizes the human factors in usability.

One criticism of large standards such as ISO 9241 is that the development of the standard takes such a long time that it becomes overtaken by changes in technology. ISO 13407 is designed to avoid this by following the human-centered design process described in the standard and the idea is that project managers may thereby ensure that the product is effective, efficient, and satisfying for its users by following the design process.

The standard requires that the procedures used, information collected, and the use made of results be specified. The standard includes a checklist to assist with this. Four key principles of human-centered design are specified in ISO 13407:

Table 7.14: Principles of Human Centred Design (ISO 13407)

Principle	Description
User Involvement	Active user involvement in project.
Human Skills	Appropriate allocation of Human Resources to tasks.
Iteration	Iterations planned in project schedule and user review of iteration.
Multi Disciplines	Multi disciplinary design with user involvement in design.

The standard lists four key human-centered design activities:

Table 7.15: Human Centred Design Activities (ISO 13407)

Activity	Description
Context of Use	This involves an explicit description of the context of use of the software.
User/Organization Requirements	This involves specifying user and organization requirements and the different viewpoints of users.
Design Solutions	Produce multiple design solutions.
Evaluate	Evaluate the designs against the requirements with user involvement/testing.

There is significant industrial interest in the ISO 13407 standard and indications suggest that it will be a powerful tool for improving software usability.

7.4.4 Usability Design

Usability, like quality, needs to be built into the software product, and therefore usability needs to be considered from the earliest stages in the software development lifecycle. Usability requires an analysis of the user population and the tasks that they perform in the targeted environment. This will help produce a more precise user requirements specification. The objective is that the system should enable its users to perform their tasks more effectively and efficiently

It is important to understand and specify the context of use and to specify user and organizational requirements. There will often be a variety of different viewpoints from different individuals in the organization and this leads to multiple design solutions and an evaluation of designs against the requirements.

An iterative software development lifecycle is generally employed and there is active user involvement during the development of the software, especially at the early stages. Prototyping is generally employed to give users a flavor of the proposed system and to provide early user feedback. User acceptance testing provides confidence that the software is correct and matches the usability and quality expectations of users.

Usability may be assessed via structured questionnaires such as the SUMI methodology as discussed earlier. The questionnaire may be completed on early prototypes or on the completed software. The usability lifecycle is described below:

Table 7.16: Usability Lifecycle

Phase	Description
Requirements	This includes the standard requirements process and interviews with different categories of users.
Prototype	The initial prototype is developed and the users provide structured feedback typically using a structured questionnaire.
Spiral Design/ Development	The prototype is reused and spiral software development with incremental changes to the design, code and testing. The completed spiral is evaluated by the users prior to the commencement of the next spiral.
Acceptance	Final acceptance testing by the users.

7.5 Formal Methods

Spivey (cf., Chapter 1 of [Spi:92]) describes "formal specifications" as the use of mathematical notation to describe in a precise way the properties which an information system must have, without unduly constraining the way in which these properties are achieved. Formal methods consist of formal specification languages or notations, and generally employ a collection of tools to support the syntax checking of the specification, and proof of properties of the specification. It is standard to distinguish between the *how* and the *what* in formal methods, in the sense that a formal specification describes *what* the system must do, as distinct from saying *how* it is to be done. This abstraction away from implementation enables questions about what the system does to be answered, independently of the implementation, i.e., the detailed code. Furthermore, the unambiguous nature of mathematical notation avoids the problem of speculation about the meaning of phrases in an imprecisely worded natural language description of a system. Natural language is inherently ambiguous and subject to these limitations, whereas mathematics employs highly precise notation with sound rules of mathematical inference.

The formal specification thus becomes the key reference point for the different parties concerned with the construction of the system. This includes determining customer needs, program implementation, testing of results, and program documentation. It follows that the formal specification is a valuable means of promoting a common understanding for all those concerned with the system. The term formal methods is used to describe a formal specification language and a method for the design and implementation of computer systems. The term has its roots in mathematics and logic, for example, the word *formal* is derived from *form* as distinct from *content*. The terminology goes back to a movement in mathematics in the early twentieth century which attempted to show that all mathematics was reducible to symbols with rules governing the generation of new symbols from existing terms. The movement arose out of the paradoxes in set theory as identified by Russell and the objective of the formalists was to develop a formal system which was both *consistent* and *complete*. Completeness indicates that all true theorems may be proved within the formal system, and consistency indicates that only true results may be proved. The objectives of the formalist program were dealt a fatal blow in 1931 by the Austrian logician Kurt Goedel [Goe:31] when he demonstrated that any formal system powerful enough to include arithmetic would necessarily be incomplete, and in fact the consistency of arithmetic is not provable within the formal system.

Formal software development was defined by Mícheál Mac an Airchinnigh in [Mac:90] as

A formal specification derived from requirements.
A formal method by which one proceeds from the specification
to the ultimate concrete reality of the software.

The specification is written in a mathematical language, and this ensures that the problem of ambiguity inherent in a natural language specification is avoided, owing to the precision of mathematics. The derivation of the implementation from the specification is achieved via step-wise refinement. The refinement step makes the specification more concrete and closer to the actual implementation. There is an associated proof obligation that the refinement is valid, and that the concrete state preserves the properties of the more abstract state. Thus, assuming that the original specification is correct and the proofs of correctness of each refinement step are valid, then there is a very high degree of confidence in the correctness of the implemented software. Step-wise refinement is illustrated as follows: the initial specification S is the initial model M_0; it is then refined into the more concrete model M_1, and M_1 is then refined into M_2, and so on until the eventual implementation $M_n = E$ is produced.

$$S = M_0 \ll M_1 \ll M_2 \ll M_3 \ll \ldots\ldots \ll M_n = E$$

Requirements are the foundation stone from which the system is built and the objective of requirements validation is to confirm that the requirements are correct and are actually those required by the customer. Formal methods may be employed to model the requirements, and the model exploration yields further desirable or undesirable properties. The ability to prove that certain properties are true of the specification is very valuable, especially in safety critical and security critical applications. These properties are logical consequences of the definition of the requirements, and, if appropriate, the requirements may need to be amended appropriately. Thus, formal methods may be employed in a sense to debug the requirements.

The main advantage of formal methods is that the mathematical models useful for studying properties of the system and the use of formal methods generally leads to more robust software, which in turn leads to increased confidence in the software. The challenges involved in the deployment of formal methods in an organization include the education of staff in formal specification, as formal specification and the use of mathematical techniques may be a culture shock to many staff.

Formal methods have been applied to a diverse range of applications, including circuit design, artificial intelligence, security critical field, the safety critical field, railways, microprocessor verification, the specification of standards, and the specification and verification of programs. The objective here is to describe a selection of state of the art methodologies in formal methods. The literature on formal methods is quite vast, and as a wide variety of methodologies are practiced, space constraints dictate that a small subset of the available methodologies be presented. An important distinction (cf. [Mac:93]) must be made between the two distinct classes of formal methods: i.e., the *model-oriented* approach of which VDM [BjJ:78} and Z [Spi:92, Wrd:92] are examples, and the *property oriented* approach, i.e., those which are not based on explicit models, including those based on the axiomatic approach and the process algebras. These two approaches will be discussed in more detail later. The differences may be illustrated by a stack: in VDM it is explicitly modeled by a sequence, whereas in an algebraic axiomatic approach, axioms such as $pop(push(x, s)) = s$ are given.

7.5.1 Why should we use formal methods?

There is a very strong motivation to use best practices in software engineering in order to produce software adhering to high quality standards. Flaws in software may at best cause minor irritations to customers, and in a worst case scenario could potentially cause major damage to a customer's business or loss of life. Consequently, companies will employ best practices to mature their software processes. Formal methods is one leading-edge technology which studies suggest may be of benefit to companies who wish to minimize the occurrence of defects in software products.

The use of formal methods is mandatory in certain circumstances. The Ministry of Defense in the UK issued two safety-critical standards in the early nineties related to the use of formal methods in the software development lifecycle. The first is Defense Standard 0055, i.e., Def Stan 00-55, *The Procurement of safety critical software in defense equipment* [MOD:91a]. This standard makes it mandatory to employ formal methods in safety-critical software development in the UK; and, in particular, it mandates the use of formal mathematical proof that the most crucial programs correctly implement their specifications. The other defense standard is Def Stan 00-56 *Hazard analysis and safety classification of the computer and programmable electronic system elements of defense equipment* [MOD:91b]. The objective of this standard is to provide guidance to identify which systems or parts of systems being developed are safety-critical and thereby require the use of formal methods. This is achieved by subjecting a proposed system to an initial hazard analysis to determine whether there are safety-critical parts. The reaction to these defense standards 00-55 and 00-56 was quite hostile initially as most suppliers were unlikely to meet the technical and organization requirements of the standard, and this is described in [Tie:91]. The standard indicates how seriously the ministry of defense takes safety, and Brown in [Bro:93] argues that

> Missile systems must be presumed dangerous until shown to be safe, and that the absence of evidence for the existence of dangerous errors does not amount to evidence for the absence of danger.

It is quite possible that a software company may be sued for software which injures a third party, and it is conjectured in [Mac:93] that the day is not far off when

> A system failure traced to a software fault and injurious to a third party, will lead to a successful litigation against the developers of the said system software.

This suggests that companies will need a quality assurance program that will demonstrate that every reasonable practice was considered to prevent the occurrence of defects. One such practice for defect prevention is the use of formal methods in the software development lifecycle, and in some domains, e.g., safety critical domain, it looks likely that the exclusion of formal methods in the software development cycle may need to be justified.

There is evidence to suggest that the use of formal methods provide savings in the cost of the project, for example, an independent audit of the large CICS transaction processing project at IBM demonstrated a 9% cost saving attributed to the use of formal methods. An independent audit of the Inmos floating point unit of the T800 transputer project confirmed that the use of formal methods led to an estimated 12 month reduction in testing time. These savings are discussed in more detail in chapter one of [HB:95].

The current approach to providing high-quality software on time and within budget is to employ a mature software development process including inspections and testing; and models such as the CMM, Bootstrap, SPICE or ISO 9000:2000 are employed to assist the organization to mature its software process. The process-based approach is also useful in that it demonstrates that reasonable practices are employed to identify and prevent the occurrence of defects, and an ISO 9000:2000-approved software development organization has been independently verified to have reasonable software development practices in place. A formal methods approach is complementary to these models, and for example, it fits comfortably into the defect prevention key process area and the technology change management key process area on the Capability Maturity Model described earlier in chapter 4.

7.5.2 Applications of Formal Methods

Formal Methods is used in academia and in industry, and the safety-critical and security critical fields are two key areas to which formal methods has been successfully applied in industry. Several organizations have piloted formal methods with varying degrees of success. These include IBM, which actually developed VDM at the IBM laboratory in Vienna. IBM (Hursley) piloted the Z formal specification language in the UK, and it was employed for the CICS (Customer Information Control System) project. This is an on-line transaction processing system with over 500,000 lines of code. This project generated valuable feedback to the formal methods community, and although it was very successful in the sense that an independent audit verified that the use of formal methods generated a 9% cost saving, there was a resistance to the deployment of the formal methods in the organization. This was attributed to the lack of education on formal methods in computer science curricula, lack of adequate support tools for formal methods, and the difficulty that the programmers had with mathematics and logic.

Formal methods has been successfully applied to thehardware verification field; for example, parts of the Viper microprocessor were formally verified, and the FM9001 microprocessor was formally verified by the Boyer Moore theorem prover [HB:95]. There are many examples of the use of formal methods in the railway domain, and examples dealing with the modeling and verification of a railroad gate controller and railway signaling are described in [HB:95]. The mandatory use of formal methods in some safety and security-critical fields has led to formal methods being employed to verify correctness in the nuclear power industry, in the aerospace industry, in the security technology area, and the railroad domain. These sectors are subject to stringent regulatory controls to ensure safety and security.

Formal methods has been successfully applied to the telecommunications domain, and has been useful in investigating the feature interaction problem as described in [Bou:94]. Formal methods has been applied to domains which have little to do with computer science, for example, to the problem of the formal specification of the single transferable voting system in [Pop:97], and to various organizations and structures in [ORg:97]. There is an extensive collection of examples to which formal methods has been applied, and a selection of these are described in detail in [HB:95]. Formal methods has also been applied to the problem of reuse, and this is described in the following section.

7.5.3 Formal Methods and Reuse

Effective software reuse helps to speed up software development productivity, and this is of particular importance in rapid application software development. The idea is to develop building blocks which may then be reused in future projects, and this requires that the component be of high quality and reliability, and that the domains to which the component may be effectively applied be well known, and that a documented description exists of the actual behavior of the component and the circumstances in which it may be employed.

Effective reuse is typically limited to a particular domain, and there are reuse models to assist organizations that may be employed to assess or diagnose the current reuse practices in the organization, as this enables a reuse strategy to be developed and implemented. Systematic reuse is being researched in academia and industry, and the ROADS project was an EC funded project which included the European Software Institute (ESI) and Thompson as partners to investigate a reuse approach for domain-based software.

Formal methods has a role to play in software reuse also, as it offers enhanced confidence in the correctness of the component, and provides an unambiguous formal description of the behavior of the particular component. The component may be tested extensively to provide extra confidence in its correctness. A component is generally used in many different environments, and the fact that a component has worked successfully in one situation is no guarantee that it will work successfully in the future as there could be potential undesirable interaction between it and other components, or other software. Consequently, it is desirable that the behavior of the component be unambiguously specified and fully understood, and that a formal analysis of component composition be performed to ensure that risks are minimized and that the resulting software is of a high quality

There has been research into the formalization of components in both academia and industry; the EC SCORE research project conducted as part of the European RACE II program considered the challenge of reuse. It included the formal specification of components and developed an actual component model. This project also considered the problem of feature interaction in the telecommunications environment [Bou:94], and this verified that formal methods may be successfully employed to identify and eliminate feature interaction. It is clear that formal methods also has a role to play in identifying and eliminating undesirable component interaction.

7.5.4 Tools for Formal Methods

One of the main criticisms of formal methods is the lack of available or usable tools to support the engineer in writing the formal specification or in doing the proof. Many of the early tools were criticized as being of academic use only and not being of industrial strength, but in recent years better tools have become available to support the formal methods community. The expectation is that more and more enhanced tools will continue to become available to support the engineer's work in formal specification and formal proof.

There are various kinds of tools employed to support the formal software development environment, including syntax checkers to check that the specification is syntactically correct or specialized editors ensure that the written specification is syntactically correct; tools to support refinement; automated code generators to generate a corresponding high level language corresponding to the specification; theorem provers to demonstrate the presence or absence of key properties and to prove the correctness of refinement steps, and to identify and resolve proof obligations; and specification animation tools where the execution of the specification can be simulated. Such tools are available from vendors like B-Core and IFAD.

The tools are developed to support existing methods, and there is a recent trend towards an integrated set of method and tools, rather than loosely coupled tools; for example, the B-Toolkit from B-Core is an integrated set of tools that supports the B-Method. These include syntax and type checking, specification animation, proof obligation generator, an auto prover, a proof assistor, and code generation. Thus, in theory, a complete formal development from initial specification to final implementation may be achieved, with every proof obligation justified, leading to a provably correct program.

The IFAD toolbox is a well-known support tool for the VDM-SL specification language, and it includes support for syntax and type checking, an interpreter and debugger to execute and debug the specification, and a code generator to convert from VDM-SL to C++. It also includes support for graphical notations such as the OMT/UML design notations.

SDL is a specification language which is employed in event driven real time systems. It is an object-orientated graphical formal language, and support for SDL is provided by the SDT tool from Telelogic. The SDT tool provides code generation from the specification into the C or C++ programming languages, and the generated code can be used in simulations as well as in applications. Telelogic provides the ITEX tool which may be used with, or independently of SDT. It allows the generation of a test suite from the SDL specification, thereby speeding up the testing cycle.

The RAISE tools are an integrated toolset including the RAISE specification language (RSL) and a collection of tools to support software development including editors and translators from the specification language to Ada or C++. There are many other tools available, including the Boyer Moore theorem prover, the FDR tool for CSP, the CADiZ tool for the Z specification language, the Mural tool for VDM, the LOTOS toolbox for LOTOS specifications, and the PVS tool.

7.5.5 Model-Oriented Approach

There are two key approaches to formal methods: namely the model-oriented approach of *VDM* or *Z*, and the algebraic, or axiomatic approach, which includes the process calculii such as the calculus communicating systems (CCS) or communicating sequential processes (CSP).

A model oriented approach to specification is based on mathematical models. A mathematical model is a mathematical representation or abstraction of a physical entity or system. The representation or model aims to provide a mathematical explanation of the behavior of the system or the physical world. A model is considered suitable if its properties closely match the properties of the system, and if its calculations match and simplify calculations in the real system, and if predictions of future behavior may be made. The physical world is dominated by models, e.g., models of the weather system, which enable predictions or weather forecasting to be made, and economic models in which predictions on the future performance of the economy may be made.

It is fundamental to explore the model and to consider the behavior of the model and the behavior of the real world entity. The extent to which the model explains the underlying physical behavior and allows predictions of future behavior to be made will determine its acceptability as a representation of the physical world. Models that are ineffective at explaining the physical world are replaced with new models which offer a better explanation of the manifested physical behavior. There are many examples in science of the replacement of one theory by a newer one: the replacement of the Ptolemaic model of the universe by the Copernican model or the replacement of Newtonian physics by Einstein's theories on relativity. The revolutions that take place in science are described in detail in Kuhn's famous work on scientific revolutions [Kuh:70].

A model is a foundation stone from which the theory is built, and from which explanations and justification of behavior are made. It is not envisaged that we should justify the model itself, and if the model explains the known behavior of the system, it is thus deemed adequate and suitable. Thus the model may be viewed as the starting point of the system. Conversely, if inadequacies are identified with the model we may view the theory and its foundations as collapsing, in a similar manner to a house of cards; alternately, we may search for amendments to the theory to address the inadequacies.

The model-oriented approach to software development involves defining an abstract model of the proposed software system. The model acts as a representation of the proposed system, and the model is then explored to assess its suitability in representing the proposed system. The exploration of the model takes the form of model interrogation, i.e., asking questions and determining the effectiveness of the model in answering the questions. The modeling in formal methods is typically performed via elementary discrete mathematics, including set theory, sequences, and functions. This approach includes the Vienna Development Method (VDM) and Z. VDM arose from work done in the IBM laboratory in Vienna in formalizing the semantics for the PL/1 compiler, and was later applied to the specification of software systems. The Z specification language had its origins in the early 1980s at Oxford University.

VDM is a method for software development and includes a specification language originally named Meta IV (a pun on *metaphor*), and later renamed VDM-SL in the standardization of VDM. The approach to software development is via step-wise refinement. There are several schools of VDM, including VDM⁺⁺, the object oriented extension to VDM, and what has become known as the *"Irish school of VD*M", i.e., VDM*, which was developed at Trinity College, Dublin.

7.5.6 Axiomatic Approach

The axiomatic approach focuses on the properties that the proposed system is to satisfy, and there is no intention to produce an abstract model of the system. The required properties and underlying behavior of the system are stated in mathematical notation. The difference between the axiomatic specification and a model-based approach is illustrated by the example of a stack. The stack is a well-known structure in computer science, and includes stack operators for pushing an element onto the stack and popping an element from the stack. The properties of *pop* and *push* are explicitly defined in the axiomatic approach, whereas in the model-oriented approach, an explicit model of the stack and its operations are constructed in terms of the effect the operations have on the model. The specification of an abstract data type of a stack involves the specification of the properties of the abstract data type, but the abstract data type is not explicitly defined; i.e., only the properties are defined. The specification of the *pop* operation on a stack is given by axiomatic properties, for example, $pop(push(s,x)) = s$. The "property oriented approach" has the advantage that the implementer is not constrained to a particular choice of implementation, and the only constraint is that the implementation must satisfy the stipulated properties. The emphasis is on the identification and expression of the required properties of the system and the actual representation or implementation issues are avoided, and the focus is on the specification of the underlying behavior. Properties are typically stated using mathematical logic or higher-order logics, and mechanized theorem-proving techniques may be employed to prove results.

One potential problem with the axiomatic approach is that the properties specified may not be satisfiable in any implementation. Thus whenever a "formal theory" is developed a corresponding "model" of the theory must be identified, in order to ensure that the properties may be realized in practice. That is, when proposing a system that is to satisfy some set of properties, there is a need to prove that there is at least one system that will satisfy the set of properties. The model-oriented approach has an explicit model to start with and so this problem does not arise. The constructive approach is preferred by some groups of formal methodists, and in this approach whenever existence is stipulated *con-*

structive existence is implied, where a direct example of the existence of an object can be exhibited, or an algorithm to produce the object within a finite time period exists. This is different from an existence proof, where it is known that there is a solution to a particular problem but there is no algorithm to construct the solution.

7.5.7 The Vienna Development Method

As stated previously, VDM dates from work done by the IBM research laboratory in Vienna. Their aim was to specify the semantics of the PL/1 programming language. This was achieved by employing the Vienna Definition Language (VDL), taking an operational semantic approach; i.e. (cf. chapter 1 of [BjJ:82]) the semantics of a language are determined in terms of a hypothetical machine which interprets the programs of that language. Later work led to the Vienna Development Method (VDM) with its specification language, Meta IV. This concerned itself with the denotational semantics of programming languages; i.e. (cf. chapter 1 of [BjJ:82]) a mathematical object (set, function, etc.) is associated with each phrase of the language. The mathematical object is the *denotation* of the phrase.

VDM is a *model-oriented approach*, and this means that an explicit model of the state of an abstract machine is given, and operations are defined in terms of this state. Operations may act on the system state, taking inputs, and producing outputs and a new system state. Operations are defined in a precondition and postcondition style. Each operation has an associated proof obligation to ensure that if the precondition is true, then the operation preserves the system invariant. The initial state itself is, of course, required to satisfy the system invariant. VDM uses keywords to distinguish different parts of the specification, e.g., preconditions, postconditions are introduced by the keywords *pre* and *post* respectively. In keeping with the philosophy that formal methods specifies **what** a system does as distinct from *how*, VDM employs postconditions to stipulate the effect of the operation on the state. The previous state is then distinguished by employing *hooked variables*, e.g., $v^\urcorner$, and the post condition specifies the new state *(defined by a logical predicate relating the pre-state to the post-state)* from the previous state.

VDM is more than its specification language Meta IV (called VDM-SL in the standardization of VDM) and is, in fact, a development method, with rules to verify the steps of development. The rules enable the executable specification, i.e., the detailed code, to be obtained from the initial specification via refinement steps. Thus, we have a sequence $S=S_0, S_1, ..., S_n = E$ of specifications, where S is the initial specification, and E is the final (executable) specification. Retrieval functions enable a return from a more concrete specification, to the more abstract specification. The initial specification consists of an initial state, a system state, and a set of operations. The system state is a particular domain, where a domain is built out of primitive domains such as the set of natural numbers, etc., or constructed from primitive domains using domain constructors such as Cartesian product, disjoint union, etc. A domain-invariant predicate may further constrain the domain, and a *type* in VDM reflects a domain obtained in this way. Thus a type in VDM is more specific than the signature of the type, and thus represents values in the domain defined by the signature, which satisfy the domain invariant. In view of this approach to types, it is clear that VDM types may not be "statically typed checked".

VDM specifications are structured into modules, with a module containing the module name, parameters, types, operations etc. Partial functions are the norm in computer science, and formal methods in particular. The problem is that many functions, especially recursively defined functions can be undefined, or fail to terminate for some arguments in their domain. VDM addresses partial functions by employing non-standard logical operators, namely the logic of partial functions (LPFs) which can deal with undefined operands. The Boolean expression T or $\perp = \perp$ or T = true, i.e., the truth value of a logical or operation is true if at least one of the logical operands is true, and the undefined term is treated as a don't care value.

Example 1

The following is a very simple example of a VDM specification and is adapted from [InA:91]. It is a simple library system which allows borrowing and returns of books. The data types for the library system are first defined and the operation to borrow a book is then defined. It is assumed that the state is made up of three sets and these are the set of books on the shelf, the set of books which are borrowed, and the set of missing books. These sets are mutually disjoint. The effect of the operation to borrow a book is to remove the book from the set of books on the shelf and to add it to the set of borrowed books. The reader is referred to [InA:91] for a detailed explanation.

types
    Bks = *Bkd-id* set

state *Library* of
    On-shelf : Bks
    Missing : Bks
    Borrowed : Bks

inv *mk-Library* (*os, mb, bb*) $\underline{\Delta}$ *is-disj*({*os,mb,bb*})
end

borrow (*b:Bkd-id*)
ex wr *on-shelf, borrowed* : *Bks*
pre b $\in$ *on-shelf*

post *on-shelf = on-shelf* ⌐ – *{b}* ∧
  borrowed = borrowed ⌐ U *{b}*

VDM is a widely used formal method and has been used in industrial strength projects as well as by the academic community. There is tool support available, for example, the IFAD toolbox. There are several variants of VDM, including VDM⁺⁺, the object-oriented extension of VDM, and the Irish school of the VDM, which is discussed in the next section.

7.5.8 VDM*, The Irish School of VDM

The Irish School of VDM is a variant of standard VDM, and is characterized by [Mac:90] its constructive approach, classical mathematical style, and its terse notation. In particular, this method combines the *what* and *how* of formal methods in that its terse specification style stipulates in concise form *what* the system should do; and furthermore the fact that its specifications are constructive (or functional) means that that the *how* is included with the *what*. However, it is important to qualify this by stating that the how as presented by VDM* is not directly executable, as several of its mathematical data types have no corresponding structure in high level programming languages, or functional languages. Thus a conversion or reification of the specification into a functional or higher-level language must take place to ensure a successful execution. It should be noted that the fact that a specification is constructive is no guarantee that it is a good implementation strategy, if the construction itself is naive. This issue is considered (cf. pp. 135-7 in [Mac:90]), and the example considered is the construction of the Fibonacci series.

The Irish school follows a similar development methodology as in standard VDM, and is, of course, a model-oriented approach. The initial specification is presented, with initial state and operations defined. The operations are presented with preconditions; however, no postcondition is necessary as the operation is "functionally", i.e., explicitly constructed. Each operation has as associated proof obligation; if the precondition for the operation is true and the operation is performed, then the system invariant remains true after the operation. The proof of invariant preservation normally takes the form of *constructive proofs*. This is especially the case for *existence proofs*, in that the philosophy of the school is to go further than to provide a theoretical proof of existence; rather the aim is to exhibit existence constructively.

The emphasis is on constructive existence and the implication of this is that the school avoids the existential quantifier of predicate calculus. In fact, reliance on logic in proof is kept to a minimum, and emphasis instead is placed on equational reasoning. Special emphasis is placed on studying algebraic structures and their morphisms. Structures with nice algebraic properties are sought, and such a structure includes the monoid, which has closure, associativity, and a unit element. The monoid is a very common structure in computer science, and thus it is appropriate to study and understand it. The concept of isomorphism is powerful, reflecting that two structures are essentially identical, and thus we may choose to work with either, depending on which is more convenient for the task in hand.

The school has been influenced by the work of Polya and Lakatos. The former [Pol:57] advocated a style of problem solving characterized by solving a complex problem by first considering an easier sub-problem, and considering several examples, which generally leads to a clearer insight into solving the main problem. Lakatos's approach to mathematical discovery (cf. [Lak:76]) is characterized by heuristic methods. A primitive conjecture is proposed and if global counter examples to the statement of the conjecture are discovered, then the corresponding "hidden lemma" for which this global counter example is a local counter example is identified and added to the statement of the primitive conjecture. The process repeats, until no more global counter examples are found. A skeptical view of absolute truth or certainty is inherent in this.

Partial functions are the norm in VDM* and as in standard VDM, the problem is that recursively defined functions may be undefined, or fail to terminate for several of the arguments in their domain. The logic of partial functions (LPFs) is avoided, and instead care is taken with recursive definitions to ensure termination is achieved for each argument. This is achieved by ensuring that the recursive argument is strictly decreasing in each recursive invocation. The $\perp$ symbol is typically used in the Irish school to represent *undefined or unavailable* or *do not care*. Academic and industrial projects have been conducted using the method of the Irish school, but at this stage tool support is limited.

Example 2

The following is the equivalent VDM* specification of the earlier example of a simple library presented in standard VDM.

Bks = P Bkd-id
Library = (Bks X Bks X Bks)

Os ∈ Bks
Ms ∈ Bks
Bw ∈ Bks

Inv- *Library (Os, Ms, Bw)* Δ *Os n Ms = Ø*
$\qquad\qquad\qquad\qquad$ ∧ *Os n Bw = Ø*
$\qquad\qquad\qquad\qquad$ ∧ *Bw n Ms = Ø*

Bor: Bkd-id -> (Bks X Bks) -> (Bks X Bks)
Bor «b» (Os, Bw) Δ *(← «b» Os, Bw U {b})*

pre- *Bor «b» (Os, Bw)* Δ *«b» Os*

There is, of course, a proof obligation to prove that the Borrow operation preserves the invariant, i.e., that the three sets of borrowed, missing, or on the shelf remain disjoint after the execution of the operation. Proof obligations require a mathematical proof by hand or a machine-assisted proof to verify that the invariant remains satisfied after the operation.

7.5.9 The Z Specification Language

Z is a formal specification language founded on Zermelo set theory. It is a model oriented' approach with an explicit model of the state of an abstract machine given, and operations are defined in terms of this state. Its main features include a mathematical notation which is similar to VDM, and the schema calculus. The latter is visually striking, and consists essentially of boxes, with these boxes or schemas used to describe operations and states. The schema calculus enables schemas to be used as building blocks and combined with other schemas.

The schema calculus is a powerful means of decomposing a specification into smaller pieces or schemas. This decomposition helps to ensure that a Z specification is highly readable, as each individual schema is small in size and self-contained. Exception handling may be addressed by defining schemas for the exception cases, and then combining the exception schema with the original operation schema. Mathematical data types are used to model the data in a system, these data types obey mathematical laws. These laws enable simplification of expressions, and are useful with proofs.

Operations are defined in a precondition / postcondition style; however the precondition is implicitly defined within the operation; i.e., it is not separated out as in standard VDM. Each operation has an associated proof obligation to ensure that if the precondition is true, then the operation preserves the system invariant. The initial state itself is, of course, required to satisfy the system invariant. Postconditions employ a logical predicate which relates the pre-state to the post-state, the post-state of a variable being distinguished by priming, e.g., v'. Various conventions are employed within Z specification, for example $v?$ indicates that v is an input variable; $v!$ indicates that v is an output variable. The $\Xi\,Op$ operation indicates that the operation Op does not affect the state; $\Delta\,Op$ indicates that Op is an operation which affects the state.

Many of the data types employed in Z have no counterpart in standard programming languages. It is therefore important to identify and describe the concrete data structures which ultimately will represent the abstract mathematical structures. As the concrete structures may differ from the abstract, the operations on the abstract data structures may need to be refined to yield operations on the concrete data which yield equivalent results. For simple systems, direct refinement (i.e., one step from abstract specification to implementation) may be possible; in more complex systems, deferred refinement is employed, where a sequence of increasingly concrete specifications are produced to yield the executable specification eventually.

Example 3

The following is the equivalent Z specification of the operation to borrow a book in the library system. Z specifications are visually striking with the schema notation.

–Library————
  on-shelf, missing, borrowed : P Bkd-Id

————
  on-shelf n missing = Ø
  on-shelf n borrowed = Ø
  borrowed n missing = Ø
—————————

—Borrow————
Δ Library
b?:Bkd-Id

————
  b? Є on-shelf
  on-shelf' = on-shelf\ {b?}
  borrowed' = borrowed U {b?}
—————————

VDM and Z are the two most widely used formal methods; their similarities and differences are summarized below:.

Table 7.17: VDM and Z

Similarites and Differences of VDM/Z
VDM is a development method including a specification language whereas Z is a specification language only.
Constraints may be placed on types in VDM specifications but not in Z specifications.
Z is structured into schemas and VDM into modules.
Schema calculus is part of Z.
Relations are part of Z but not of VDM.
Preconditions are not separated out in Z specifications.

7.5.10 The B Method

The *B-Technologies* (cf. [McD:94]) consist of three components; a method for software development, namely the *B*-Method; a supporting set of tools, namely, the *B*-Toolkit; and a generic program for symbol manipulation, namely, the *B*-Tool (from which the *B*-Toolkit is derived). The *B*-Method is a model-oriented approach and is closely related to the Z specification language. Every construct in the method has a set theoretic counterpart, and the method is founded on Zermelo set theory. Each operation has an explicit precondition, and an immediate proof obligation is that the precondition is stronger than the weakest precondition for the operation.

One key purpose [McD:94] of the *abstract machine* in the *B*-Method is to provide encapsulation of variables representing the state of the machine, and operations which manipulate the state. Machines may refer to other machines, and a machine may be introduced as a refinement of another machine. The abstract machine are specification machines, refinement machines, or implementable machines. The *B*-Method adopts a layered approach to design where the design is gradually made more concrete by a sequence of design layers, where each design layer is a refinement that involves a more detailed implementation in terms of abstract machines of the previous layer. The design refinement ends when the final layer is implemented purely in terms of library machines. Any refinement of a machine by another has associated proof obligations and proof may be carried out to verify the validity of the refinement step,

Specification animation of the AMN specification is possible with the *B*-Toolkit and this enables typical usage scenarios of the AMN specification to be explored for requirements validation. This is, in effect, an early form of testing and may be used to demonstrate the presence or absence of desirable or undesirable behavior. Verification takes the form of proof to demonstrate that the invariant is preserved when the operation is executed within its precondition, and this is performed on the AMN specification with the *B*-Toolkit.

The *B*-Toolkit provides several tools which support the *B*-Method, and these include syntax and type checking; specification animation, proof obligation generator, auto prover, proof assistor, and code generation. Thus, in theory, a complete formal development from initial specification to final implementation may be achieved, with every proof obligation justified, leading to a provably correct program.

The *B*-Method and toolkit have been successfully applied in industrial applications and one of the projects to which they have been applied is the CICS project at IBM Hursley in the UK. The *B*-Method and toolkit have been designed to support the complete software development process from specification to code. The application of *B* to the CICS project is described in [Hoa:95], and the automated support provided has been cited as a major benefit of the application of the *B*-Method and the *B*-Toolkit.

7.5.11 Propositional and Predicate Calculus

Propositional calculus, in which a truth value is associated with each proposition, is widely employed in mathematics and logic. There are a rich set of connectives employed in the calculus for truth functional operations, and these include $A \Rightarrow B, A \wedge B, A \vee B$ which denote, respectively, the conditional if A then B, the conjunction of A and B, and the disjunction of A and B. A truth table of the truth value of the functional operation may be constructed, and truth values are normally the binary values of *true* and *false*, although there are other logics, for example, the 3 valued logics, which are more than the normal binary truth values for the proposition.

A formula in predicate calculus (cf. pp. 39-40 of [Gib:90]) is built up from the basic symbols of the language; these symbols include variables; predicate symbols, including equality; function symbols, including the constants; logical symbols, e.g., $\exists$, $\wedge$, $\vee$, $\neg$, etc.; and the punctuation symbols, e.g., brackets and commas. The formulae of predicate calculus are then built from terms, where a *term* is a key construct, and is defined recursively as a variable or individual constant or as some function containing terms as arguments. A formula may be an atomic formula or built from other formulae via the logical symbols. Other logical symbols are then defined as abbreviations of the basic logical symbols.

An interpretation gives meaning to a formula. If the formula is a sentence (i.e., does not contain any free variables) then the given interpretation is true or false. If a formula has free variables, then the truth or falsity of the formula depends on the values given to the free variables. A free formula essentially describes a relation say, $R(x_1, x_2, \ldots x_n)$ such that $R(x_1, x_2, \ldots x_n)$ is true if $(x_1, x_2, \ldots x_n)$ is in relation R. If a free formula is true irrespective of the values given to the free variables, then the formula is true in the interpretation.

A valuation (meaning) function is associated with the interpretation, and gives meaning to the connectives. Thus associated with each constant c is a constant c_Σ in some universe of values Σ; with each function symbol f, we have a function symbol f_Σ in Σ; and for each predicate symbol P a relation P_Σ in Σ. The valuation function in effect gives a semantics to the language of the predicate calculus L The truth of a proposition P with respect to a model M is then defined in the natural way, in terms of the meanings of the terms, the meanings of the functions, predicate symbols, and the normal meanings of the connectives (cf. p. 43 of [Gib:90].

Mendelson (cf. p. 48 of [Men:87]) provides a rigorous though technical definition of truth in terms of satisfaction (with respect to an interpretation M). Intuitively a formula F is *satisfiable* if it is *true* (in the intuitive sense) for some assignment of the free variables in the formula F. If a formula F is satisfied for every possible assignment to the free variables in F, then it is *true* (in the technical sense) for the interpretation M. An analogous definition is provided for *false* in the interpretation M.

A formula is *valid* if it is true in every interpretation; however, as there may be uncountably many interpretations, it may not be possible to check this requirement in practice. M is said to be a model for a set of formulae if any only if every formula is true in M.

There is a distinction between proof theoretic and model theoretic approaches in predicate calculus. *Proof theoretic* is essentially syntactic, and we have a list of axioms with rules of inference. In this way the theorems of the calculus may be logically derived and thus we may logically derive (i.e., |- A) the theorems of the calculus. In essence the logical truths are as a result of the syntax or form of the formulae, rather than the *meaning* of the formulae. *Model theoretical*, in contrast is essentially semantic. The truths derive essentially from the meaning of the symbols and connectives, rather than the logical structure of the formulae. This is written as $\vdash_M A$.

A calculus is *sound* if all the logically valid theorems are true in the interpretation, i.e., proof theoretic $\Rightarrow$ model theoretic. A calculus is complete if all the truths in an interpretation are provable in the calculus, i.e., model theoretic $\Rightarrow$ proof theoretic. A calculus is *consistent* if there is no formula A such that $\vdash A$ and $\vdash \neg A$.

7.5.12 Predicate Transformers and Weakest Preconditions

The precondition of a program S is a predicate, i.e., a statement that may be true or false, and it is usually required to prove that Q is true if Q is the precondition of a program S; i.e., ($\{Q\}$ S $\{R\}$), then execution of S is guaranteed to terminate in a finite amount of time in a state satisfying R.

The weakest precondition (cf. p. 109 of [Gri:81]) of a command S with respect to a postcondition R represents the set of all states such that if execution begins in any one of these states, then execution will terminate in a finite amount of time in a state with R true. These set of states may be represented by a predicate Q', y, so that $wp(S,R) = wp_S(R) = Q'$, and so wp_S is a predicate transformer, i.e., it may be regarded as a function on predicates. The weakest precondition is the precondition that places the fewest constraints on the state than all of the other preconditions of (S,R). That is, all of the other preconditions are stronger than the weakest precondition.

The notation $Q\{S\}R$ is used to denote partial correctness and indicates that if execution of S commences in any state satisfying Q, and if execution terminates, then the final state will satisfy R. Often, a predicate Q which is stronger than the weakest precondition $wp(S,R)$ is employed, especially where the calculation of the weakest precondition is non-trivial. Thus a stronger predicate Q such that $Q - > wp(S,R)$ is sometimes employed in these cases.

There are many properties associated with weakest preconditions and these are used in practice to simplify expressions involving weakest preconditions, and in determining the weakest preconditions of various program commands, e.g., assignments, iterations, etc. Weakest preconditions are useful in developing a proof of correctness of a program in parallel with its development.

An imperative program may be regarded as a predicate transformer. This is since a predicate P characterizes the set of states in which the predicate P is true, and an imperative program may be regarded as a binary relation on states, which may be extended to a function F, leading to the Hoare triple $P\{F\}Q$. That is, the program F acts as a predicate transformer. The predicate P may be regarded as an input assertion, i.e., a Boolean expression which must be true before the program F is executed. The Boolean expression Q is the output assertion, and is true if the program F terminates, having commenced in a state satisfying P.

7.5.13 The Process Calculi

The objectives of the process calculi [Hor:85] are to provide mathematical models which provide insight into the diverse issues involved in the specification, design, and implementation of computer systems which continuously act and interact with their environment. These systems may be decomposed into subsystems which interact with each other and their environment. The basic building block is the *process*, which is a mathematical abstraction of the interactions between a system and its environment. A process which lasts indefinitely may be specified recursively. Processes may be assembled into systems, execute concurrently, or communicate with each other. Process communication may be synchronized, and generally takes the form of a process outputting a message simultaneously to another process inputing a message. Resources may be shared among several processes. Process calculi enrich the understanding of communication and concurrency, and elegant formalisms such as CSP [Hor:85] and CCS [Mil:89] which obey a rich collection of mathematical laws have been developed.

The expression *(a -> P)* in CSP describes a process which first engages in event *a,* and then behaves as process *P*. A recursive definition is written as $(\mu X) \bullet F(X))$, and an example of a simple chocolate vending machine is

$$VMS = \mu X:\{coin, choc\}.(coin->(choc->X))$$

The simple vending machine has an alphabet of two symbols, namely, *coin* and *choc*, and the behavior of the machine is that a coin is entered into the machine and then a chocolate selected and provided.

CSP processes use channels to communicate values with their environment, and input on channel *c* is denoted by *(c?.x -> P_x)*, which describes a process that accepts any value *x* on channel *c*, and then behaves as process P_x. In contrast, *(c!e -> P)* defines a process which outputs the expression *e* on channel *c* and then behaves as process *P*.

.Calculus is a calculus which is based on names. Communication between processes takes place between named channels, and the name of a channel may be passed over a channel. Thus in .calculus, as distinct from CCS, there is no distinction between channel names and data values. The output of a value *v* on channel *a* is given by av, i.e., output is a negative prefix. Input on channel a is given by a(x), and is a positive prefix. Private links or restrictions are given by *(x)P* in the calculus and *P\x* in CCS.

7.5.14 Miscellaneous Specification Languages

The RAISE (Rigorous Approach to Industrial Software Engineering) project was an ESPRIT-funded project (1985-90). Its objective [Geo:91] was to produce a method for the rigorous development of software, based on a wide-spectrum specification language, and accompanied by tool support. It considered standard VDM to be deficient, in that it lacked modularity, and was unable to deal with concurrency. The RAISE specification language (RSL) is designed to address these deficiencies, and an algebraic approach is adopted. Comprehensive support is available from the RAISE tools.

The RAISE method (as distinct from its specification language) covers the software lifecycle, from requirements analysis to code generation. This is achieved via a number of design steps, in which the specification is gradually made more concrete, until ultimately a specification that may be transferred into code is reached. The RAISE toolset includes library tools for storing and retrieving modules and translators from subsets of RSL into Ada and C++.

SDL was developed specifically for the specification and description of the behavior of telecommunications system. It may be used at several levels of abstraction, ranging from a very broad overview of a system to detailed design. The behavior of the system is considered as the combined behavior of the processes in the system, and the latter is considered to be an extended finite state machine, i.e., a finite state machine that can use and manipulate data stored in variables local to the machine. Processes may cooperate via signals, i.e., discrete messages and exhibit deterministic behavior.

A graphical language is employed to describe processes and this involves graphical representation of states, input, output, and decisions. Channels enable communication between blocks (containing processes) and the system (containing blocks connected by channels) and its environment. SDL supports time constraints via the timer construct. The graphical language has a corresponding equivalent textual representation.

SSADM is a structured systems analysis and design method. It presents three distinct views of an information system. These include logical data structures, data flow diagrams, and entity life histories. The behavior of the system is explained by employing a graphical language of symbols; these symbols may indicate a one-to-many relationship, an optional occurrence, mutually exclusive choices, etc. The method is data driven, with emphasis placed on the processes which manipulate the data. User involvement and commitment to the development is emphasized from the earliest stage of the project.

7.5.15 Proof and Formal Methods

The word *proof* has several connotations in various disciplines; for example, in a court of law, the defendant is assumed innocent until proven guilty. The proof of the guilt of the defendant may take the form of certain facts in relation to the movements of the defendant, the defendant's circumstances, the defendant's alibi, statements from witnesses, rebuttal arguments from the defense and certain theories produced by the prosecution or defense. Ultimately, in the case of a trial by jury, the defendant is judged guilty or not guilty depending on the extent to which the jury has been convinced by the arguments proposed by prosecution and defense.

A mathematical proof typically includes natural language and mathematical symbols; often many of the tedious details of the proof are omitted. The strategy of proof in proving a conjecture tends to be *a divide and conquer* technique, i.e., breaking the conjecture down into sub-goals and then attempting to prove the sub-goals. Most proofs in formal methods are concerned with cross-checking on the details of the specification or validity of refinement proofs, or proofs that certain properties are satisfied by the specification. There are many tedious lemmas to be proved and theorem provers assist and are essential. Machine proof needs to be explicit and reliance on some brilliant insight is avoided. Proofs by hand are notorious for containing errors or jumps in reasoning, as discussed in chapter 1 of [HB:95], while machine proofs are extremely lengthy and unreadable, but generally help to avoid errors and jumps in proof as every step needs to be justified.

One well-known theorem prover is the "Boyer/Moore theorem prover" [BoM:79], and a mathematical proof consists of a sequence of formulae where each element is either an axiom or derived from a previous element in the series by applying a fixed set of mechanical rules. There is an interesting case in the literature concerning the proof of correctness of the VIPER microprocessor [Tie:91] and the actual machine proof consisted of several million formulae.

Theorem provers are invaluable in resolving many of the thousands of proof obligations that arise from a formal specification, and it is not feasible to apply formal methods in an industrial environment without the use of machine assisted proof. Automated theorem proving is difficult, as often mathematicians prove a theorem with an initial intuitive feeling that the theorem is true. Human intervention to provide guidance or intuition improves the effectiveness of the theorem prover.

The proof of various properties about the programs increases confidence in the correctness of the program. However, an absolute proof of correctness is unlikely except for the most trivial of programs. A program may consist of legacy software which is assumed to work, or be created by compilers which are assumed to work; theorem provers are programs which are assumed to function correctly. In order to be absolutely certain one would also need to verify the hardware, customized-off-the-shelf software, subcontractor software, and every single execution path that the software system will be used for. The best that formal methods can claim is increased confidence in correctness of the software.

7.6 Summary

This chapter considered advanced topics in the software quality field, including software configuration management, the unified modeling language, and formal methods.

The section on software configuration management was concerned with identifying the configuration of a system, controlling changes to the configuration, and maintaining integrity and traceability. The configuration items are generally documents in the early part of the development of the system, whereas the focus is on source code control management and software release management in the later parts of the system.

The unified modeling language is a visual modeling language for software systems. The advantage of a visual modeling language is that it facilitates the understanding of the architecture of the system by visual means and assists in the management of the complexity of large systems. It allows the same information to be presented in many different ways, and there are nine main diagrams with the standard.

Software usability is an important aspect of quality and usability needs to be built into the software product. This requires a focus on usability from the earliest phases of the lifecycle and there are guidelines from ISO to assist organizations in the implementation of usable software. It is essential to have active user participation and feedback on early prototypes to enable usable software to be produced.

Formal methods is a mathematical approach to the correctness of software. The objective is to specify the program in a mathematical language and to demonstrate that certain properties are satisfied by the specification using mathematical proof. The ultimate objective is to provide confidence that the implementation satisfies the requirements. Formal methods offers increased precision but cannot provide a guarantee of correctness.

Some well-known formal methods were discussed, including VDM and Z. The safety-critical field is a domain to which formal methods is quite suited as it may be applied to verify that stringent safety and reliability properties hold. Tool support is essential for formal methods to be taken seriously by industrialists, and better tools have been provided in recent years by organizations such as B-Core and IFAD.

The role of proof in formal methods was discussed and tool support is essential for industrial proof. The proofs may of invariant preservation of operations or proof of validity of the refinement step. However, the first step in implementing formal methods is to consider formal specification, and the use of mathematical proof and theorem provers belongs to a more advanced deployment of formal methods.

References

Bas:88   The TAME project: Towards improvement-oriented software environments. Victor Basili and H. Rombach. IEEE Transactions on software Engineering 14(6). 1988.

Bha:93   A case study of software process improvement during development. Inderpal Bhandari. IEEE Transactions on software Engineering, 19(12). 1993.

BjJ:78   The vienna development method. The meta language. Dines Bjorner and Cliff Jones. *Lecture Notes in Computer Science* (61). Springer Verlag.1978.

BjJ:82   Formal Specification and software Development. Dines Bjorner and Cliff Jones. Prentice Hall International Series in Computer Science. 1982.

Boe:81   Software engineering economics. Barry Boehm. Prentice Hall. New Jersey. 1981.

Boe:88   A spiral model for software development and enhancement. Barry Boehm. *Computer*. May 1988.

BoM:79   A computational logic. The Boyer Moore Theorem Prover. Robert Boyer and J.S. Moore. Academic Press. 1979.

Bow:00   Which comes first, the Process or the Tool? John Bowman. Software Research Institute. San Francisco. June 2000.

Bou:94   Formalization of properties for feature interaction detection. Experience in a real life situation. Wiet Bouma et al. in: Towards a Pan-European Telecommunications Service Infrastructure. Editors: Hans-Jurgen Kugler, Al Mullery, and Norbert Niebert. Springer Verlag. 1994.

BR:94   The Memory Jogger. A Pocket Guide of Tools for Continuous Improvement and Effective Planning. Michael Brassard and Diane Ritter. Goal / QPC. Methuen, MA. 1994.

Brk:75   The Mythical Man Month. Fred Brooks. Addison Wesley. 1975.

Brk:86   No silver bullet. Essence and accidents of software engineering. Fred Brooks. *Information Processing*. Elsevier. Amsterdam, 1986.

Bro:93   Rational for the Development of the U.K. Defence Standards for Safety Critical software. COMPASS Conference, June 1990. Ministry of Defence.

Bux:75   Software Engineering. Petrocelli. 1975. J.N. Buxton, P.Naur and B.Randell. Report on two NATO Conferences held in Garmisch, Germany (October 1968) and Rome, Italy (October 1969).

Byr:96   Software Capability Evaluation (V3.0).Paul Byrnes and Mike Phillips. Technical Report (CMU/SEI/SEI-96-TR-002). Software Engineering Institute. 1996.

Cas:00   SpiCE for Space. A Method of Process Assessment for Space software Projects. Ann Cass in: SPICE 2000 Conference. Software Process Improvement and Capability Determination. Editor: T.P. Rout. Limerick. June 2000.

Chi:95   Software Triggers as a Function of Time. ODC on Field Faults. Ram Chillarege and Kathryn A. Bassin. Fifth ISIP Working Conference on Dependable Computing for Critical Applications. September 1995.

CJ:96   software Systems Failure and Success. Capers Jones. Thomson Press, Boston, MA. 1996.

Crs:80   Quality is Free. The Art of Making Quality Certain. Philip Crosby. Penguin Books. 1980.

CSE:00   Unified Modeling Language. Technical Briefing No. 8. Centre for Software Engineering. Dublin City University. Ireland. April 2000.

Dem:86   Out of Crisis. W. Edwards Deming. M.I.T. Press. 1986.

Dij:72   Structured Programming. E.W. Dijkstra. Academic Press. 1972.

Dun:96   CMM Based Appraisal for Internal Process Improvement (CBA IPI): Method Description. Donna K. Dunaway and Steve Masters. Technical Report CMU/SEI-96-TR-007. Software Engineering Institute. 1996.

Fag:76   Design and code inspections to reduce errors in software development. Michael Fagan. *IBM Systems Journal* 15(3). 1976.

Fen:95   Software Metrics: A Rigorous Approach. Norman Fenton. Thompson Computer Press. 1995.

Geo:91   The RAISE Specification language: A tutorial. Chris George. *Lecture Notes in Computer Science* (552). Springer Verlag. 1991.

Ger:00   Risk-Based E-Business Testing. Paul Gerrard. Technical Report. Systeme Evolutif. London. 2000.

Gib:90   PhD Thesis. Department of Computer Science. Trinity College Dublin. 1990.

Glb:94   Software Inspections. Tom Gilb and Dorothy Graham. Addison Wesley. 1994.

Glb:76   Software Metrics. Tom Gilb. Winthrop Publishers, Inc. Cambridge. 1976.

Goe:31   Kurt Goedel. Undecidable Propositions in Arithmetic. 1931.

Gri:81   The Science of Programming. David Gries. Springer Verlag. Berlin. 1981.

HB:95   Applications of Formal Methods. Edited by Michael Hinchey and Jonathan Bowen. Prentice Hall International Series in Computer Science. 1995.

Hoa:95   Application of the B-Method to CICS. Jonathan P. Hoare in: Applications of Formal Methods. Editors: Michael Hinchey and Jonathan P. Bowen. Prentice Hall International Series in Computer Science. 1995.

Hor:85   Communicating Sequential Processes. C.A.R. Hoare. Prentice Hall International Series in Computer Science. 1985.

Hum:89   Managing the Software Process. Watts Humphry. Addison Wesley. 1989.

Hum:87   A Method for Assessing the Software Engineering Capability of Contractors. W. Humphrey and W. Sweet. Technical Report. CMU/SEI-87-TR-023. Software Engineering Institute. 1987.

IEEE:829   IEEE Standard for Software Test Documentation.

InA:91   Practical Formal Methods with VDM. Darrell Ince and Derek Andrews. McGraw Hill International Series in Software Engineering. 1991.

ISO:98   Information Technology. Software Process Assessment. ISO/IEC TR 15504 – SPICE - Parts 1 to 9. Technical Report (Type 2). 1998.

ISO:98a   ISO 9241 (Parts 1 – 17). Ergonomic Requirements for Office Work involving Visual Display Terminals. International Standards Organization. 1998.

ISO:99   ISO 13407:1999. Human Centred Design Processes for Interactive Systems. International Standards Organization. 1999.

ISO:00   ISO 9000:2000. Quality Management Systems – Requirements. ISO 9004:2000. Quality Management Systems – Guidelines for Performance Improvements. December 2000.

ISO:91   ISO/IEC 9126: Information Technology.- Software Product Evaluation: Quality Characteristics and Guidelines for their Use. 1991.

Jur:51   Quality Control Handbook. Joseph Juran. McGraw-Hill. New York. 1951.

Kee:00   The evolution of quality processes at Tate Consultancy Services. Gargi Keeni et al. *IEEE Software* 17(4). July 2000.

Kir:00   The SUMI Methodology for Software Usability. Jurek Kirakowski. Human Factors Research Group. University College Cork, Ireland.

KpN:96   The Balanced Scorecard. Translating Strategy into Action. Kaplan and Norton. Harvard Business School Press. 1996.

Kuh:70   The Structure of Scientific Revolutions. Thomas Kuhn. University of Chicago Press. 1970.

Kuv:93   BOOTSTRAP: Europe's assessment method. P.Kuvaja et al. *IEEE Software*. 10(3). May 1993.

Lak:76   Proof and Refutations. The Logic of Mathematical Discovery. Imre Lakatos. Cambridge University Press. 1976.

Lio:96   ARIANE 5. Flight 501 Failure. Report by the Inquiry Board. Prof. J.L. Lions (Chairman of the Board). 1996.

Mac:90   Conceptual Models and Computing. PhD Thesis. Micheal Mac An Airchinnigh. Department of Computer Science. University of Dublin. Trinity College. Dublin. 1990.

Mac:93   Formal Methods and Testing. Micheal Mac An Airchinnigh. Tutorials of the 6th International software Quality Week. Software Research Institute. 1993.

MaCo:96   Software Quality Assurance. Thomas Manns and Michael Coleman. Macmillan Press Ltd. 1996.

Mag:00   The Role of the Improvement Manager. Giuseppe Magnani et al in: Proceedings of SPICE 2000. Software Process Improvement and Capability Determination. Editor: T. Rout. Limerick, Ireland.

Man:95   Taurus: How I lived to tell the tale. Elliot Manley. *American Programmer: Software Failures.* July 1995.

McD:94   MSc Thesis. Eoin McDonnell. Department of Computer Science. Trinity College, Dublin. 1994.

Men:87   Introduction to Mathematical Logic. Elliot Mendelson. Wadsworth and Cole/Brook, Advanced Books & Software. California, 1987.

Mil:89   A Calculus of Mobile Processes. Part 1. Robin Milner et al. LFCS Report Series. ECS-LFCS-89-85. Department of Computer Science. University of Edinburgh.

MOD:91a   00-55 (PART 1) / Issue 1, The Procurement of Safety Critical software in Defence Equipment, PART 1: Requirements. Ministry of Defence, Interim Defence Standard, U.K. 1991.

MOD:91b   00-55 (PART 2) / Issue 1, The Procurement of Safety Critical software in Defence Equipment, PART 2: Guidance. Ministry of Defence, Interim Defence Standard, UK. 1991.

OHa:98   Peer Reviews – The Key to Cost Effective Quality. Fran O'Hara. European SEPG. Amsterdam. 1998.

ORg:97   Applying Formal Methods to Model Organizations and Structures in the Real World. PhD Thesis. Department of Computer Science. Trinity College, Dublin. 1997.

Pau:93   Key Practices of the Capability Maturity Model, V1.1. Mark Paul et al. CMU/SEI-93-TR-25. 1993.

Pet:95   The IDEAL Model. Software Engineering Institute. Bill Peterson. Software Process Improvement and Practice (Pilot Issue). August 1995.

Pol:57   How to Solve It. A New Aspect of Mathematical Method. Georges Polya. . Princeton University Press. 1957.

Pop:97   The single transferable voting system: Functional decomposition in formal specification. Michael Poppleton in: 1st Irish Workshop on Formal Methods (IWFM'97). Editors: Gerard O'Regan and Sharon Flynn. Springer Verlag Electronic Workshops in Computing, Dublin, 1997.

Pre:94   Human Computer Interaction. Jenny Preece et al. Addison Wesley Publishing Company. 1994.

Pri:00   The SPIRE Handbook. Better, Faster, Cheaper software Development in Small Organizations. The SPIRE Partners. Editor: Jill Pritchard. Centre for Software Engineering, Dublin.

Rot:00   The influential test manager. Johanna Rothman. *Software and Internet Quality Week*. Software Research Institute. San Francisco. June 2000.

Roy:70   The Software Lifecycle Model (Waterfall Model). Managing the Development of Large Software Systems: Concepts and Techniques. W. Royce in: Proc. WESCON. August 1970.

Rou:00   Evolving SPICE – the future for ISO 15504. Terry Rout. SPICE 2000. International Conference on Software Process Improvement and Capability Determination. Limerick, Ireland. June 2000.

Rum:99   The Unified Modeling Language: User Guide. James Rumbaugh, Ivar Jacobson, and Grady Booch. Addison Wesley, 1999.

Ryn:00   Managing requirements: A new focus for project success. Kevin Ryan and Richard Stevens. *Software in Focus* (10) 2000. Centre for Software Engineering, Dublin.

SEI:00a   The CMM Integration Model (CMMI[SM]) CMMI SE/SW v1.02. CMM/SEI-2000/TR018. Staged Version of the CMM. Technical Report, Software Engineering Institute, Carnegie Mellon University, Pittsburg. July 2000.

SEI:00b   The CMM Integration Model (CMMI^{SM}) CMMI SE/SW v1.02. CMM/SEI-2000/TR019. Continuous Version of the CMM. Technical Report, Software Engineering Institute. Carnegie Mellon University, Pittsburg. July 2000.

Shw:31   The Economic Control of Manufactured Products. Walter Shewhart. Van Nostrand. 1931.

Spi:92   The Z Notation. A Reference Manual. J.M. Spivey. Prentice Hall International Series in Computer Science. 1992.

Std:99   Estimating: Art or Science. Featuring Morotz Cost Expert. Standish Group Research Note. 1999.

Sub:00   Performance testing. A methodical approach to E-commerce. B.M. Subraya and S.V. Subrahmanya. *Software and Internet Quality Week*. Software Research Institute. San Francisco. June 2000.

Tie:91   The Evolution of Def Stan 00-55 and 00-56 : An Intensification of the 'Formal Methods debate' in the UK. Margaret Tierney. Research Centre for Social Sciences. University of Edinburgh, 1991.

Voa:90   Prototyping. The Effective Use of CASE Technology. Roland Voan. Prentice Hall. 1990.

Wrd:92   Formal Methods with Z. A Practical Approach to Formal Methods in Engineering. J.B. Wordsworth. Addison Wesley. 1992.

Glossary

AMN	Abstract Machine Notation
AQL	Acceptable Quality Level
BSC	Balanced Score Card
BSI	British Standards Institute
CAF	CMM Appraisal Framework
CBA IPI	CMM Based Appraisal for Internal Process Improvement
CCS	Calculus of Communicating Systems
CICS	Customer Information Control System
CMM®	Capability Maturity Model
CMMI^{SM}	Capability Maturity Model Integration
COPQ	Cost of Poor Quality
COTS	Commercial-Off-The-Shelf Software
CSE	Centre for Software Engineering
CSP	Communicating Sequential Processes
DOD	Department of Defence
DSDM	Dynamic System Development Method
EFQM	European Foundation for Quality Management
ESA	European Space Agency
ESI	European Software Institute
ESPRIT	European Strategic Programme for Research and Development in Information Technology.
FAR	Functional Area Representative
FMEA	Failure Model Effects Analysis
GQM	Goal, Question, Metric
GUI	Graphical User Interface
HCI	Human Computer Interface
IDEAL^{SM}	Initiate, Diagnose, Establishing, Acting, Leveraging
IEEE	Institute of Electrical Electronic Engineers
ISO	International Standards Organization
JAD	Joint Application Development
LPF	Logic of Partial Functions
KLOC	Thousand Lines Of Code

KPA	Key Process Area
LPF	Logic Partial Functions
MOD	Ministry of Defense
MSG	Management Steering Group
MTBF	Mean Time Between Failure
MTTR	Mean Time to Repair
NASA	National Aeronautics and Space Administration
NATO	North Atlantic Treaty Organization
ODC	Orthogonal Defect Classification
OMG	Object Management Group
OSSP	Organization Standard Software Process
PCE	Phase Containment Effectiveness
P-CMM	People CMM
PDCA	Plan, Do, Check, Act
QCC	Quality Control Circle
QMS	Quality Management System
RACE	Research Advanced Communications Europe
RAD	Rapid Application Development
RAISE	Rigorous Approach to Industrial software Engineering
ROADS	Reuse-Oriented Approach for Domain Based software
RSL	RAISE Specification Language
S4S	SpiCE for Space
SCE	Software Capability Evaluation
SCM	Software Configuration Management
SCORE	Service Creation in an Object Reuse Environment
SDL	Specification and Description Language
SEI	Software Engineering Institute
SEPG	Software Engineering Process Group
SLA	Service Level Agreement
SPI	Software Process Improvement
SPICE	Software Process Improvement and Capability determination
SQA	Software Quality Assurance
SUMI	Software Usability Measurement Inventory
TQM	Total Quality Management
UML	Unified Modeling Language
VDM	Vienna Development Method
ZD	Zero Defects

Index